ESSAYS
of an
EX-LIBRARIAN

ESSAYS
of an
EX-LIBRARIAN

by
Richard Garnett, 1835- 1906

Essay Index Reprint Series

originally published by
DODD, MEAD & COMPANY

BOOKS FOR LIBRARIES PRESS
FREEPORT, NEW YORK

First Published 1901
Reprinted 1970

STANDARD BOOK NUMBER:
8369-1503-8

LIBRARY OF CONGRESS CATALOG CARD NUMBER:
74-107702

PRINTED IN THE UNITED STATES OF AMERICA

PREFACE

THE twelve essays comprised within this volume have been written at various times within the last fourteen years; some without external prompting, others at the invitation of editors or publishers. The acknowledgment of the author's obligations for permission to reprint will perhaps be best made by a brief statement of the circumstances attending the original publication of each essay.

The first in the volume, "On Translating Homer," appeared in 1889 in *The Universal Review*, edited by Harry Quilter, Esq. The versions from the Iliad included in it were reprinted in the following year along with the author's dramatic poem, "Iphigenia in Delphi," published in Mr. Fisher Unwin's "Cameo Series."

The essay on the date and occasion of "The Tempest" appeared in the same periodical in the same year. Its substance had been previously imparted *viva voce* to the New Shakespeare Society, and in 1890 its arguments were re-stated in the literary and critical portions of the introduction to "The Tempest" in "The Henry Irving Shakespeare." They found little acceptance in this country; mainly, as the writer conceives, from the morbid prejudice against James the First prevalent in so many quarters. Abroad, however, the author's view was warmly advocated by no less distinguished a critic than Dr. Brandes; and the essay has enjoyed the almost unique honour of a translation in the *Jahrbuch* of the German Shakespeare Society, vol. xxxv. Some improvements made on this occasion are repeated in the present republication.

The essay on Coleridge is the introduction to the selection from Coleridge's poetical works edited by the writer for Messrs. Lawrence & Bullen's "Muses' Library" (1898). "Shelley and Lord Beaconsfield" is a paper read to the Shelley Society in 1887, a very few copies of which were printed. "The Story of Gycia" was contributed to *The English Historical Review* for January 1897; and "The Love Story of Luigi Tansillo" to Vol. I. of *The Yellow Book* (1894). Four introductions follow. The essay on Beckford's "Vathek" was prefixed to Messrs. Lawrence & Bullen's edition of the book (1893); that on Moore to the "Thomas Moore Anecdotes," edited by Mr. Wilmot Harrison, and published by Messrs. Jarrold & Sons in 1899; that on Thomas Love Peacock to Messrs. Dent & Co.'s edition of Peacock's works (1891); and that on Matthew Arnold to Messrs. Ward, Lock, and Bowden's edition of "Alaric at Rome, and other Poems," 1896—a volume of the "Nineteenth Century Classics" edited by Mr. Clement Shorter.

The essay on Emerson was written in 1896 for "The Library of the World's Best Literature," edited at New York by Mr. Charles Dudley Warner. That on "Shelley's Views on Art" is in fact a lecture, delivered in April 1899 at the house of the late Lord Leighton, in aid of the movement for its acquisition by the community. When the discourse was printed in *The Anglo-Saxon Review* for September 1900, everything indicative of its original character was omitted, a circumstance only mentioned in apology for a didactic attitude less appropriate to an essay than to an address *ex cathedra*.

It will be seen that the obligations thus involved and cordially acknowledged are numerous, as is inevitable in the case of a volume which, reversing the antique precept, proffers "non multum, sed multa." The sole bonds of union among its contents are their belonging with but one exception to the domains of literary history and criticism, and their having preluded their appeal to public interest by interesting the author himself.

R. GARNETT.

April 20, 1901.

CONTENTS

ON TRANSLATING HOMER

ON TRANSLATING HOMER

EVER and anon the world receives from some bright spirit a tiny golden book—some Longinus on the Sublime, or Mill on Liberty—to which little can be added, and from which little can be taken away, in which the main outlines of the subject are perceived to have been traced for all time by the hand of a master. Such—but for a few unfortunate infringements of literary decorum —is Matthew Arnold's trio of lectures "On Translating Homer," where the main conditions of success in Homeric translation are laid down with such clearness, decision, and demonstrative cogency that the translator who fails through neglect of them is without excuse. Let him, says Mr. Arnold, be above all penetrated by a sense of four qualities in his author. Homer is (1) eminently rapid; (2) eminently plain and direct, both in his syntax and his words; (3) eminently plain and direct in his matter and ideas; and (4) eminently noble. These are indeed the four cardinal points, like the four swans

3

which, in Pope's "Temple of Fame," upbear the chariot of Pindar.

Since the publication of Mr. Arnold's lectures in 1861 few translators of the "Iliad," it may be hoped, have gone to work without pondering his precepts, while the number of attempts must have astonished him. He seems to think it somewhat remarkable that within the last ten years before he wrote two fresh translations of the "Iliad" should have appeared in England. From 1861 to 1888, twelve were published, some of which, especially those by Way, Blackie, and Worsley, are in various respects an advance upon anything accomplished before. And yet, with all the native power of these real poets, and all the aid Mr. Arnold has given them, Pope is not dethroned. A version which is in many respects a travesty of the "Iliad" remains the national version. Landor, Keats, Shelley, Tennyson, Mr. Arnold himself, have imbued our literature with the Hellenic spirit, and made it notorious to all that whatever else Pope may be, he is not a Greek. And yet his verses continue the possession of the nation, while the rest are only for scholars and amateurs. Surely this is not creditable. Pope's "Iliad," indeed, neither should, nor can, sink into oblivion; it will always live as a great example of the energy and resource of the English language. But it is not a satisfactory reflection that while the standard versions of most other languages approximate more or less closely to the spirit of Homer, that of our own is hopelessly and ostentatiously alienated from it. Several reasons have been assigned, but their collective force is only adequate to a partial solution of the problem. It is no doubt true that, with all his faults, Pope is the greatest English poet who has as yet essayed Homeric translation on any considerable scale. It is also true that his best qualities, fire and vigour, are those beyond all others essential to the translator of Homer, the absence of which can be compensated by no other virtue, and whose presence covers a multitude of sins. Much must also be allowed for the prestige of his great name and the long period during which he reigned without a rival. But all these considerations scarcely account for, much less do they excuse, the supremacy of a work so entirely in the spirit of the age of Queen Anne, long after we have learned what really is the spirit of Homer.

The host of translators, then, who have arisen since Pope, differing among each other in so many respects, agree in this, that they have failed to supersede him. If any other circumstance in which they all agree could be found, it might be worth considering whether the latter fact did not afford the key to the former.

Is there such a circumstance? There is. With the single exception of Sotheby, who is such a mere echo of Pope that Mr. Arnold justly refuses his version the right to exist, Pope's successors have been unanimous in one respect—they have repudiated his metre. They have tried blank verse, hexameter rhymed and unrhymed, ballad measures, nondescripts, the metre of Spenser and the metre of Scott, but never the heroic couplet. This alone might justify the conjecture that the cause of failure lies here, and we believe that this proposition can be established as firmly as is possible in the case of a merely æsthetic question. To effect this we must show that objections lie against the metrical forms preferred by modern translators, which incapacitate each and all of these from properly representing Homer. We must next show that these objections do not apply to heroic rhyme, and that the disesteem under which it labours is owing to its being confounded with the particular form of it exhibited by Pope. This latter proposition is evident when once pointed out; but Pope's form not being the one we advocate, and no specimen of a freer treatment existing except Chapman's antiquated version of the "Odyssey," we shall be constrained to follow Mr. Arnold's example, and essay translation ourselves.

It would be impossible to examine every metrical form which translators may have chosen to adopt, and some are manifestly incapable of being discussed to any useful purpose. Supposing, for instance, which we utterly refuse to admit, that the ideal translation were one in the manner of Spenser or of Scott, it would still be apparent that a Spenserian or Scottish translation was not a feat that could bear repetition. Worsley's Spenserian version leaves no room for rivalry, and an equally perfect example of Scott's manner, should such ever be produced, will bar the way against every other. These and similar forms, therefore, may be left out of consideration. There are only four forms at once legitimate in themselves and admitting of indefinitely varied experiment — blank verse, the English hexameter, whether on the Greek model or in Mr. Way's adaptation, the ballad Alexandrine, and the heroic couplet.

At first sight plain blank verse would seem the easiest metre in which Homer can be translated and the best adapted to reflect his dignity and simplicity. It is unquestionably true that the bare meaning of Homer can be better conveyed in this than in any rhymed metre. But, on the other hand, although blank verse is the easiest metre to write, it is the most difficult to write well. What is still more to the point, bad blank verse is in our language a better medium for rendering Homer's manner than good blank verse. The reason is, that the majesty and music of good English blank verse (and in skilful hands no metrical form is more majestic or more musical) depend in great measure upon variety of pause. To be frequently varied the pauses must themselves be frequent; hence the movement of the finest English blank verse is slow. Homer, on the other hand, as Mr. Arnold truly tells us, is "eminently rapid." To render Homer into the blank verse of Milton or Coleridge, therefore, is to transpose him into another key, and a key as unsuitable for his subject as the burden of "In Memoriam" would be for the substance of "Ye Mariners of England." The Homeric hexameter cannot be better described and exemplified than in Schlegel's couplet, thus rendered by Coleridge—

" Strongly it bears us along in swelling and limitless billows ;
    Nothing before and nothing behind but the sky and the
    ocean."

How does this description agree with an average specimen of noble English blank verse ?

            " Though ne'er yet
    Thou hast unveiled thy inmost sanctuary,
    Enough from incommunicable dream,
    And twilight phantasms, and deep noon-day thought,

Has shone within me, that, serenely now,
And moveless, as a long-forgotten lyre
Suspended in the solitary dome
Of some mysterious and deserted fane,
I wait thy breath, Great Parent ; that my strain
May modulate with murmurs of the air,
And motions of the forests and the sea,
And voice of living beings, and woven hymns
Of night and day, and the deep heart of man."

The ear accustomed to harmony like this will be
satisfied with nothing inferior, but to demand it is
to demand something quite un-Homeric. If, on
the other hand, blank verse is not thus artfully
solemnised with variety of cadence, it becomes mere
prose cut into lengths. The blank verse translator
of Homer, therefore, is in an inextricable dilemma.
If, like Cowper, he frames his verse on the Miltonic
model, he may write finely, but he cannot write
Homer; he may give Homer's verbal meaning
with perfect accuracy, but he steeps it in a colour
most alien to its own. If, on the other hand,
like Lord Derby, he writes a plain, straightforward blank verse, neither harsh nor musical, he
does not, indeed, hide Homer from the reader;
on the contrary, he disarrays him of his singing
robes.

The English hexameter, advocated and exemplified by Mr. Arnold himself, has several obvious
advantages. It is the best adapted of any metre

to reproduce the movement of Homer's verse and
his syntax; it usually admits of line being rendered
for line; and it seems to be Homer's own metre.
It must be granted that a poet should be rendered
in his own metre whenever possible; but the
truth is, that in the case of Homer this is not
possible, that the English hexameter, unless when
converted, as Mr. Way converts it, into a semi-lyrical
metre, resembles the Greek as draughts resemble
chess, or a Jew's harp the harp hung upon the
willows of Babylon.   The Greek hexameter consists of two descriptions of metrical feet—the dactyl,
composed of one long syllable followed by two
short ones; and the spondee, composed of two
consecutive long syllables.   One long syllable being
equal to two short ones, the time occupied by these
feet is the same.   In English, accent takes the place
of metrical quantity, and the definition of the
dactyl becomes one accented syllable followed by
two unaccented ones; and of the spondee, two
strongly accented syllables in succession.   Now
the English hexameter cannot, like the Greek,
consist of dactyls and spondees, for the conclusive
reason that there are hardly any spondees in the
language.   Mr. Arnold says that "the translator
must learn to use spondees freely"; but, sub-
joins Mrs. Glasse, first catch your spondee.   It
requires infinite care and art to bring two equally

accented syllables together in English.   How difficult it is we may see by the very lines with which Coleridge endeavoured to exemplify the spondee—

> " From long to long in solemn sort
> Slow Spondee stalks, strong foot, yet ill able
> Ever to come up with dactyl trisyllable."

In the first line not one foot is a spondee, all are iambi.   In the second the poet does manage to get three spondees and a half together, after which unexampled feat he skips with alacrity into the dactyl.   The place of the spondee in the English hexameter is generally occupied by the trochee, consisting in English of one accented syllable followed by an unaccented one.   Of all feet this is the most saltatory ("Trip it lightly as you go, On the gay fantastic toe"), and its usurpation of the place of the weighty spondee bereaves the measure of its dignity, and destroys the isochrony, or equivalence of the feet in time, which is the very life of it.   "This is a galloping measure, a hop, and a trot, and a gallop," says Coleridge of his own hexameters.   Even the dactyl, though congenial to our language, is continually getting transformed into something else by the conflux of monosyllables in this monosyllabic tongue, on which the stress will not fall as the poet means it to fall.   In the few specimens presented by Mr.

Arnold we have many such juxtapositions as
"Woman, I," "if like a," "sees thy tears," none
of which are dactyls. The German translators, it
must be admitted, have succeeded well, notwithstanding similar metrical disabilities,[1] but they
have the vast advantage of a polysyllabic language,
which gives something of the grand roll and boom-
ing music of the Homeric hexameter. These are
the most vital points, and, in our judgment, the
indispensable effect can only be obtained by
recourse to a music unknown to Homer, the
music of rhyme.

Blank verse is obviously incapable of this music,
but is the hexameter? It is not; by simply
removing the last syllable we convert the English
hexameter into a lyrical measure of fine quality.
The discovery, or at least the first important
application of it, is Tennyson's. Scores of lines
in "Maud" are on this pattern—

"Cold and clear-cut face, why come you so cruelly meek?"

If instead of "meek" the poet had written "placid,"

---

[1] The German hexameter, nevertheless, has been severely
criticised in its own country—

"In Weimar und Jena macht man die Hexameter wie den :
    Und die Pentameter sind noch viel erbärmlicher."

"In Weimar and Jena they write their hexameters like this :
    And the pentameters are still more wretched affairs."

he would have given us a perfect English hexameter; as it is, his lyrical line is nothing but the
hexameter, deemed so especially epic, deprived of
its final syllable, and made to rhyme with the next
line but one. Mr. Way, by far the most spirited
and, except Worsley, the most poetical among the
recent translators of Homer, has adopted this hint,
largely profiting at the same time by the example of
our great modern master of impetuous and sonorous
versification, Mr. Swinburne. He has immensely
augmented the sonority and compass of the verse by
giving it rhyme, which usually involves the docking
of the final syllable, and by no longer trying to
avail himself exclusively of dactyls and spondees,
but using anapæsts or any other foot which takes
an equal time in pronunciation. When such feet
creep into a professedly dactylic hexameter the
effect is bad, for we know that they are there in
spite of the poet; when the necessity is frankly
accepted it is quite another thing. Mr. Way's
rhymed and curtailed hexameter, which is substantially the metre of Mr. Morris's " Sigurd " and
his translation of the " Odyssey," but more con-
sistently polysyllabic, and hence more sonorous
and musical, is not only an improvement upon
the hexameter of the classical pattern, but also
upon another leading candidate for public favour,
the old Alexandrine or ballad metre, so frequently

recommended as the best for Homeric translation, and which undoubtedly possesses strong claims. The superiority of Mr. Way's form, nevertheless, becomes apparent upon comparison with the best representatives of the ballad form, Chapman and Professor Blackie—

> " The spirit I first did breathe
> Did never teach me that ; much less, since the contempt
> of death
> Was settled in me, and my mind knew what a worthy was,
> Whose office is to lead in fight, and give no danger pass
> Without improvement.   In the fire must Hector's trial
> shine;
> Here must his country, father, friends, be in him made
> divine."

Fine lines, but whose strength is less like the free sweep of the rolling sea itself than the energy of the strong swimmer who buffets it.   Professor Blackie is smoother, but gets perilously near sing-song—

> "Thus he ; and stout Tydides his broad shoulders flung
> around
> A huge and tawny lion's hide that reached down to the
> ground ;
> Then seized his spear, and forth he went, and round the
> warlike pair
> Whom Nestor named, and through the camp with urgent
> feet did bear."

Each of these lines might perfectly well be divided

into two, and would then appear fitter for the
guitar than the harp. But Mr. Way's line is like
the hexameter it represents, a metrical unit—

"Alas, 'tis one of the gods which abide on Olympus' height,
    That in shape of the prophet commandeth that here by the
        galleys we fight.
Of a truth no Kalchas is this, no bird-seer taught by a god,
For I followed the gleam of his ankles, the flash of his feet
        as they trod,
When he turned him away—the signs of a God no man
        may mistake.
Yea, and within this breast of mine is my spirit awake,
And it yearneth for fight, and battleward straineth yet
        more than before ;
In my feet is the fury of onset ; mine hands are afire for
        the war."

Lines like these have indeed the clash and ring of
the original, and half the effect is due to the happy
employment of rhyme.

Mr. Way has thus made a great advance upon
hexametric and ballad metre, and yet if, with all
his fire and passion, an undeniable tinge of eccen-
tricity detracts from the merit of his noble version,
the fault appears to us to lie in this very point of
metre. His is a dangerous form, because it almost
inevitably suggests to the translator that Homer is
more archaic than is really the case. Writing in
a style so nearly akin to that of the ballad, he is
tempted to make Homer rather a minstrel than a

poet. What would be right if he were working upon the lays out of which the "Iliad" originated, is wrong when one is dealing with the consummate work of a great poetical artist. If the translator forgets this he becomes archaic, and if he becomes archaic he is lost. No translation will ever establish itself that is not alive with the vitality of its own age. Something of an antique cast is indeed essential, but it must never be forgotten that Homer is a bard for all time; and that if in one sense the oldest of the poets, he is in another the youngest. The rust of antiquity, happily, has not eaten very deeply into Mr. Way's diction, but the charm of his version is undoubtedly impaired by the constant recurrence of such oddities as " onset - yell," " maddened up," " battle - stay," " outrage-wild," " get them aback," and the affectation of such comparatively legitimate, still local or obsolescent expressions as " garth," " forthright." These blemishes would not have existed if Mr. Way had been writing in blank verse or heroic rhyme; and if his metre really tends to generate them, this is a heavy deduction from its incontestable merits.

We have now arrived by an exhaustive process at the rhymed heroic metre, which Mr. Arnold allows to be one of the possible metres for a translator of Homer. We will not say the heroic couplet, for the neglect of this noble and national form of verse, not merely in translation but in original composition, is probably due to its association with the couplet of Pope. Pope's versification is, indeed, an affair of couplets; he strictly confines the verse to the distich, and not only rejects the variety he might have obtained by the free use of the triplet and Alexandrine, but strives to make every couplet the counterpart of its fellows. If he had not been a great poet, endowed with more fire and animation than any other Homeric translator except Chapman and Way, the result would have been a dull monotony; as it is, he is spirited enough, but with the spirit of a Dryden rather than of a Homer, not so much epic as epigrammatic. But why assume that Pope's polished pattern has superseded every other form of the heroic couplet, when it has been rejected by the more distinguished of his successors? If Byron copied him in the " Corsair," Keats went to Dryden for a model when writing "Lamia," and the versification of Mr. Morris's "Jason" is nearly the same as that one of the first examples of English Homeric translation, Chapman's "Odyssey." It is not generally remembered that in this, his second attempt, Chapman replaced the Alexandrine by the heroic line, and that the greatest of English critics, Coleridge, commended him for doing so,

B

and wished that he had executed his "Iliad" on the same plan. "When," says his editor, Hooper, "the ear has become habituated to the rhythm, there is a dramatic power about Chapman's 'Odyssey' that has not been attained by any subsequent translator." It is indeed true that Chapman and Morris's pattern of the heroic metre (which is substantially the same as that of "Endymion"), however admirable for metrical romance, does not quite attain the dignity of epic. It is too picturesquely vagrant, too free and easy, carries variety of pause to excess, is not sufficiently concentrated and energetic. What we want is something intermediate between it and the sonorous passion of Mr. Swinburne's "Anactoria," unsurpassable as poetic declamation, but fitter for the translator of Lucan and Juvenal than of Homer. Could we have such a form, varied with the triplet and Alexandrine, which Dryden used so effectively, and wielded by a translator not inferior to Pope or Way in poetical spirit, we should have something possessing all the claims to popularity which keep Pope's at the head of English versions, and admitting of strict fidelity to that Greek spirit of which Pope had not the most remote perception. Nothing in our language is or can be more deeply imbued with this spirit than Shelley's versions of the minor Homeric hymns, executed in heroic metre. It must be admitted that the movement of the Homeric verse is imperfectly represented by English heroics, and that the recurring rhymes tend to confine, as with river-banks, what in the original is limitless as ocean. But the alternative thus presented to us, the use of the English hexameter on the Greek model, we have already seen to be unacceptable; and if Mr. Way's semi-lyrical hexameter version does not establish itself, a question which we admit to be still *sub judice*, it will at least not easily be superseded by another on the same plan. The field for the translator in heroic verse is more open.

Of the specimens appended we shall not be expected to say much. It will be remembered that they are mainly offered as contributions to the metrical department of the subject, and that their right to existence is vindicated if they are satisfactory on this point alone. If we endeavoured to enumerate the other requisites of a successful version we should speedily affect the reader as Imlac's definition of a poet affected Rasselas. Mr. Arnold's four points are the main ones; for the rest, the style to be recommended to the Homeric translator cannot be better expressed than by Pope's description of the style of Homer himself—

> "A strong expression most he seemed to affect,
> And here and there disclosed a brave neglect."

THE ENCOUNTER OF THE HOSTS

As when on some loud coast the wind impels
The thronging waters, vast the billow swells,
And o'er all other sea a moment towers,
Then, furiously flung forward on the shores,
Curves its surmounting crest, and far away
Hurls with a roar the lavish-scattered spray :
So streamed in one huge host the gathered bands
Of Greeks incessant to the war.   Commands
Their leaders gave ; silently moved along
The others ; dumb seemed all that serried throng,
So deep the awe their chieftains did inspire :
They marched, and as they marched their armour flashed
    forth fire.
But as when, gathered in a rich man's stall,
Unnumbered ewes stand at the milking, all
With ceaseless bleats replying to their young,
Uproar prevailed the Trojan host among :
From various lands, of stranger tribes who came,
Unlike their accent, nor their speech the same.
Their bosoms blazed with fire from Ares caught ;
Like passion mid the Greeks Athene wrought :
And Terror stalked around, and with him Dread ;
And Strife insatiate mid the armies sped.
Sister and mate of Ares, who appears
Pigmy at first, then on the sudden rears
Her head in heaven's eminence, while yet
Her feet upon the nether earth are set.
There mid the hosts woe-working was she found,
Strewing the fire of battle all around.

THE TROJAN CAMP AT NIGHT

But they, full of high thoughts, by battle's gate,
Burning huge fires, all night encamping sate ;

As when the bright stars gloriously gird
The radiant moon, and aether sleeps unstirred.
And boldly stand forth headland, cliff, and grove,
And heaven immeasurable is rent above,
And every constellation manifest,
And gladness fills the gazing shepherd's breast :
So many fires 'twixt stream and navy shone
Before the massy walls of Ilion—
A thousand fires !   By each upon the plain
Sat fifty warriors, flashing forth amain
Fire from their arms, and, champing the white corn,
Their steeds stood by the cars, awaiting fair-throned Morn.

POSEIDON GOING TO THE AID OF THE GREEKS

Zeus, having led up Hector and his might
Unto the navy, left them there to fight
Incessantly with toil and wear of war,
But turned himself his radiant eyes afar ;
The many-steeded plains of Thrace he scanned,
And close-ranked Mysians, fighters hand to hand ;
The milk-fed Hippomolgians viewed he then,
And Abii, most just of mortal men.
But unto Ilion looked he not at all,
Not deeming that it ever could befall
That any God would aid or those who bled
For Troy, or who against her combated.

But great Poseidon kept not watch in vain.
Marvelling he marked the battle on the plain,
Throned upon Samothrace's woody crest,
Whence was the whole of Ida manifest,
And Troy's towers and the navy clear-exprest.

There sat he, risen from the main's profound,
Grieving to see his Grecians giving ground,
And greatly wroth with Zeus.   Sudden at last
He rose, and swiftly down the steep he passed ;
The mountain trembled with each step he took,
The forest with the quaking mountain shook.
Three strides he made, and with the fourth he stood
At Aegae, where is founded 'neath the flood
His hall of glorious gold that cannot fade ;
Entering therein, beneath the yoke he laid
His steeds with feet of brass and manes of gold,
Swift as the wind, and his own frame did fold
In golden weeds, and grasped within his hand
The well-wrought golden scourge, and took his stand
Behind the coursers, and immediately
Wended upon the surface of the sea ;
And all the whales and monsters knew their king,
And rose up from the bottom frolicking ;
And the sea's face was parted with a smile,
And rapidly the horses sped the while ;
The brazen axle was not wet below ;
And to the Grecian navy did they go.

ACHILLES RECOVERS THE BODY OF PATROCLUS

These words swift Iris spake, then flew above,
And straight uprose the chieftain dear to Jove.
Divine Athene on his shoulders laid
Her many-tasselled aegis, and displayed
A gold cloud round his head, and caused intense
Effusion of bright fire to issue thence.
And as aerial flame is seen afar,
Ascending from some isle where men of war
Have all day long assailed with shafts and spears
The lone and unassisted islanders,

But at sunsetting these along their shores
Light frequent beacons ; swift the signal soars
Summoning their neighbours in fleet ships to speed
Thither, and bring them succour in their need ;
Thus streamed the splendour of Achilles' brow
To heaven, as he arose and stood below
Behind the trench, nor with the rest did stand,
Observant of his mother's wise command.
He stood and shouted.   Pallas too did swell
His shout with hers, and straight unutterable
Tumult and terror on the Trojans fell.
And as when loud war-music thrilling clear
Rings from the clarion of a trumpeter
When a town's walls are compassèd with foes,
So thrillingly Achilles' voice arose.
When then their ears rang with that brazen shout
Great dread fell on them all, the steeds about
Turned with the chariots, for they did forecast
Ruin, and they that drove beheld aghast
The fire that unabatingly was shed
By Pallas from Aeacides's head.
Thrice did Achilles lift his voice's might,
Thrice Trojans and allies recoiled in flight,
And twelve great champions, famous in the wars,
Died, pierced by their own spears and crushed by their
        own cars.
But, triumphing, the Greeks Patroclus dead
Drew from amid the javelins ; on a bed
Bestowed the corpse ; and every Myrmidon
Stood by it, weeping bitter tears thereon.
Sadly mid these Achilles also bent,
Wailing his mate beloved, gory and rent,
Stretched on the bier, whom he himself had sent
With his own car and coursers to the plain,
But not with them had welcomed back again.

ACHILLES ARMS HIMSELF

Eager Athene thus did Zeus incite
Yet more, from heaven she suddenly took flight ;
In figure like an osprey long of wing
She darted where the Greeks apparelling
Themselves in arms were stationed, there imbued
Achilles' breast with nectar, lest he should
Faint in the battle, for refreshment fain,
Then flew up to her father's dome again :
But from the ships they poured and swarmed upon the plain,
And thick as Zeus' cold flakes, when forth they fare,
Borne of the north wind through the crystal air,
Legions innumerable landward flowed
Of many-glancing helms, and mail that glowed
With over-lapping plates, and bossy shields,
And ashen spears.   Their splendour from the fields
Flashed up to heaven, and all the earth about
Laughed luminous with lustre they cast out,
And quaked beneath the infinite footfall,
And high Achilles armed him mid them all.
Raging he gnashed his teeth, flame in his eye
Lightened, but on his heart weighed misery ;
And wrath and sadness shared him as he stood,
And bright Hephaestus' battle-garb indued.
First in his greaves his legs he did enclasp,
Well riveting the silver ankle-hasp ;
His bosom in his cuirass next arrayed ;
Then hung his shining, silver-studded blade
Athwart his shoulder ; then his shield he took,
Massy and huge ; whose beam was as the look
Of the broad moon from heaven ; or as when
Fire blazes on the hills where shepherds pen
Their flocks at night, and splendour streams to sea,
Discerned of them who toss unhappily

On the great waters, who may not arrive
At land, but with the wind unwilling drive ;
Such light the fair elaborate buckler shed.
Then his huge crested helmet on his head,
Which shone as if a star his brows had crowned,
He set, and all the golden plumes around
Danced thrilling, on the helm by deft Hephaestus bound.
Then did he prove the armour, if it might
Be truly fashioned, fitting him aright,
And felt as he were winged with feathers light,
So aptly did it sheathe him.   Next the spear
He grasped which Peleus anciently did bear,
Tough, long and heavy, which not any one
Of Greeks could brandish, saving him alone ;
The shaft by Chiron felled on Pelion, then
To Peleus given, doom to warrior men.
But Alcimus and bold Automedon
Wrought by the steeds, fitting the harness on.
The horses' mouths with curbs they did constrain,
And to the chariot seat drew back the rein.
Automedon then mounted, in his right
Shaking the beaming scourge.   As sunshine bright,
Godlike Achilles sprang unto his side,
And loudly to his father's coursers cried :
    Xanthus and Balius, Podarge's breed,
Bring ye this day your lord with better speed
Back from the field, when from the field ye fare,
Nor leave him, as ye left Patroclus, there.

But to him audibly his steed thus said,
Swift Xanthus, from the chariot, as his head
He on a sudden drooped, and with his mane,
Unloosened from the yoke-band, swept the plain,
For white-armed Hera gave him voice—This day,
Achilles, we shall save thee from the fray,

But nigh at hand the hour when thou must fall,
For which accuse not thou thy steeds at all,
But Gods, and Fates who life and death dispense,
Not by our tardiness or indolence
Did Trojans strip the arms Patroclus wore,
But the bright God whom fair-haired Leto bore
Slew him among the first, yet Hector won
The glory.   Fleet may we as Zephyr run,
Who fleetest among winds is famed to be,
Yet slaughter and the slayers wait for thee,
Whom shall a mortal slay, and eke a Deity.

Here ceased he, for his tongue the Furies tied :
To him Achilles wrathfully replied,
Xanthus, why bode my death ? thou need'st not so ;
That I must perish here full well I know,
Far from my father, from my mother far ;
Yet verily I will not cease from war
Till I have overthrown the Trojans quite,
He said, and shouting drove into the fight.

THE GODS JOIN IN THE BATTLE

But to the Gods, coming where strove these men,
Came strife, and with the rest they battled then.
And with a mighty voice Athene cried,
Now where the moat the rampart fortified
Shouting, and now the roaring main beside.
Ares upon his part, as storms a blast,
Now crying to the Trojans his voice cast
Forth from the citadel, and now where is
Callicolone by swift Simois.

Thus cheered they on the armies, their own might
Mingling with theirs in formidable fight.

And Zeus the sire of Gods and men dismayed
The heavens with thunder, and Poseidon made
Tremor in all the immeasurable earth,
And Ida where the many springs have birth
Quaked with her peak and every mountain-spur,
And Troy's towers and the navy quaked with her.
And nether Hades, despot of the dead,
Leapt from his throne and cried aloud, in dread
Lest earth should yawn, so strong Poseidon shook,
And suffer men and heavenly Gods to look
Into the squalor of his realm unblest,
Which even the undying Gods detest.

THE DATE AND OCCASION OF "THE TEMPEST"

THE DATE AND OCCASION OF
"THE TEMPEST"

IN an essay on the Politics and Religion of Shakespeare, published in *Macmillan's Magazine* for
January 1889, Mr. Goldwin Smith commits himself
to a view of the date and purpose of "The Tempest" which will be far from commanding the
general assent which he seems to expect. "Who
Ferdinand and Miranda were," he says, "is not
doubtful. It appears from the manuscript of Vertue
that 'The Tempest' was acted by John Heminge
and the rest of the King's company before Prince
Charles, the Lady Elizabeth, and the Prince Palatine Elector, at the beginning of the year 1613.
Frederick had come over to receive his bride, the
Princess, who was the darling of all Protestant
hearts. Ferdinand, then, was Frederick, and
Miranda, Elizabeth."

Mr. Goldwin Smith's judgments on Shakespeare
are probably the result of independent study, and
he may not greatly care to acquaint himself with

the course of Shakespearian criticism. He would
otherwise have been aware that the view of the
purpose of the drama thus propounded as self-
evident is supported by only two considerable
authorities, Tieck and Meissner; and that the date
of 1613, evidently essential to its acceptance, is
absolutely rejected by every recent editor and commentator. The editors of last generation may have
been largely influenced by the alleged discovery of
a notice of the performance of the play in 1611.
But, even since this has been admitted to be a
fabrication, criticism is no less unanimous in assigning 1610 or 1611 as the date. Such is the opinion
of Halliwell, Lloyd, Dowden, Grant White, Stokes,
Furnivall, Fleay, and Hudson. It is obvious that a
piece composed two or three years before the Princess Elizabeth's nuptials can have had no relation
to them; that she cannot, in this case, be Miranda
or Frederick Ferdinand; that, if this be so, the
true interpretation of the drama must be quite
different from Mr. Goldwin Smith's, and that the
view which he almost takes for granted is, in
the present state of opinion, certain of unanimous
rejection.

Mr. Goldwin Smith, nevertheless, is to our thinking perfectly right; but proof must be found in an
elaborate investigation of the drama. In the following remarks, the substance of which was stated

verbally to the New Shakespeare Society in January 1887,[1] we hope to show—

1. That "The Tempest" was written for performance before a private audience, and on occasion of a marriage.

2. That the particular audience and the particular marriage are known from documentary evidence, and further revealed by evident allusions to the personality of the bridegroom, and to the recent death of Prince Henry, and by the introduction of King James himself into the piece.

3. That there is additional internal evidence for the date 1613, and no evidence for any other date. Our contention is substantially the same as that of Tieck and Meissner, who have, however, rather indicated the line of argument than elaborated the argument itself.

It may, in the first place, be taken as now universally admitted that "The Tempest" is one of Shakespeare's very latest plays. The theory of Hunter, assigning the date to 1598, and that of Elze, fixing it at 1604, not only have nothing solid to rest upon, but are absolutely negatived by internal evidence. Without wishing to carry metrical tests to an extreme, it is incontestable that the

---

[1] See the report of Mr. Moulton's remarkable paper on "The Tempest," and the ensuing discussion, in the *Academy* for January 22, 1887.

versification of Shakespeare's later dramas differs in a marked manner from that of the earlier, and that the versification of "The Tempest" stamps it as a late play. Nor does any play bear more obvious tokens of maturity in serene wisdom, intellectual force, and mastery of dramatic art. The date being thus approximately established on internal testimony, it would be something more than a wonder if the mention of the "still-vexed Bermoothes" were a pure accident without reference to the storm and shipwreck that made the Bermudas known to the English public through the medium of Sylvester Jourdan's pamphlet, published in October 1610. Shakespeare, indeed, could derive little of his local colouring from Jourdan, as the necessities of his plot compelled him to transfer the Atlantic island to the Mediterranean. It is nevertheless impossible to doubt that Jourdan's narrative must have been familiar to him. The numerous parallels produced by Malone leave no room for question. The error of this eminent critic is not in the identification of Shakespeare's storm with the Bermuda tempest, but in the gratuitous assumption that because the narrative on which the play was founded was published in October 1610, therefore the play must have been written immediately afterwards. We have, on the contrary, no right to assume the existence of the piece before the first notice we have of its representation, which, as already stated, took place at the marriage of the Princess Elizabeth to the Elector Palatine.

The proofs that "The Tempest" was actually written for private representation on this occasion are of the strongest. Two circumstances especially suggest that it was not intended for an ordinary audience :—

1. It is much below the ordinary length of a Shakespearian drama. The average is three thousand lines; "The Tempest" has only about two thousand. For this, on the supposition of its having been written for representation at Court at a period of general festivity, there are two excellent and indeed imperative reasons. The time of the monarch and his guests must not be unduly encroached upon; and the piece must not be on too large a scale to be written, rehearsed, and put upon the stage with great expedition. We shall see that, on our theory, the entire preparation of "The Tempest" could at most have occupied little more than two months; so that there would be the strongest motive to make the play as brief as consistent with the due exposition of the subject.

2. For the same and kindred reasons it would be an object to have as few changes of scene as possible. "The Tempest" is unique among Shakespeare's plays in this respect. After the

brief representation of the deck of the storm-tossed vessel with which the play opens, there is practically but one scene; for though the action occasionally shifts from the space before Prospero's cell to some other part of the island, everything is avoided which might necessitate a change of decoration.[1] Neither is there any change of costume except Prospero's assumption of his ducal robes in the last act which takes place on the stage. In keeping with this general restraint is the compression of the action, which, instead of stretching over a long period as usual with Shakespeare, is, as we are frequently reminded, accomplished within three hours, or about the time which the actual representation of the drama would occupy.

The strongest argument, however, is the introduction of two masques such as were in Shakespeare's age usually presented to sovereigns on occasions of ceremony. The machinery of the masque in Act iii. scene 3 is much more elaborate than would have been requisite if the scene had not been introduced for its own sake. Still more significant is the nuptial masque of Juno,

---

[1] Though the scenic resources of Shakespeare's age were limited, they were sufficient to be troublesome on a private stage. Tombs, rocks, hell-mouths, steeples, beacons, and trees are found in lists of properties.

Ceres, and Iris in the fourth act, which, when
the real purpose of the play is overlooked, appears
such a mere excrescence that it has been supposed
to be an interpolation. The untenableness of this
notion appears from two simple considerations. In
the first place, if the masque goes, the fourth act
almost disappears along with it; this act is in any
case remarkably short, and can only be made of
due proportionate length by the dance which ensues
upon the masque. In the second place, the noblest
passage in the play is inextricably associated with
the masque, and stands or falls with it. It is common to quote—

" Like the baseless fabric of a vision."

This is incorrect; Shakespeare wrote "*this*
vision," meaning the interlude which has just been
exhibited, to which a few lines farther on he
again refers as " this insubstantial pageant." Whoever wrote this speech wrote, or at least designed,
the masque also. If, as some maintain, the pageant
was interpolated by Francis Beaumont[1] upon the
revival of the piece, Beaumont must have penned
one of the most inspired passages in literature,

[1] It is perfectly possible—though we see no especial reason for
the supposition—that Beaumont or some one else may have written
the interlude under Shakespeare's direction. All we need insist
upon is, that it belongs to the scheme of the play, and was planned
and prescribed by the play's author.

and Shakespeare must have written a fourth act of disproportionate brevity. Neither of these propositions will find easy credit; but if they are not true, Shakespeare must have had some very cogent motive for introducing this apparently aimless pageantry into the very heart of his drama. This could be nothing else than the fact that, in one point of view, "The Tempest" is a spectacular play for the entertainment of princes and courtiers upon a great occasion; and that from another, the seeming impertinence enabled him to stamp his piece as a hymeneal drama. To condense our argument to a point, this nuptial interlude is either a mere idle excrescence or pregnant with significance. The former it cannot be, for if it is removed the fourth act tumbles to pieces, and the finest passage in the drama goes along with it. If, on the other hand, it has a significance, this must relate to something in the situation of the spectators, who must have been aware of some circumstance justifying its introduction, and this could be nothing else than a marriage deeply interesting to some persons among the audience.

This much might have been inferred if the occasion of the first recorded performance of the play had been unknown; when, however, we learn from Vertue's MS. what it was, and who the audience were, the purpose of the drama becomes perfectly clear. It is not credible that so many marks of a play intended for Court representation—brevity, unity of time and place, a brilliant spectacle apparently unconnected with the plot, and to which nevertheless everything is made to lead up—should combine in a mere revival of a play written for the ordinary stage. Much less can the piece be a revival of one which had already done duty as a hymeneal drama, for Shakespeare never produced anything unfitting the occasion; and it is safe to affirm that before the espousals of Frederick and Elizabeth no marriage had taken place in his time to which "The Tempest" could be in the least degree appropriate. Everything bespeaks a royal marriage, and everything corresponds with the royal marriage of 1613. The foreign prince come from beyond sea, the island princess who has never left her home, the wise father who brings about the auspicious consummation by his policy—all found their counterparts among the splendid company that watched the performance on that February night. The perception of the absolute appropriateness of the piece to the occasion must have heightened their enjoyment to a degree which, even with our vastly enhanced reverence for the genius of Shakespeare, we cannot reproduce. Every point would be new and bright, every allusion would be taken as soon as made. What a smile, for instance, must have gone round at Gonzalo's speech :—

> "Would they believe me
> If I should say I saw such islanders?"

But that assembly numbered shadows as well as men. "The Tempest" would hardly have existed in its present form, and certainly would have been far from exemplifying Shakespeare's courtly tact and tender humanity, but for the gloom thrown upon the marriage festivities by the recent death of the king's eldest son. Some attention to dates will here be requisite. The first apparent allusion to the marriage treaty in the State Papers is in December 1611, when Frederick is named among possible candidates for the Princess's hand. On August 3, 1612, the arrival of an envoy from him is mentioned, "who has gone post-haste to the King." But another candidate is in the field. On October 9 Sir Dudley Carleton is informed that the "Savoy match is nearly concluded. All approve it except the churchmen." It probably had the support of the Queen, who was secretly a Roman Catholic. On October 22, however, the Palatine arrives in person, and is presented by the King with a ring worth £1800. His suit must have prospered immediately : for the Prince had arranged to conduct his sister to Germany before his sudden and startling death on November 6 ensuing. The situation was most embarrassing for the Palatine, most grievous for the Court. Death and life were joint inmates of the palace, where the Prince's body lay for a month ere the arrangements for the public funeral could be completed. Yet the bridegroom was in England, and the marriage could not be long delayed.

> " The funeral baked meats
> *Must* coldly furnish forth the marriage tables."

On December 2 the Palatine came back to visit his mistress, but the marriage must have been regarded as settled somewhat earlier, for on December 10 we hear of a wedding present of £20,000 from Scotland. On December 27 the pair were solemnly affianced. On January 6 Sir Thomas Lake writes, " The black is wearing out and the marriage pomps preparing." Among these, as we have seen, was the preparation of " The Tempest," which may have been commissioned about the end of November. Shakespeare thus found himself in a position as trying as ever tested the dexterity of a courtier or the humanity of a man. How to reconcile the demands of sorrow and joy on this unparalleled occasion ? To ignore the late affliction would be heartless and an insult to the King, but how to recognise it without darkening the nuptial joy and suggesting omens as sinister as Marie Antoinette's tapestry ? In the entire range of Shakespeare's art there is nothing more exquisite than the skill with which he has solved this problem. The recent calamity is not unrecognised; on the contrary, the supposed death of the drowned prince is a most vital incident, kept continually in view. But, by a consummate stroke of genius, the woe is taken away from Prospero, the representative of James, and transferred to the house of his enemy. The lost prince is duly mourned, but not by his real father. James is reminded of his bereavement, but it is not obtruded upon him. The sense of loss mingles, a fine and almost imperceptible element, with the general cheerfulness. In the end, the hitherto sonless Prospero gains a son, as the be-reaved James is gaining one in the Palatine; while, a compliment within a compliment, delicate allusion is made to the promise of Prince Charles. If this be refined flattery, it is also refined humanity. To ignore it is to miss the key to the interpretation of the play. We should also lose the best evidence we possess of the speedy working of Shakespeare's imagination; how, in quite another sense than Johnson's, " panting Time toiled after him in vain." The supposed death of Ferdinand is so vital a portion of the plot that the play cannot have been undertaken without it. We have seen, however, that the incident which suggested it did not occur until November 6 preceding the marriage, which was solemnised on February 14. The representation must have preceded the wedding, otherwise Prospero's exhortation at the beginning of the fourth act to pre-nuptial chastity would have lost all force. This marvellous work must accordingly have been planned, written, and put upon the stage within less than three months. Nothing can give a higher idea of the activity of Shakespeare's genius; while at the same time we discern cogent reasons for the comparative brevity of the play.

If Frederick and Elizabeth are Ferdinand and Miranda, it follows, as long ago pointed out by Tieck, that Prospero is James. The conclusion may appear strange and unwelcome; it met no support when propounded by the present writer to the New Shakespeare Society. The current conception of James is one of a grotesque, preposterous figure, more like a bat flown forth after the setting of "the bright occidental star" than the sun to whose arising on that occasion his accession is compared by the translators of our Bible. Even were this estimate well founded, to have passed the sovereign by without notice in a piece written for the nuptials of the sovereign's daughter would have been an impoliteness which Shakespeare would

never have perpetrated. But it is exceedingly
unjust. It was James's misfortune that his defects were mostly of an unkingly sort, and such as
easily lend themselves to ridicule. Shakespeare's
own words are fulfilled in him :—

> "All give to dust that is little gilt
> More laud than gilt o'er-dusted."

"Those," says Mark Pattison, "whose impressions
of character have been chiefly derived from modern
histories, will find that as they become better acquainted with contemporary memoirs their estimate
of James's abilities will be raised." "We are ready
to take a long stride beyond Mr. Pattison's eulogy,"
comments the *Quarterly* reviewer, and proceeds to
assign excellent reasons, concluding, "That un-
gainly figure was the mask of a very considerable
personality. Behind those rough and lazy features
worked a big and versatile brain, and a most observant and discriminating intellect. One has to
take into account the irony of Nature toward him,
the pedantic externals of his manners and character." That is the point. With all his talents
James certainly was a pedant, and gave to all
about him the impression that he was fitter for
books than for business. And it is just this infirmity at which Shakespeare glances, in lines

which it is difficult to believe were not expressly
intended for the King's admonition :—

> " For the liberal arts
> Without a parallel : those being all my study,
> The government I cast upon my brother,
> And to my state grew stranger, being transported
> And rapt in secret studies."

This and much else to the same effect Prospero
recounts without apparent suspicion how strongly
it tells against himself, a circumstance fatal to M.
Emile Montegut's specious theory that Shakespeare
idealised himself in Prospero. The character is
full of dramatic irony. Prospero is wise and good
indeed, but not so much of either as he thinks
himself. He betrays fretfulness, irritability, and
self-importance, reminding us of the limitations of
the highest humanity, and contrasting sharply with
his preternatural power. But these traits do not
lie upon the surface, and upon a broad view of the
character it is impossible to conceive one more
completely embodying James's ideal of himself, or
more dexterously and at the same time truthfully
bringing the really strong sides of his personality
into view. A wise, humane, pacific prince, gaining
his ends not by violence but by policy; devoted to
far-off purposes which none but himself can realise,
much less fathom; independent of counsellors,

safely contemptuous of foes, and controlling all about him by his superior wisdom; keeping in the background till the decisive hour has struck, and then interfering effectually; devoted to lawful knowledge, but the sworn enemy of black magic—such was James in James's eyes, and such is Prospero.

Except in the particular of supernatural power, the portrait here presented bears the strongest resemblance to another of Shakespeare's characters, whose affinity to James has been already remarked by Chalmers, and there is every reason to believe that James was not in "The Tempest" idealised for the first time. In "Measure for Measure" we have the same controlling and supervising agent, with the same ironic touch of affected mystery and self-consciousness; and, as in "The Tempest," the intention of the poet is revealed by the circumstances of the time. The plot of the play is mainly taken from Whetstone's "Promus and Cassandra," itself founded on a novel of Cinthio's; but neither in Whetstone nor in his original is there the least hint of Shakespeare's central incident, the disguise of the Duke. What suggested this incident? The peculiar situation of the King. According to unanimous opinion, and the internal evidence of several passages, "Measure for Measure" was written no long time after the accession of James, and the accession of James was immediately followed by a furious outbreak of pestilence. The coronation took place in July 1603, "in the midst of a raging plague" which drove the Court from London, and James did not re-enter the capital till March following. The assembling of Parliament, which had been fixed for September, was necessarily postponed, and, of course, the theatres were closed. Yet the machinery of Government worked as usual; the King, absent in body, was present in spirit, and the season of apparent interregnum was that of one of his most characteristic measures, the conference at Hampton Court. That the drama contains some apologies for unpopular features in James's deportment is generally admitted; what more natural than that advantage should be taken of the joyful re-opening of the theatres to extenuate and embellish his absence from the capital, and represent him in the character he so much affected of the wise ruler invisibly guiding events to their desired consummation by his superiority of intellect? We are convinced that the coincidence is no accident, and that the more the characters of the Duke and Prospero are studied together, the more apparent it will become that they were drawn from the same model.

Some additional evidence in favour of the date of 1613 should not be omitted, though we may not be disposed to lay great stress upon it. The autumn

and winter of 1612 were unusually tempestuous:
there were in particular tremendous storms on
October 22nd and November 4th, the latter of
which was especially remarked from its occurring
only two days before the death of Prince Henry.
More weight is due to the curious atmosphere of
discovery and colonisation which invests "The
Tempest"—rather to be felt than proved, but admirably perceived and expressed by Mr. Watkiss
Lloyd:—

"The wonders of new lands, new races: the
exaggerations of travellers, and their truths more
strange than exaggeration: new natural pheno-
mena, and superstitious suggestions of them: the
perils of the sea and shipwrecks, the effect of
such fatalities in awakening remorse for ill deeds,
not unremembered because easily committed: the
quarrels and mutinies of colonists for grudges
new and old: the contests for authority of the
leaders, and the greedy misdirection of industry
while even subsistence is precarious: the theories
of government for plantations, the imaginary and
the actual characteristics of man in the state of
nature: the complications with the indigenæ: the
resort, penally or otherwise, to compelled labour:
the reappearance on new soil of the vices of the
older world: the contrast of moral and intellectual
qualities between the civilised and the savage,

and the gradual apprehension of the wondrous stranger by the savage, with all the requirements of activity, promptitude, and vigour demanded for the efficient and successful administration of a settlement—all these topics, problems, and conjunctures came up in the plantation of Virginia by James I.; and familiarity with their colonial dependency would heighten the sensibility of the audience to every scene of a play which presented them in contrasted guise, but in a manner that only the more distinctly brought them home to their cardinal bearings in the philosophy of Society—of man."

As true as well expressed, but requiring a later date for "The Tempest" than Mr. Lloyd assigns. The first American settlement was only made in May 1607, and by only one hundred and five colonists. The Virginia company was not incorporated till 1609; but little news from the more numerous emigrants sent out by it had reached England by 1610, and it is not until 1612 that "R. J." can write, "Our colony consisteth now of seven hundred men." In this year, however, several accounts of Virginia appeared, not always of the most encouraging nature. On July 9, 1612, Chamberlain tells Carleton: "The Virginia plantation likely to come to nothing, through the idleness of the

D

English. Ten men, sent to fish for their relief,
have slipped off to England, and fill the town
with ill reports about it."

> " Had I plantation of this isle, my lord " . . .
> " He'd sow it with nettle seed."

We may therefore, if we like, revert to the old
belief that in " The Tempest" Shakespeare took
a formal leave of the stage, that his magic staff
was broken along with Prospero's, and that the
wondrous book drowned "deeper than did ever
plummet sound," was no other than his own. A
worthier consummation of the great magician's
career cannot be desired ; and though " Henry the
Eighth " was probably later than "The Tempest,"
being described as a new play in June 1613,
Fletcher's share in it is so considerable that it
hardly counts.

None of Shakespeare's pieces stands so near
to " The Tempest " in style, metre, and general
cast of thought as does. " The Winter's Tale,"
and hardly any literary historian now doubts that
they were written nearly at the same time. In
one point of view, indeed, " The Midsummer
Night's Dream " presents a greater superficial
analogy to " The Tempest," that marvellous poetical invention which creates in Puck and Ariel
supernatural beings " more real than living man ; "

but this is not a gift indicative of any particular period in Shakespeare's career. It was rather an integral constituent of his genius, capable of being called into activity at his will. The points which really do assign "The Tempest" and "The Winter's Tale" to the same period are those characteristic traits of a veteran poet, a cheerful and reconciled view of life, and an especial complacency in traits of girlish innocence. After Imogen, also a creation of the poet's latter years, Perdita and Miranda are perhaps the most attractive of any of his female characters. But this especial charm is realised by an especial method, betokening a profound acquaintance with theatrical art, and a mastery only attainable by continual practice. Without apparent effort he grasps a character, indelibly fixed, so to speak, in the very moment of disappearance. Nothing more frail, fleeting, and apparently unimportant can be conceived than Perdita and Miranda, and yet they are more winning than the elaborately portrayed female personages of his earliest plays. The seeming artlessness is in truth the perfection of art. This characteristic trait, taken in connection with the metrical tests, not always reliable, but here convincing, establishes both the late and the contemporaneous composition of both pieces.

It would have been needless to dwell upon a

point so generally admitted if the light which it throws upon the date of "The Tempest" had not been invariably overlooked. Editors continue to assign both dramas to 1610, and to ascribe priority now to one, now to the other, as it may happen, as though the question were insoluble. It admits, nevertheless, of proof that "The Tempest" must have been the later of the two. We have seen that it cannot have been produced before the storm at the Bermudas in 1610 was known in England, and that there is not the smallest necessity for supposing it to have been written immediately upon the publication of a pamphlet which Shakespeare may not have seen until long afterwards. The date of "The Winter's Tale," however, may be brought within narrow limits. It is universally considered to be later than "Cymbeline," and "Cymbeline" is with equal unanimity ascribed to 1609 or 1610. The first testimony of the existence of "The Winter's Tale" is that of Simon Forman, who was present at a performance of it in May 1611. The title of the piece bears no reference to any incident in the action, and unquestionably alludes to its production in the season of winter. It must therefore have appeared soon before or soon after the end of 1610. The composition of "The Tempest" could not have been begun before October in this year, and the supposition of its having been written, rehearsed, acted, and withdrawn between this date and Christmas is wholly untenable. It is not probable that Shakespeare would have commenced a new play before "The Winter's Tale" had run its course, and this was still on the stage in May 1611. "The Tempest," therefore, cannot have been produced before the latter half of 1611 at the earliest; and the interval between this date and the end of 1612 is assuredly not sufficient to constitute any objection to the date which we have advocated.

More important, however, than the question of date is the question of interpretation. If the composition of any of Shakespeare's dramas was prompted by an impulse from without, the knowledge of the cause is essential to the understanding of the effect. In the present instance, if the final cause of the existence of "The Tempest" were, indeed, the celebration of a royal wedding, much that was obscure becomes plain, much that seemed plain appears in a new light. All parties concerned rise in our estimation. We obtain more light than ever on the ready affluence of Shakespeare's imagination and the swift magic of his mind's inner workings. We discover in him not merely the inspiration of the bard, but the tact and dexterity of the courtier, and see him moreover in his proper place as the national poet, chosen to celebrate a public event of the first importance. James rises in our opinion inasmuch as, having to choose a chief poet, he chose so well; and Frederick and Elizabeth acquire a surer title to immortality as the unconscious originators of Ferdinand and Miranda than war and policy were destined to bestow upon the unlucky pair who lost an electorate in seeking a crown. Nor is the marvel of Shakespeare's creations diminished by the actual existence of their faint prototypes; nor are the serene wisdom and moral grandeur of the play less admirable because it does not exist for their sake, but for the sake of a young couple, as even better things have existed, and will exist.

THE POETRY OF COLERIDGE

THE POETRY OF COLERIDGE[1]

THE principle of this edition of Coleridge is intimated by the title, which promises not his poems but his poetry. He is no exception to the almost universal rule that the works of even the greatest poets include much which might be consigned to oblivion without detriment to their reputation. Such a course, however, is neither recommendable on all accounts, nor practicable on all occasions. The pebble of poetry is sometimes the pearl of biography; nor is it easy to recall what has once been given to the world under the auspices of a great name. The judgment of editors cannot be implicitly trusted; and the most judicious retrenchment exposes the publisher to the charge of having mutilated an author. Coleridge's wood, hay, and stubble must consequently continue along with his fine gold; and, by a curious paralogism, the only editions esteemed standard will be those where the abstract standard of excellence is dis-

[1] The Introduction to the writer's edition of Coleridge's poems in "The Muses' Library," published by Messrs. Lawrence & Bullen: 1898.

regarded. The only alternative hitherto attempted has been that of an anthology, and one has been prepared by the incomparably competent hands of Mr. Swinburne. Such a miniature collection, however, though proffering "infinite riches in a little room," cannot include everything on which the poet might rest his fame, or that the lovers of his poetry would wish to have in their hands. There is room for something intermediate—for an ampler and more generous collection where the rule is not so much the inclusion of the most beautiful as the exclusion of the most defective. Coleridge is a peculiarly favourable subject for an experiment of this nature, for an unerring test is supplied by himself. His poems lie as it were in two strata, which may be conveniently distinguished as eighteenth and nineteenth century deposits. Much of his early poetry is insignificant, not from want of genius but because composed under the influence of misleading and conventional precedents. Marvellous as was his intellectual power, he was still more eminent as a critic than as an original thinker ; and he did not discover what a world of inspiration lay around him until his meeting with Wordsworth. From that time Coleridge wrote like a poet by the grace of God : and all that the retrenching editor need do is to cancel all poems previous to this epoch, some few excepted which deserve preservation on special grounds; and to detach certain "dead leaves in the bay-leaf crown" of later years, in the shape of merely trivial or occasional pieces, or serious efforts to which the poet's failing energies were unequal. It is also necessary in an edition thus abridged to omit the original and translated dramas, in themselves most worthy of preservation, inasmuch as they would exact an entirely disproportionate space.

Coleridge's eventful life and varied genius do not admit of satisfactory treatment within moderate limits. Either the man must give way to the poet or the philosopher, or both of these must make room for the man. Coleridge's editors have usually preferred biography to criticism, and to this preference literature is indebted for three very able memoirs. Mr. Shepherd's is satisfactory in every respect. Mr. Ashe's would be more than satisfactory but for an abruptness conveying the impression of want of finish, with which in fact it is not chargeable. The last editor, the late lamented Mr. Dykes Campbell, has excelled his predecessors by the production of a perfect masterpiece of condensed biography. It seems useless to do again what has so recently been so excellently done. We shall assume the reader to be already fairly well acquainted with the leading incidents in Coleridge's life, and shall refer to

these merely as they illustrate his place as a poet.
His equally important position as a philosopher
does not concern us; nor have we at present much
to say upon him in his character as critic — the
character in which, with all our reverence for him
as a poet, we should on the whole be inclined to
pronounce him most memorable.

In all these capacities Coleridge presents himself
eminently as a *Bahnbrecher*, one who, although
receiving his own original impulse from another,
makes a way for successors. He might say with
his own "Ancient Mariner"—

> "I was the first that ever burst
> Into that silent sea."

If the application is not precisely appropriate, it
is because it seems to imply more energetic action
and more deliberate adaptation of means to ends
than lay in Coleridge. He was rather an avenue
for invasive light than a fire-bringing Prometheus;
or his relation to the world of thought and poetry
might be even better compared with that which
Shelley attributes to Phœbus in his character of
the Sun—

> "I am the eye with which the Universe
> Beholds itself, and knows itself divine."

He was not only an exemplar of the new age,

but its hierophant. Better than any contemporary
except Wordsworth, whose critical writings are too
much confined to the enforcement of particular
principles, he could expound as well as exhibit
the mighty change which had come over English
poetry since the proclamation of a new dispensa-
tion by the significant, though to most invisible,
apparition of Blake's " Poetical Sketches " in 1783.
Other poets seem, as indeed they were, the unconscious productions of an age of ferment, the
instruments and vehicles of irresistible forces,
"building better than they knew." Coleridge,
while as immediately inspired as any of them,
knows better whence he has come and whither
he is going. His frailties and his misfortunes
deprived him of the glory he might have attained
of being the supreme poet of his age, but he
remains its supreme critic. In another point of
view he is more interesting still. Decisively as
he has broken with conventional poetry in his
more important writings, no contemporary poet of
his rank has left so much verse composed in
obedience to conventional canons, and reproduc-
tive of the tone and spirit of the preceding age.
This is indeed mere accident, explicable by the
fact that his poetical vein flowed most freely in
early youth, and that, although, as he himself
informs us, guarded against the stock conven-

tionalities by the precepts of his master at Christ's
Hospital, he nevertheless produced a great amount
of verse before he had learned to discriminate
between subjects proper and improper for poetry.
The result is important, for it allows the comparison
of the schools of the eighteenth and the nineteenth
century as exhibited in the same person.

Of late years a reaction in favour of the
eighteenth century style in poetry has been ob-
servable in several quarters; among other indications of which may be named the preference
recently avowed on a public occasion by no less
a person than Mr. Balfour.   To a certain extent
this is perfectly legitimate, and indeed inevitable.
Every age treats its immediate predecessor as the
Roman miners treated the ore of Sardinia, gets
all it can out of it, and leaves a valuable residuum
to the ages to come.   The ore, once deemed exhausted, is taken up again, and found to be teeming
with unexpected wealth; hence a reaction astonishing to the dominant school of criticism of the
day, but entirely sane and laudable.   The revival
of interest in the old English drama in Coleridge's
time is a signal instance; and a similar revival
in favour of Dryden, Pope, and Addison would be
equally welcome.   But to exalt these eminent
writers at the expense of their successors, to represent them as the models of taste and the

pontiffs of an orthodox creed in art from which
these successors have apostatised, raises quite
another contention, which compels us to inquire
of its advocates, what is their definition of poetry?
Is it to them what, *teste* Shelley, it was to our
Coleridge—

> " He spoke of poetry, and how
>   Divine it was—a light, a love—
> A spirit which like wind doth blow
> As it listeth, to and fro,
>   A dew rained down from God above ;
>
> A power which comes and goes like dream,
>   And which none can ever trace—
> Heaven's light on earth—Truth's brightest beam.
> And when he ceased, there lay the gleam
>   Of those words upon his face."

Or is their ideal of poetry strong sense vigorously
expressed in resonant verse ?   That the poetry of
the eighteenth century, as a whole, belongs to this
latter class, is evident from the fact that the injury
which it suffers from conversion into prose is more
detrimental to its form than to its spirit.   Pope's sentences, divested of their rhymes and their cadences,
would certainly have suffered much ; but the loss
would be purely one of literary form, not of the
spiritual aroma which they never possessed.   But
turn Coleridge, or Shelley, or Keats into prose,
and we shall at once be conscious of having lost

something besides literary form, and obtained an infinitely less valuable residuum than the same process would have given in the case of Pope or Dryden. The conclusion is inevitable, that nineteenth century poetry has a soul, an essence, an aroma which eighteenth century poetry has not; and that the panegyrists of the latter at the expense of the former deceive themselves in imagining that their homage is given to poetry, while it is really rendered to intellect.

We have remarked that no writer upon Coleridge need hope to render full justice to his theme. Not only was Coleridge, as he has been most justly termed, a myriad - minded man, but the various branches of his intellectual activity so interlace that it is difficult to consider him long in any point of view without being insensibly led to another. Severe limitation is necessary if anything is to be effected in an essay of moderate length. We shall select a vein hitherto but little wrought in confining our attention to Coleridge's place in poetical literature as the incarnate transition, so to speak, from the eighteenth to the nineteenth century, summing up in his own person in the restricted field of English poetry that description of spiritual evolution which Goethe has exhibited on a large scale in his symbolical representation of Faust's and Helena's passage from the classical

into the mediæval age. The poetry of the eighteenth and the nineteenth centuries lie associated
within the covers of his writings, and the impressiveness of the contrast is enhanced by the absence
of any intermediate period. The transition from
Coleridge's first to his second manner is almost
instantaneous. An accurate discrimination between
what, for brevity's sake, we may term his inspired
and his uninspired work, is of the utmost importance to his fame as a poet. Most interesting too
are the inquiries under what influences this meta-
morphosis was effected with such suddenness ;
and why so brilliant an outburst was followed by
relapse, not indeed into his original manner, but
into almost absolute silence as a poet. These
questions cannot be overlooked, and are specially
appropriate for discussion in the preface to a
volume of selected poetry, although it may not
be possible to offer any entirely satisfactory reply
to them. The one point absolutely certain, and
it is one of supreme importance, is that the verdict of the greatest of English critics, evinced by
the surest of tests, his own practice, has been
given in favour of the poetry of the nineteenth as
compared with that of the eighteenth century.

No greater service could be rendered to Coleridge's poetical fame than to bring this fact clearly
into light. Like all his great contemporaries, except

E

Shelley, he suffers from the large proportion of inferior matter among his really exquisite and divine work. The same is the case with Byron, Wordsworth, and Keats; but the explanation is different in every instance. With Byron it is mainly the fitfulness and frequent lapse of genuine inspiration. It was only now and then that his imagination was sufficiently ardent to fuse and kindle the matter cast into its furnace. The great inequality of Wordsworth may be attributed partly to his having continued writing during nearly the whole of his life; partly to the inherent defects of plan in his long poems; chiefly, perhaps, to the self-esteem which forbade him to conceive that anything which he had touched could be devoid of value. Few poets have amended or tried to amend more; but few have retrenched less. The cause of the inequality of Keats is merely the youthful inexperience inseparable from his first poetical ferment. Had he spent a life of average duration in the full exercise of poetical activity, the crudities of his first attempts would be no more remembered than the similar extravagances or insipidities of Tennyson; but his early death, by magnifying their proportion to the general bulk of his writings, has invested them with a factitious importance. Coleridge's less interesting poetry might also be described as the product of youthful inexperience; but its genesis and its substance differ widely from Keats's. The latter's failures are the failures of inspiration trying its unfledged wings. Coleridge's shortcomings cannot be justly described as failures, for they fully attain the writer's standard of excellence, but that standard is low. The immature Keats is an innovator and iconoclast, bent on destroying the models which the immature Coleridge follows with dutiful humility. Keats has nothing of the eighteenth century about him; Coleridge begins as an eighteenth - century poet. Keats pursues a gradual course of development, harmonious and consistent with itself; Coleridge undergoes a sudden conversion and a complete regeneration. Hence, while Keats's " first blights," as he called them, though made by accident to appear more important than they really are, can never be wholly dissociated from the general body of his work, Coleridge's early poetry need not be taken into account at all in our estimate of his poetical genius. It greatly concerns Coleridge to bear this in mind, for clearly it makes the greatest difference to any writer's fame whether he is regarded as the fountain of an ocean of verse of the most various degrees of merit, or whether our estimate of him is formed entirely by a consideration of a phial of some of the most quintessential poetry in the world. This is not now contested by any one. When we think of Coleridge as a poet we think of " The Ancient Mariner," of " Christabel," of " Kubla Khan," of "Genevieve," of " The Nightingale " and its companion blank verse idylls. We do not think in the least of " Religious Musings," and the other poems produced before the days of the Lake School. But many of our ancestors thought very differently. At the beginning of the nineteenth century the taste of the eighteenth century was naturally still in the ascendant, and would, in all probability, have continued to rule much longer but for the influence of Scott and Byron. These poets, though not so deeply or truly inspired as some of their contemporaries, irresistibly commanded attention by their vigour and their successful extension of the sway of poetry over the adjacent domain of fiction. They compelled the old-fashioned critics to praise where on their own principles they ought to have condemned, and thus made a breach for Wordsworth and Coleridge to enter in their wake, as Shelley and Keats afterwards in theirs. But there was a time when the criticism which had inconsistently recognised Scott and Byron was so far from consenting to go any further, that these productions of Coleridge which afford the present age the most exquisite delight, and upon which his claim to poetical greatness is

now entirely and universally based, were singled
out as proofs that he was no poet at all.   Said the
Edinburgh Review :—

"Upon the whole, we look upon this publication
(containing 'Christabel,' 'Kubla Khan,' and 'The
Pains of Sleep') as one of the most notable pieces
of impertinence of which the press has lately been
guilty, and one of the boldest experiments that
has as yet been made upon the patience or understanding of the public.   The other productions of
the Lake School have generally exhibited talents
thrown away upon subjects so mean that no power
of genius could ennoble them ; or perverted and
rendered useless by a false theory of poetical
composition.   But even in the worst of them, if
we except the 'White Doe' of Mr. Wordsworth
and some of the Laureate odes, there were always
some gleams of feeling or of fancy.   But the thing
now before us is utterly destitute of value.   It
exhibits from beginning to end not a ray of genius ;
and we defy any man to point out a passage of
poetical merit in any of the three pieces which it
contains, except, perhaps, the following lines, and
even these are not very brilliant."

If Hazlitt was really the writer of this astound-
ing deliverance it cannot have been wholly sincere,
and must have been largely inspired by spite and
animosity.   Yet he must have felt that he was

expressing an opinion not likely to provoke the dissent of the generality, and in fact his review passed the editorial censorship of Jeffrey, and excited few complaints except from the luckless victim. Men clearly perceived that a new element had come into poetry irreconcilable with the traditional standard of excellence, and that there was no room for both. Coleridge, then, has the unique distinction among the poets of his time, of himself exemplifying the antagonistic styles within the compass of his own writings. This justifies the reprint of some of his poetry, which, at first sight, according to the standard of the present day, hardly seems to deserve the distinction. It is of quite another order to the inferior poetry of Wordsworth or Byron, its inferiority is not that of high power impaired by old age, or mere iteration of a message already delivered, or of brilliant talent striving to fill the place of genius, it is that of genius as yet unawakened, and syllabling the old tongue from ignorance of the new. Hence, though worthless as poetry, it is of permanent value as a document, and possesses an importance far exceeding the inferior work of the poets just named. We see in it what we do not see in them, how men of true genius would have written if the great awakenings of the Romantic School and the French Revolution had never taken place, and are able to gauge in some degree our intellectual indebtedness to these mighty mutations. The contrast is the more instructive, as the early poems are by no means unpoetical. There is scarcely one which does not give evidence of having proceeded from a true poet. The cause of their unquestionable inferiority is the inferiority of the language, not so much in particular phrases as in the general cast of diction. It is as though a painter had sought to express a subject which required to be painted in oil through the medium of water-colours. The distinction cannot be accurately conveyed in a phrase, but we should not be far wrong if we said that here, and here only, Coleridge is conventional. He writes in the manner which he found to prevail when he commenced poetical composition. His originality had not carried him to the length of fashioning a new style for its expression. Individuality he certainly has: one can always be sure that the poems are Coleridge's and not another's; but the peculiar impress of the author is much less distinct than that of even so imitative a poet as Tennyson's upon his early writings. The same may be remarked in a field where he was more original still, 'his prose criticism. Coleridge's individuality may always be recognised here, but it is not the robust individuality of a Macaulay or a Carlyle.

Perhaps in this comparative inability to assert himself forcibly, while lavishing the most exquisite poems and the most subtle criticisms, we find the secret of Coleridge's strength, as well as of his weakness. Splendid as was his imagination, potent as was his intellect, these were not in the highest sense creative. Rather was he receptive and susceptible. It is significant that of all great English poets he should have been the greatest critic. Dryden, Wordsworth, Shelley, Arnold, all excelled in this department, but all must yield the palm to Coleridge. Now, although the highest criticism is in a sense original, as bringing to light what was previously unseen, it is unoriginal in this, that it must be waked into activity by another mind. Criticism, like hope, cannot live without an object. It is, of course, possible that the passionate conviction of a very independent and self-sufficing poet may throw him upon criticism, but he will hardly, like Coleridge, take to it as a congenial element. One can scarcely imagine Dante jotting down criticisms on the margins of his books, though his footprints might possibly have been sometimes tracked by the vestiges of rent leaves. Coleridge annotated everything, with most charming and profitable results, but in so doing showed that his was one of the class of minds which require to be impregnated. What he was as a commentator, he also was in original composition. He slid naturally into the style which he found current around him, and required to be emancipated from it by a mind of more inventiveness and vigour, and nearer than his to the essential truth of things. There can be no doubt that this influence proceeded from William and Dorothy Wordsworth. Coleridge's poems, in a revised form and with many retrenchments, had appeared very shortly before he came to know Wordsworth, otherwise than by a casual *rencontre*. "Nothing in the volume," says Mr. Dykes Campbell, "gives the least hint that Coleridge's hand was already on the latch of the magic casements which were to open on the perilous seas sailed by the 'Ancient Mariner,' and the fairy lands of 'Christabel' and 'Kubla Khan.'" Neither, it may be added, is there anything to suggest the less daringly imaginative, but not less beautiful, blank verse performances of Coleridge's best period, "The Nightingale," "Frost at Midnight," "Fears in Solitude," and so many more. The capacity for such composition came to him after he became acquainted with the Wordsworths.

Wordsworth assuredly did not teach Coleridge out of a book, and Coleridge's regeneration can be ascribed to nothing else than the perception that his friend was leading where he could follow him.

He came after Wordsworth as one bird might follow another through an open window—a bird of more gorgeous plumage certainly, though not of sweeter voice. In truth a great revolution had been wrought in imaginative literature, and the only question was how long it would take the new ideas to become dominant. It would be interesting, but beyond our present scope, to trace them back to their germs in Rousseau and others; it will be more to the purpose to inquire under what aspect the reform presented itself to the men who initiated it, Wordsworth and Coleridge. Briefly, their object may be said to have been to enforce a return to Nature. The most obvious announcement of this principle to the ordinary reader was the revolution in poetic diction, the discarding of merely conventional poetic language, and the reversion to a natural simplicity of speech which, especially in Wordsworth, frequently wore the semblance of baldness. But this was merely a symptom : the essential fact was that English poetry, with a few exceptions, had drifted away from Nature, and that the reformers wished to bring them together again. It had ceased to be what Milton declares poetry ought to be—sensuous ; and become intellectual, and intellect stands a remove further from Nature than sense does. Throughout Coleridge's early poems there is hardly a trace of any joy in Nature

for her own sake, or any use for her except as
affording ornaments for human emotions and
abstract thoughts. Stars and flowers are indeed
introduced, but in such language as might have
been equally well used by one who had seen
neither. There is a total absence of that minute
observation which may indeed be carried too far
when the detail is suffered to become more important than the object, but which is at all events
welcome as a proof that the poet has seen what
he describes. But the later pieces are full of
exquisite description clearly derived from actual
contact with the object. He tells us in " Frost at
Midnight " that when a boy at school he had
often gazed intently at the film upon the fire-
bar which was supposed to announce the advent
of a stranger, but never before 1797 had it
occurred to him to find poetical worth in anything so trivial. And now, with what felicity it
is introduced to heighten the impression of perfect
stillness !

> " The thin blue flame
> Lies on my low-burnt fire, and quivers not ;
> Only that film which fluttered in the grate
> Still flutters there, the sole unquiet thing."

Never until very recently had he imagined a
training up with Nature for himself or others.

Now, after deploring his own education "mid cloisters dim," he exclaims:—

> " But thou, my babe ! shalt wander like a breeze
> By lakes and sandy shores, beneath the crags
> Of ancient mountain, and beneath the clouds,
> Which image in their bulk both lakes and shores
> And mountain crags : so shalt thou see and hear
> The lovely shapes and sounds intelligible
> Of that eternal language, which thy God
> Utters, who from eternity doth teach
> Himself in all, and all things in himself."

Once more, Coleridge might at any time have predicted "therefore all seasons shall be sweet to thee," though it may be doubted whether he would have expressed the thought so simply, tersely, and musically.   But it is not probable that before coming under Wordsworth's influence, he would have thought of so expanding it as to wind up " Frost at Midnight" with a general panorama in miniature of the whole year, produced by a dexterous selection of striking picturesque circumstances, and enabling him to conclude the poem with no less dignity than it began:—

> " Whether the summer clothe the general earth
> With greenness, or the redbreast sit and sing
> Betwixt the tufts of snow on the bare branch
> Of mossy apple-tree, while the nigh thatch
> Smokes in the sun-thaw ; whether the eave-drops fall

Heard only in the trances of the blast,
Or if the secret ministry of frost
Shall hang them up in silent icicles,
Quietly shining to the quiet moon."

The dry bones now live indeed. If we compare this with even the best descriptive verse of the eighteenth-century school, or such as Coleridge himself was writing a year or two previously, we are conscious of a great deliverance, an emergence into a higher and purer region. It is not a mere advance in a normal development, like the successive volumes of Tennyson, but is an absolute elevation of the entire poetic personality into "an ampler æther, a diviner air." Previously the poet has excelled in those departments which would have equally befitted a good writer of prose; his present performances have so little in common with prose that, were they even despoiled of their metrical form, they would still be poetry. They are better adapted than anything else in our language to exhibit the fundamental distinction between poetry in its purest form and the thought or narrative whose claims to the title of poetry are metrical expression and artificial diction. They have thus the merit of bringing to the plainest issue the question between the poetry of the intellect and the poetry of the imagination. Was Kingsley right or wrong in deploring that

"Pope and plain sense had gone out, and Shelley and the seventh heaven come in?"

Coleridge enables us to answer this question decisively. He has set both the old and the new wine before us, and we find the new better. This is now undisputed. There was an admirable consistency about the Edinburgh Reviewer who could see no merit whatever in Coleridge's later poetry. Such a person had a perfect right to prefer the poetry of the eighteenth century. But this position is no longer tenable. The man who seriously thought "Religious Musings" finer than "Christabel" would not be argued with, he would be ignored. All, whatever their school or their sympathies, concur in allowing that the poems which Coleridge composed in perfect emancipation from conventional restraints are much better than those which he wrote while still in subjection to them. It is inconceivable that he should have been an ordinary writer as long as he composed on correct principles, and inspired as soon as he began to go wrong. To admit—and everybody does—the vast superiority of the poetry which he produced after his acquaintance with Wordsworth to that which he had composed prior to that date, is virtually to surrender the cause of the pseudo-classic school.

This conclusion, unimpeachable as regards the
merits of the rival schools, may be perverted if
it is made an index to the personal merits of
their chief representatives. It does not follow
that Wordsworth and Coleridge were endowed
with more powerful minds than Dryden and
Pope because they have given us greater poetry.
From one point of view it may be argued that
the poet is the creature of his age—that as
Shakespeare himself must have found another
manifestation for his genius than the drama if
he had lived in the time of Augustus — so
Dryden and Pope would have been greater Cole-
ridges and Wordsworths if they had flourished
at the beginning of the nineteenth century, and
vice versâ. When it is considered how great a
Dryden Byron would have made, and what
curious affinities exist between the genius of
Pope and the genius of Tennyson, this view
cannot be dismissed as purely fanciful. It may
also be contended that poetical genius is not
the highest conceivable endowment, and that the
powers of reasoning and pointed expression
evinced in the writings of Pope and kindred
poets, set them above writers admittedly superior
to them in melody, fancy, and imagination. This
view deserves attention because it pervades much
of what is enforced and more of what is taken

for granted on the subject of poetry, and is not
without support from the critical writings of
Wordsworth and Coleridge themselves.   It may be
briefly defined as the utilitarian view of poetry, the
distinct preference of the *prodesse* to the *delectare*.

Is not this still the unacknowledged principle
of much of our poetical criticism ?   Few, it must
be feared, care for poetry as poetry and nothing
else.   We find poets eulogised or censured for
their views of life, for their speculative opinions,
for the supposed influence of their writings, salutary or otherwise, not at all for their poetry.
It does not seem to be recognised that poetry
is an entity as real and as independent of other
entities as form or colour are independent of
weight and size.   It seems to be overlooked that
while the merit of a poem is undoubtedly enhanced if the writer's ideas are true as well as
poetical, just as, *cæteris paribus*, the embodiment
of a fine conception in marble is preferable to
an equally fine embodiment in wax, the standard
of merit is not the truth but the poetry.   Poetry
in a poem, though it can never be forgiven for
infidelity to the truth of nature or of human
nature, can exist perfectly well with a very moderate amount of conformity to truth as ascertained
by the speculative intellect.   The charm, other
than that of its verbal merits, of the induction

to Tennyson's "Lotus Eaters," for example, would disappear if the drowsy Libyan afternoon were other than the poet has painted it; but the most complete demonstration of the vanity of belief in personal immortality would leave the poetical beauty of "Crossing the Bar" exactly where it is. One of the great poems of the world is founded upon an absurd belief, the generation of the universe by the fortuitous collision of atoms, yet the merit of Lucretius as a poet is not in the least impaired by the fallacies of his philosophy. It may be true that he would have been a still better poet with a sounder cosmogony; but the criticism does not affect his genius, but the material in which it wrought. Conversely, Plato's "Republic" and Darwin's "Origin of Species" would have been contemptible compositions if they had been expressed in sorry verse, although their intellectual power might have been exactly the same. This should be perfectly obvious, yet how rarely do we see a poet judged as a poet! Wordsworth is preferred to Shelley by those who regard his ideas as more profound and sane than his rival's, not as a thinker or a moralist, which, granting the premises, would be legitimate, but as a poet. Shelley in his turn is preferred to Keats, because he expressed views and sympathies to which Keats was a stranger,

F

a circumstance which indeed renders him more interesting as a man and more important as a writer, without in the least proving that he was the better poet. Goethe endured quarantine until a very obtuse set of readers tardily satisfied themselves that "Faust" was neither immoral nor impious; and we have just seen Shakespeare excommunicated by Tolstoi for tepidity as a democrat. It is quite possible to protest against such vagaries without becoming committed to the opposite and equally pernicious theory of "art for art." It is by no means true that the intellectual outfit of a poet and the moral purpose of his work are matters of indifference. Let two writers of equal genius work on the same topic, and the finer work will indubitably be produced by him whose moral tone is the higher, and whose moral purpose is the more intense. But suppose them of unequal gifts—let one be endowed with divine madness from the Muses, and the other with nothing but moral enthusiasm, and the work of the former, whatever its shortcomings, will be great and precious, and that of the other, in so far as concerns its claim to rank as poetry or art, absolutely worthless.

If this is the case it is obvious that the claims of the Dryden-Pope school to precedence on the ground of poetry are invalid, and that the supe-

riority which their admirers claim for them can
only be asserted, if at all, in the sphere of intellect. This is not to affirm that Dryden and
Pope were not very considerable poets, but poetry
is not the first consideration with them. Their
most splendid passages owe their splendour to
exactly the same qualities as confer the same distinction upon Macaulay's prose—judicious choice
of words, skilful disposition of them for rhetorical
effect, sonorous utterance, cogent sense. All admirable qualities, but present in an even greater
degree in the Philippics of Demosthenes. We
cannot, therefore, accept them as models for an
age that follows after poetry. Their useful function
is the subordinate one of schoolmasters, not pre-
ceptors of the eternal principles of art, but powerful curbs on the extravagances of enthusiasm, and
monitors of the importance of good style and good
sense. The essential spirit of poetry cannot be
imbibed from any human teacher, but it can be
displayed, and probably no poet exhibits it so
clearly as Coleridge in his most exquisite poems.
Here we have, so to speak, the chemical rays
the spectrum of poetry, intense and subtle beyond
the rest, but less capable of being yoked to useful ends. As the photographic power inherent in
the chemical ray slumbers until it falls on the
right material, so the charms of Coleridge's best

verse are wasted on all save delicate and sensitive minds, and their most fervent admirers can point to no such tangible influences from them as accompany the study of Wordsworth and Shelley. Few, indeed, have more profoundly influenced their epoch than Coleridge, but this influence does not proceed from the best and highest, and, in truth, his criticisms excepted, the only quite satisfactory part of his literary activity, but from his comparatively feeble utterances in prose, mere fragments and suggestions of what he might have achieved as a thinker. These have nevertheless produced important effects, while his really inspired and perfect work has given the world little else than pleasure. There cannot well be a stronger proof that the place of a poet is not to be determined by its conformity to an utilitarian standard. Coleridge possessed a magnificent intellect, and his writings have been most serviceable to mankind; yet his greatest performances, those on which his fame must in the main rest, are those in which there is least of utility, and least of merely intellectual power. We must therefore conclude that poetry is neither exalted utility nor sublimated intellect, but an entity of itself, distinct from and independent of both, though capable of harmonious and advantageous alliance with them; and must come back to Shelley's definition, already cited, as expressing the sober sense, no less than the imaginative aspect of the matter. It is, of course, evident, and this Coleridge and Shelley would have fully granted, that the poet cannot always dwell in a realm of pure imagination, and that in proportion as he stoops to sublunary things he must approve himself conversant with the ordinary affairs of the world. It would, for example, have been idle for Goethe to have written his "Tasso," or Shelley his "Cenci," without some knowledge of the Italy of the end of the sixteenth century. But this power would have been just as much needed by the historian who should have essayed to present a picture of the time. It is consequently not poetry, but a gift essential to the manifestation of poetry in certain departments, especially the dramatic. It is also manifest that this faculty of vivid realisation, although a most valuable endowment, is not pre-eminently an intellectual one, since Wordsworth and Coleridge, the deepest thinkers of their age, possessed it in but a limited measure, while it is conspicuous in Scott and Byron.

Coleridge sometimes persuaded himself that his poetry was the product of serious and deliberate effort. "With this view," he says, "I wrote 'The Ancient Mariner.'" This may be read in the light of Mr. Dykes Campbell's dry comment on a similar asseveration, "In *Biographia Lite-raria*, Coleridge gave what he was then willing to believe were his reasons for writing these parodies." Coleridge would have us believe that he and Wordsworth had formed a scheme of joint action, in which his own part would have been "to transfer from our inward nature a human interest and semblance of truth sufficient to procure for shadows of imagination that willing suspension of disbelief for the moment which constitutes poetic faith." Writing, however, to Davy near the very time (October 1800), he accounts for the non-appearance of "Christabel" in the second volume of "Lyrical Ballads" on the ground that the poem was in direct opposition to the very purpose for which "Lyrical Ballads" were published, which is defined to be "the application of extraordinary passions to the incidents of common life." We learn from the matter-of-fact and veracious Words-worth that the impulse to composition, so far as tangible, was the *magister artis, ingenique largitor :* —"We had both determined to write some poetry for a monthly magazine, the profits of which were to defray the expenses of a little excursion we were to make together." There is no reason to doubt that this prosaic need actually prompted the com-position of one of the most inspired poems in our language, but it was the mere casual accident which

liberated forces long slowly accumulating. The
need returned, but the inspiration did not accompany it. In 1800, Coleridge, by his own account,
was unable to make any progress with the second
part of "Christabel" until, dining out, "somehow
or other" he "drank so much wine that I found
some effort and dexterity requisite to balance
myself on the higher edge of sobriety." It is to
be hoped that his dexterity was as successful in
the estimation of others as in his own. However
this may have been, the next day "Christabel"
started afresh, on a lower level than of old, yet
not unsuccessfully; although, "seeing double,"
Coleridge persuaded himself that he had written
twice as many verses as he really had. These
anecdotes are not very compatible with a preconceived purpose either of elevating ordinary things
or of bestowing reality upon the creatures of the
imagination. Coleridge was simply a great lyrical
poet, who, throughout his *annus mirabilis* of 1797,
and for some time afterwards, was in a state of
joyous exaltation from the new world of poetry
which had been disclosed to him by Wordsworth.
As the force of the new influence waned, his powers
waned with it : though never entirely forsaken by
inspiration, he was never again the poet of that
glorious time. But one thing he never did, he
never recurred to the style of his early composi-

tions.   He always wrote as the Coleridge of 1797, if fitfully and with diminished power :

> "For he on honeydew had fed
> And drunk the milk of Paradise."

The loss which English poetry has sustained by the collapse of Coleridge's poetical productiveness is beyond calculation, almost beyond conception.   He lived until 1834.   If every year of his life had yielded such a harvest as 1797, he would have produced a greater amount of high poetry than all his contemporaries put together.   In so far as his impoverishment resulted from actual desertion by the inward impulse, no blame can be imputed to him, "the wind bloweth where it listeth."   But external causes certainly co-operated, which might have been eluded.   One was his growing devotion to philosophy, and what was worse, his constant indecision whether he would be a philosopher or a poet.   He never perceived that he was, in a sense, more of a critic than a thinker, and that, just as he had required a Wordsworth, a man on the whole less gifted than himself, to impregnate his mind with the germs of a higher poetry than he had hitherto known, so his best powers of thought were called forth by assent or antagonism to the opinions of others, frequently texts of little worth in comparison with the commentary. He was not content to inscribe the margins of musty folios with penetrating criticism, or to lavish the unconsidered opulence of his table-talk, but he was for ever planning, and persuading himself that he had all but executed, some marvellous reconciliation of all contradictory systems which would leave no one any excuse for differing from anybody else. This visionary project was responsible for much of Coleridge's unproductiveness in poetry and other departments; preoccupation with it was an upas, which suffered nothing else to spring up in its neighbourhood. It is remarkable that two of the greatest geniuses of the age were also fascinated by it, and were preserved from wasting their time, one by ill-health, the other by the second of the causes which to so great an extent paralysed Coleridge— opium. " I consider poetry," says Shelley, "very subordinate to moral and metaphysical science, and but for my health," &c. De Quincey in his youth planned a philosophical treatise on a larger scale than Coleridge's to which he intended to devote his whole life. His talent for metaphysical research was probably at least equal to Coleridge's, but who that knows his caprice and fastidiousness can doubt that the result would have been a mass of extracts and memoranda for an unwritten book ? Opium came to the rescue, bracing up De Quincey's energies by depriving him of his little independence, and compelling him to work or starve. Necessity forced him upon just the kind of work which suited him best. Obliged to write for periodicals, the needs of the situation debarred him from the endless research and dismaying prolixity so dear to his natural inclinations, and enriched our literature with a series of cabinet pictures which would have remained unfinished if attempted on heroic scale. But no necessity could cure Coleridge of forming schemes beyond his capacity to execute, and the time wasted in dreaming over them, and the discouragement and self-reproach begotten of their continual failure, must be reckoned among the causes which impeded the full exertion of his powers. In so far as opium contributed to this everlasting reverie and chronic impotence of will, it was assuredly among his enemies. This need not have been so; there was no fatality in the matter. Another important cause of the comparative torpidity of Coleridge's poetical power was, in our opinion, a step which he need not have taken. If a period could be fixed for the duration of his flourishing epoch, his pride and prime of genius, it would begin with his acquaintance with Wordsworth and end with his final depart from Nether Stowey, June 1800. He assigned various reasons for the step, but the true reason was that

given by Mrs. Sandford, "Coleridge would never
have been content to live in the West of England
while Wordsworth was living in the North," supplemented perhaps by another, his admiration for
Dorothy Wordsworth, who would in all probability
have become his wife but for the unfortunate pre-
cipitation, under strong pressure from well-meaning
and much-mistaken Southey, which had already
made him the husband of an excellent woman
entirely unsuited to him. Had this union taken
place it is safe to affirm that Coleridge's history
would have been entirely different, that the finest
of his poems would not be exquisite fragments,
and that his mind would not be best discerned in
the mirror of other intellects. But it was too
late; Dorothy could now at best be but a dis-
turbing influence; Wordsworth's chary sympathy
was a poor substitute for Tom Poole; one instinctively feels the warm, genial son of opulent Devon
misplaced in the stern though grand environment
of the lakes where Wordsworth was so perfectly
at home. From this time ill-health, opium, pecuniary embarrassment, domestic jars, and painful
estrangements increase and multiply, and although
Coleridge's genius remains essentially as great as
ever, its power of adequate manifestation dwindles
more and more.

The period which we have signalised as that of

Coleridge's most brilliant poetical activity comprises " The Ancient Mariner," " Christabel," " Kubla Khan," " Genevieve," " The Nightingale," " Frost at Midnight," " This Lime-Tree Bower my Prison," " Fears in Solitude," " Ode to France," " Lines in the Hartz Forest," and " The Wanderings of Cain." Were these removed from his works he would lose all title to be esteemed a great poet. The translation of " Wallenstein " falls within the same period. Never again did he rise to an equal height, except in two exquisite but very brief poems, the inspiration of his advanced years. Still, Coleridge's long third period (1800–1834) is not senility, and is not decadence. Save in the two beautiful pieces just alluded to (" Youth and Age," and " Work without Hope ") he remains upon a lower level than of old, his wing has lost the power to upbear him to the seventh heaven of poetry. But within his own sphere he is still perfect. If we knew nothing of him but " The Garden of Boccaccio " (1828), we should still say that a poet of rare elegance and charm had graced the latter days of George IV. Poems more exquisitely finished and absolutely perfect in their way than " The Butterfly " (1815), and " Love, Hope, and Patience in Education " (1829), will not be found in English literature. They are, moreover, not mere intellectual exercises, but genuine inspirations, showing that Coleridge's poetical faculty remained undebased, though it had no longer the energy for any conspicuous manifestation of its existence.

It will be understood that any regrets here expressed for the limited and fragmentary character of Coleridge's performances as poet or thinker have reference not to the merit of the work in itself, but to its amount in comparison with what it lay in him to have achieved. Any one of his best poems would suffice for the immortality of any poet : taken altogether, they place him upon an eminence inferior to none of his great contemporaries. But the man's powers were gigantic, and it would have been easy for him to have been the central sun of the constellation of his brilliant period. That he failed to be this is perhaps as much the fault of others as of himself. An ingenious attempt has been made in our time to classify the souls of poets as either masculine or feminine ; and although the principles adopted cannot have been sound—for the impetuous and indomitable Shelley is petticoated under its operation—a species of sex in souls is hardly to be disputed. Among the poets those may with justice be described as feminine who more or less require to be impregnated by contact with other minds, whether spirits of old speaking through books, or spirits incarnated in living men. The very sensitiveness of Keats's poetical temperament rendered him in a measure dependent: he usually wrote under the influence of some famous old poet—first Spenser, afterwards Milton, at the last, Dante. Coleridge is rarely imitative of another author, but his Muse required to be wooed by the sympathy of a kindred spirit. Wordsworth sufficed him for a time, but sympathy alone will not flourish without admiration; and although Coleridge was by no means exacting, Wordsworth, who thought " The Ancient Mariner " needed some apology, was honestly unable to enter into the airy and spiritual graces of his poetry. Dorothy Wordsworth, who might have been everything to him, was tied up from him by an iron knot; and it is most pathetic to see Coleridge, dimly conscious of his want, turning blindly about for his satisfaction to the most unlikely quarters, even to Alsop. He had the most sympathetic of friends in Charles Lamb, but the smaller minds of his day could not, with every good intention, satisfy his craving, and the greater men, except Shelley, who only knew him afar off, had no proper conception of his rank as a man of surpassing genius. One there was who might—or who might not—have supplied the lack of all the rest. If Coleridge, when in Germany, instead of spending his time at Hanover, had gone

straight to Weimar, the consequences might have
been momentous to himself and to English literature. It is by no means certain; Goethe could
be very blind and very unsympathetic. But had
it proved otherwise, had he appreciated Coleridge
at his worth, he might by admiration, by reproof,
by example, above all by the contagion of a common interest in the highest things, have infused
the needful fire and confidence into him, have
checked his self-indulgence and self-deception, and
prevented the misuse of his powers. Coleridge's
very weakness and dependence would have insured the triumph of Goethe's salutary influence.
" Faust" would have been rendered into English
with as great success as "Wallenstein"; and it
might have come to be said that not even Goethe's
" Faust" was so great a work as Goethe's Coleridge.

But although Coleridge's poetical production fell
in quantity far below what might have been hoped
from him, the better portion of it surpassed all
reasonable expectation in its quality. Before him,
there seemed no probability that English poetry
would be enriched by "Christabel" and "The
Ancient Mariner." It might have been predicted,
especially after the appearance of Burns, Blake,
and Chatterton, that the reaction from the formality
and artificiality of the reigning taste must evolve
an antagonistic type somewhat resembling Words-

worth's; the revival of interest in the Elizabethans betokened the appearance of a Keats; and the Revolution could hardly fail to find laureates of the stamp of a Byron or a Shelley. But Coleridge could not have been foretold; his best vein is in the main independent of these and other contemporary movements; it is quintessential poetry, and that is all. As a consequence he has founded no school. There are no tendencies to imbibe, no mannerisms to copy. The only abiding trace of his influence, perhaps, is the English blank verse idyll as subsequently perfected by Tennyson, who would hardly have achieved such success if, while elaborating his verse to the last degree of artistic polish, he had not kept his comparatively artless predecessor continually in mind. It is, however, the greatest of mistakes to speak of Coleridge as a wasted force, the recipient of misused gifts, a man who accomplished little. As a prose writer, though achieving no one great work, he deposited the seeds of thought in innumerable minds. As a poet, to speak only of the aspect under which we have principally considered him, he has shown within the compass of his own writings what is and what is not poetry, and forced all professed admirers of poetry to consider whether she can exist without inspiration, and whether in speaking of poetic excellence they do not really mean the excellence of the ethical teacher, the advocate, the stylist, or some other merit equally capable of manifestation in prose. It is right to honour Dryden and Pope for what they were, but the man who would place them along with or above Coleridge as poets, must admit that he dissents from the opinion of the Greeks respecting poetry, and regards it as a form of intellectual exercise. Coleridge's themes, except in his early and now and then in his late period, are distinctly poetical; and none understand like him to create a perpetual feeling of enchantment by the constant but unobtrusive employment of the most beautiful and melodious words. As a painter and musician in speech he is surpassed by none of his contemporaries; and his "Ancient Mariner" and the first part of "Christabel" are related to the bulk of nineteenth-century poetry, down to the time of Rossetti, as "The Tempest" and "A Midsummer Night's Dream" are to the other plays of Shakespeare.[1]

[1] It has not been thought necessary to reprint the concluding paragraphs of this essay, which chiefly refer to the arrangement of Coleridge's poems adopted in the edition to which it was originally prefixed.

SHELLEY AND
LORD BEACONSFIELD

SHELLEY AND
LORD BEACONSFIELD[1]

SHELLEY undoubtedly possessed every quality necessary to constitute a perfect hero of romance, and it is a matter of some surprise that writers of fiction have not hitherto made more use of him. It is far from improbable that he will still figure in many works of imagination, but if so, it will probably be as the centre of ideal groups widely different from the actual environment of his life. The time when his actual history could be made the subject of a novel has gone by, the real incidents of his life are too well known for the romancer to tamper with, even if—which is not the case— he could hope by so doing to render them more romantic. There was a time of twilight, when they were so obscure or variously related as to invest a true history with some of the prerogatives of fiction. It was then that a man of genius, whose own career, if less adventurous than Shelley's was even more exceptional, essayed to shadow the

---

[1] A paper read to the Shelley Society, 1887.

poet forth to the public through the medium of a
romance. This was no less a person than Lord
Beaconsfield; and it is a matter of considerable
interest to ascertain how he performed his task,
and what qualifications he possessed in the shape
of special sympathy or special information. A
further inquiry worth making is how far his study
of Shelley reacted upon this remarkable man himself, and what traces, if any, it has left in his
writings.

It must at first sight seem a visionary endeavour
to establish any sort of affinity between Shelley
and Lord Beaconsfield. The differences between
the characters of the two men are so palpable that
they cast the actual though partial resemblance
entirely into the shade. The dissimilarity of their
respective careers is so great that it appears useless
to look for any likeness. We do not sufficiently
remember that Shelley's was merely the beginning
of a career, and that, though nothing could have
prevented Lord Beaconsfield from being a distinguished man, the particular kind of distinction he
attained might have been metamorphosed by circumstances. If the elder Disraeli had not forsaken
the faith of his fathers, the younger Disraeli would
not have entered Parliament until far advanced in
middle life, when the Corn Law question had been
solved, and there would have been no leap to

power for him from the prostrate body of Sir
Robert Peel, as the fox sprang out of the well on
the goat's shoulders. Debarred from practical politics, Disraeli might have given free course to those
revolutionary tendencies of his nature which the
necessities of political life suppressed, and been
famous as the keen, steady, and ruthless assailant
of many things which, as matters turned out, his
destiny enlisted him to defend. Shelley, on his
part, would very probably have entered Parliament
if he had lived to the period of the Reform Bill,
and though he could no more have been a great
parliamentary tactician than Disraeli could have
been a great poet, he would have been equally
eminent as an orator; his parliamentary career
would have been distinguished by just that persis-
tent indomitable resolution which made Disraeli
what it would never have made Shelley. If the
ideals of the two men seem at first sight almost
antagonistic, there is one very important point in
which they coincide. Which of the heroines of
modern fiction would Shelley have most admired?
We learn from Peacock that his favourite among
the heroines he did know was Brockden Brown's
Constantia Dudley; and the same qualities which
fixed his preference on her would have guided him
to the Theodora of Disraeli's "Lothair." She is in
truth one of the noblest creations of a modern

novelist; she impersonates all the traits which Shelley specially valued in woman; she is a maturer Cythna, a Cythna of flesh and blood. What is equally to the point, she is her creator's ideal also. Disraeli usually deals with his characters with easy familiarity, and, except when he is depicting a personal enemy, with amiable indulgence. He sees their foibles, nevertheless, and takes care that these shall not escape the reader. In Theodora alone there is nothing of this. She has captivated her creator, as Galatea captivated Pygmalion. There is not a single touch of satire in the portrait; it plainly represents the artist's highest conception of woman, which proves to be essentially the same as Shelley's.

More might be said on the points of contact between the poet and the statesman, but time is short and criticism long. We must confine ourselves to facts capable of verification, and consider—(1) The external evidence of Disraeli's acquaintance with Shelley. (2) Disraeli's estimate of Shelley as deduced from the portrait of the latter which he has given in "Venetia." (3) Traces of Shelley's influence on Disraeli's writings.

There is one great contemporary poet whom Lord Beaconsfield undoubtedly admired with enthusiasm. It is known with what eagerness he exerted himself in his latter days to promote the erection of a monument to Byron. In so doing he both expressed a conviction and discharged a debt. Byron had prompted " Contarini Fleming," a higher and purer ideal than " Vivian Grey." Byron had seen much in his Eastern wanderings, and by his " Hebrew Melodies " had constituted himself in some sort the laureate of Disraeli's own race. Whoever is interested in Byron, is interested in Shelley, if only as a member of the former's circle; and although Disraeli's knowledge of the real relations of the two poets was no doubt defective, he knew enough to be aware that they consorted as intellectual peers. But in truth he had special means of information. Readers of Shelley's letters will remember his account of Byron's valet, Tita Falcieri, " a fine fellow with a prodigious black beard, who has stabbed two or three people, and is the most good-natured looking fellow I ever saw." This personage had actually come into the service of the elder Disraeli. He had remained with Byron until his master's death, had then commanded a regiment of Albanians, and successively passed into the service of the younger and the elder Disraeli, closing his life in the enjoyment of *otium cum dignitate* as messenger at the India Office.[1] He was with Shelley at Lerici for a time, and is

---

[1] A portrait of him by Maclise will be found in Mr. Prothero's edition of Byron's Letters and Journals, vol. iv.

recorded to have had many anecdotes of him; and we may be sure that his master would not neglect such a source of information when writing the remarkable novel of which we are to speak immediately, in which Byron and Shelley are introduced. One other Shelleyan influence on Disraeli must not be omitted. This is Bulwer Lytton, intimately connected with Disraeli for several years after the latter's return from the East. Bulwer's estimate of Shelley, though too far in advance of the period to be termed conventional, was still shallow and inadequate. "You evidently admire him as a poet," he wrote to Jefferson Hogg, "far more than I think criticism warrants us in doing. He is great in parts; but, the 'Cenci' excepted, does not, in my opinion, effect a great whole." As editor of the *New Monthly*, however, Bulwer was the means of giving Hogg's reminiscences to the world; he was also on very friendly terms with Mrs. Shelley, and he cannot have failed to stimulate the curiosity which his friend and contributor Disraeli had already begun to entertain on the subject.

To these sources of information may be added another, of which it will be more convenient to speak further on.

When therefore, about the middle of 1836, Disraeli sat down to write "Venetia," he was not ill prepared to speak of Shelley, in so far as knowledge of his history and character went; and, as will be shown by-and-by, he possessed no inconsiderable acquaintance with his writings. In drawing Shelley's portrait, however, he resorted to a device which may almost be said to have been habitual with him. He did not wish his personages to appear mere servile transcripts of reality, and as invention was by no means his forte, and he actually was indebted for the pith and marrow of his novels to the observation of life, he was accustomed to avoid this imputation by fusing two characters into one, or rather by borrowing traits from one personage which he somewhat inartificially joined on to another. Thus in " Endymion," one of the leading characters is compounded of Cobden and Bright, certainly in unequal proportions. Having, therefore, in " Venetia " to introduce Byron as Lord Cadurcis, and Shelley as Marmion Herbert, he cuts Byron's relations with Lady Byron and " Ada, sole daughter of my house and heart," off from the character of Cadurcis, and superimposes them upon Herbert, leaving the rest unaltered. " The voice is the voice of Jacob, but the hands are the hands of Esau "; the situation is Byronic, but the character is Shelleyan. Looking at the character apart from the situation, we find that Herbert is drawn in conformity with the most orthodox Shelleyan tradition, precisely as

Mrs. Shelley and Trelawny and Hogg and Medwin
have agreed to represent the poet.   Not only is
Shelley thus delineated with substantial accuracy,
but the development of his mind and the history of
his writings are followed with a closeness which
shows that Disraeli has taken pains to master
the biographical information accessible to him.
The picture of Herbert's personal appearance is
Shelley's with a few picturesque touches super-
added, and representing him at a more advanced
age than he actually reached.   " His stature was
much above the middle height, though his figure,
which was remarkably slender, was bowed; not
by years, certainly, for his countenance, though
singularly pallid, still retained traces of youth.
His hair, which he wore very long, descended over
his shoulders, and must originally have been of a
light auburn colour, but was now severely touched
with grey.   His countenance was very pallid, so
colourless, indeed, that its aspect was almost
unearthly ; but his large blue eyes still glittered
with fire."   In another passage, Herbert is said to
have " looked like a golden phantom "—a phrase
which seems very likely to have been adopted from
some one who had actually seen Shelley.

Herbert, in his entrance upon life, is thus
delineated :—" Young, irresistibly prepossessing in
his appearance, with great eloquence, crude but

considerable knowledge, an ardent imagination, and
a generous and passionate soul." Like Shelley,
Herbert goes to Eton and Oxford, where "his
college life passed in ceaseless controversy with
his tutor." He is not expelled the University,
which would have interfered with the plot of the
novel; but as he is supposed to have quitted it in
his nineteenth year, he can hardly have taken a
degree. Like the Shelley of Hogg's reminiscences,
he is described as "a proficient in those scientific
pursuits which were then rare," and after leaving
the University secludes himself in his laboratory
and his dissecting-room as well as his study.
"While thus engaged, he occasionally flattered
himself that he might discover the great secret
which had perplexed generations," an evident
allusion to "Frankenstein." He thus confirms
himself in all the heresies which his Oxford tutor
supposed himself to have shaken, and becomes,
moreover, "a strenuous antagonist of marriage,
which he taught himself to esteem, not only as an
unnatural tie, but as eminently unjust towards that
softer sex who had so long been the victims of
man." But, as in Shelley's case, poetry gets the
upper hand of philosophy. The youthful poem
attributed to Herbert is a fusion of two of Shelley's
works. When we read that "he called into creation
that society of immaculate purity and unbounded

enjoyment which he believed was the natural inheritance of unshackled man," we are reminded of " Queen Mab"; but " the stanzas glittering with refined images and resonant with subtle symphony " are a description, and a very good description, of the " Revolt of Islam." With this poem also corresponds this further trait:—" In the hero he pictured a philosopher young and gifted as himself; in the heroine, his idea of a perfect woman." It is added, not unjustly as regards even the " Revolt of Islam," but with still closer application to " Prometheus Unbound": " These peculiar doctrines of Herbert, which, undisguised, must have excited so much odium, were more or less developed and inculcated in this work; nevertheless they were necessarily so veiled by the highly spiritual and metaphorical language of the poet that it required some previous acquaintance with the system enforced to be able to discover and recognise the esoteric spirit of his muse." The fate, therefore, of Herbert's early writings is represented as different from Shelley's, but not wholly unlike what Shelley's might have been if he had not begun with " Queen Mab." " The public," it is said, " read only the history of an ideal world, and of creatures of exquisite beauty, told in language that alike dazzled their fancy and captivated their ear. They were lost in a delicious maze of metaphor and music, and were proud to

acknowledge an addition to the glorious catalogue
of their poets in a young and interesting member
of their aristocracy." After, however, Herbert's
rupture with his wife, the particulars of which, as
already intimated, are borrowed from the history
of Byron, "his works were but little read and
universally decried. The general impression of the
English public was that Herbert was an abandoned
being of profligate habits; and as scarcely any one
but a sympathetic spirit ever read a line he wrote,
for, indeed, the very sight of his works was pollu-
tion, it is not very wonderful that this opinion was
so generally prevalent. A calm inquirer might
perhaps have suspected that abandoned profligacy
is not very compatible with severe study, and
might have been of opinion that a solitary sage
may be the antagonist of a priesthood without
denying the existence of a God. But there never
are calm inquirers."

This passage, as well as the general character
of the portrait, entitles, I think, Lord Beaconsfield
to a place among the honourable list of those who
have defended Shelley when the unfavourable
estimate of his character was by far the preponderating one. In fact, hardly any exception can
be taken to his portrait, except its defectiveness
in points with which it was hardly possible that
he should have been acquainted. His literary

estimate is less sound, yet even in its incomplete-
ness is in a sense welcome as proving that his
judgment of the man was not disabled by his
admiration of the poet. "There is," he makes
Herbert say, "a radical fault in my poetic mind,
and I am conscious of it. I am not altogether
void of the creative faculty, but mine is a fragmentary mind. I produce no whole. Unless you
do this you cannot last; at least you cannot
materially affect your species." This, it will be
noticed, is an echo of Bulwer's remark in his
letter to Hogg already quoted, and would seem
to indicate that the quality of Shelley's genius
had formed the subject of discussion between
Disraeli and his friend. The very conversation,
however, between Herbert and Cadurcis, from
which these observations were taken, shows that
if Disraeli was not a disciple of Shelley or an
adequate appraiser of his genius, he was yet a
student of his writings, for the most striking
passages—with a freedom which would justly have
subjected Disraeli to the imputation of plagiarism
if he had not put them into the mouth of Shelley
himself—are taken out of one of the least known
of his works. "And yet," says Cadurcis, "the age
of Pericles has passed away. Solve me the problem
why so unparalleled a progress was made during
that period in literature and the arts, and why

that progress, so rapid and so sustained, so soon received a check and became retrograde?" "It is a problem left to the wonder and conjecture of posterity," said Herbert. "Nothing of the Athenians remains except their genius; but they fulfilled their purpose. The wrecks and fragments of their subtle and profound minds obscurely suggest to us the grandeur and perfection of the whole." The conversation is pursued for some time in the same strain, and, like the above passage, is derived nearly verbatim from Shelley's "Discourse on the Manners of the Ancients," which was not published in an authorised shape for three years after the appearance of "Venetia." But a fragment, including these sentences, had, in 1833, been given to the world by Medwin in the Shelley Papers, and Disraeli must not only have studied this little ephemeral book with some care, but have had it in his possession when he wrote "Venetia." A still more striking quotation comes from the same source. The reader of Shelley who remembers that the "Defence of Poetry" was not published until 1840, may well start when he comes upon one of its most memorable dicta in the middle of "Venetia": "Poets are the unacknowledged legislators of the world." He may be thrilled, as Bertha in Tieck's wonderful tale is thrilled, when the knight to whom she has been recounting her history startles her with the name of the little dog, *Strohmian*, which she has never told, for she has herself forgotten it. But the explanation is simple. The remark which closes Shelley's " Defence of Poetry " is one which he frequently made in conversation, and Medwin, who often heard it from him, has repeated it in the Shelley Papers. Yet another citation from an unpublished work is also to be traced to Medwin's Shelley Papers. After deploring the fragmentary character of his own productions, as already mentioned, Herbert says, "What I admire in you, Cadurcis, is that, with all the faults of youth, of which you will free yourself, your creative power is vigorous, prolific, and complete; your creations rise fast and fair, like perfect worlds." This is from the "Sonnet to Byron," originally published in an imperfect form by Medwin in the Shelley Papers, where Shelley says (to use Medwin's text, the only one accessible to Disraeli) :—

> " My soul, which, as a worm may haply share
> A portion of the Unapproachable,
> Marks his creations rise as fast and fair
> As perfect worlds at the Creator's will."

About the same time that this was written, Shelley wrote to Gisborne of Byron's latest composition : "What think you of Lord Byron now? Space wondered less at the swift and fair creations of God when He grew weary of vacancy, than I at this spirit of an angel in the mortal paradise of a decaying body. So I think, let the world envy while it admires, as it may." Disraeli's representation of Herbert, then, admiring without envy the more popular productions of his friend Cadurcis, and awarding him an unmerited superiority of genius, as well as pre - eminence in contemporary reputation, is perfectly in accordance with fact. Was there any source from which he could have derived it besides the confused and not always reliable indications of Medwin? I think there may have been. There was a man then prominent in London society, who had known Byron and Shelley equally well, and had a perfect knowledge of the sentiments they respectively entertained for each other. I have been but once in the late Mr. Trelawny's company, but that single occasion was enough to convince me of the inexhaustibility of his stores of Byronic and Shelleyan anecdote, and of the general trustworthiness of his views of Shelley. I am not sure that as much could be said of his estimate of Byron, or of the members of the Pisa circle in general. But in Shelley's case no spleen or disappointment or fancied slight had marred the original clearness of his view, and I feel as sure that his report of Shelley's feelings towards Byron would be mainly correct, as that Disraeli, deeply

interested in both poets as he was, must have
turned Trelawny's acquaintance to account. Trelawny was intimate with Disraeli's friends, Lady
Blessington and Count D'Orsay, and that Disraeli
knew him about the time that he was writing
"Venetia," appears from a letter in his correspondence, dated July 1836, introducing an excellent
bon-mot of James Smith's: "What do you think
of Spain? Trelawny, who is a republican, is in
raptures. 'The Spaniards,' he says, 'are in advance of all countries; they have got their constitution of 1812.' Says James Smith, 'I wish I had
got mine.'"

The catastrophe of "Venetia" is the catastrophe
of Shelley, in which Byron also is involved. The
scene is laid at Lerici; the details are perfectly
accurate, and mainly derived from Trelawny's
account in Leigh Hunt's "Byron and his Contemporaries," supplemented, I imagine, with particulars gleaned in conversation. Byron plays the
part of Williams. "Lord Cadurcis was a fine
swimmer, and had evidently made strong efforts
for his life, for he was partly undressed. While
Captain Cadurcis leant over the body, chafing
the extremities in a hurried frenzy and gazing
intently on the countenance, a shout was heard
from one of the stragglers who had recently
arrived. The sea had washed on the beach

another corpse, the form of Marmion Herbert. It would appear that he had made no struggle to save himself, for his hand was locked in his waistcoat, where, at the moment, he had thrust the " Phaedo," showing that he had been reading to the last, and was meditating on immortality when he died."

It must, I fear, be admitted that " Venetia " is almost the weakest of Lord Beaconsfield's novels as a work of fiction, and that such interest as it possesses is mainly biographical. It is so close a copy of reality that the structure seems loose and inartificial, and the sequence of events capricious. The really artistic novelist is an eclectic artist who chooses out of life the events susceptible of treatment in fiction, and imparts to them the logical concatenation which the ordinary littlenesses of life obstruct or obscure. Disraeli has simply copied, and except by the rather clumsy device of fixing a piece of Byron upon Shelley, has made hardly an endeavour to combine or diversify. The domestic bereavement of Lord Lyndhurst, to whom the book is dedicated, has, he says, restrained him from offering any account of "the principles which had guided me in its composition." This must have been a meagre catalogue at best ; but the biographer redeems the novelist, and he is right in claiming credit for the endeavour "to shadow forth, though but in a glass darkly, two of the most renowned and refined spirits that have adorned these our latter days."

There is but one of Lord Beaconsfield's works in which it would be reasonable to seek for any considerable trace of the influence of Shelley, and in this we find it. Disraeli's "Revolutionary Epic" could hardly have been produced without some inspiration from the poet who had written the true revolutionary epic of the age in the "Revolt of Islam." Disraeli's epic bears its obligations to Shelley blazoned upon its front. Demogorgon, in Milton an anarch old, had been promoted in Shelley's "Prometheus Unbound" to the rank of a deity, the ultimate ground, in fact, of divine existence. Disraeli adopts the idea. His Demogorgon is the all-wise spirit before whom Magros and Lyridon, the contending genii of the mediæval and the modern order, Faith and Freedom, appear to plead their respective causes. The antagonism of these genii is clearly derived from the Eagle and Serpent of "The Revolt of Islam." The manner in which they present themselves, it must be owned, bears a somewhat burlesque resemblance to the contention of Michael and Satan in Byron's "Vision of Judgment." Which is Michael and which is Satan is hard to tell; nor perhaps had the author fully satisfied himself. For it is a marked peculiarity of Disraeli that to the revolutionary temperament which enabled him to write such audacious persiflage as the "Infernal Marriage" and to draw such characters as Theodora, he united a genuine reverence for the beauty of the ancient order—its chivalry, its feudalism, its monasticism; and it is to a great extent this doubleness of nature which renders his works so interesting, and earns pardon for two of the worst defects an author can have—flippancy and meretriciousness. Magros and Lyridon plead their causes before Demogorgon's throne with considerable rhetorical force, though without much poetry, the entire situation presenting a perfect analogy to that unfinished "Prologue to Hellas," in which Christ and Mahomet play the same part of advocates, but which Disraeli cannot have seen. Demogorgon informs the genii, in a line which but for its lack of melody might have been borrowed from Shelley,

"In man alone the fate of man is placed,"

and bids them mark the career of a mortal in whom, it is hinted, they will find their respective aims reconciled. This is no other than Napoleon, the child of a revolution yet the founder of an empire. Napoleon is accordingly introduced, leading the French from victory to victory up to the gates of Milan; but here Disraeli's inspiration, or rather the ambition which had simulated inspiration, deserted him. He published what he had written in the apparent hope that it might yet be revived by popular applause, but prefaced his work with a declaration which few versifiers even would make, and certainly no poets: " I am not one who finds consolation for the neglect of my contemporaries in the imaginary plaudits of a more sympathetic posterity."

The public having declined to interest itself in the " Revolutionary Epic," the author redeemed the pledge given in his preface, and, with or without a pang, "hurled his lyre to limbo." [1] He was, in truth, no poet, and in attempting an enterprise which Shelley himself would have found difficult, he had absurdly misconceived both the nature and the extent of his powers. Yet, notwithstanding frequent bombast and frequent bathos, and every possible indication of an essentially prosaic nature masquerading in the garb of verse, there is a freedom and largeness of treatment about the " Revolutionary Epic" which redeems it from contempt; and at a time when imitators of Shelley

---

[1] He says, however, in the preface to the second edition, that in 1837 he corrected the poem with the intention of completing it, but was prevented by his election to Parliament.

were generally copying his style alone, it is not unrefreshing to find another order of followers neglecting the style to lay hold of the ideas.   It is due to Disraeli to observe that the style of his verse, if less individual than that of his prose, is still distinctively his own, and that he is but rarely found deliberately imitating the diction of others.   Though few close verbal parallels can be adduced, there is, nevertheless, sufficient general resemblance in particular passages to evince that Shelley was not unfamiliar to him.   Section 21 of Book I. is clearly suggested by Shelley's description of the Coliseum, which Medwin had published in the Shelley Papers.   A passage in Section 45 is copied, consciously or unconsciously, from a corresponding passage in "Prometheus Unbound"; and the comparison affords an instructive example of the difference between false poetry and true poetry :—

DISRAELI.

"Omens dire
Struck cold the heart of man, and made all gaze
With silent speech upon each other's face,
Waiting who first should tell the thought all feared.
Steeples were blasted by descending fire ;
Ancestral trees, that seemed the types of Time,
Were stricken by strong winds, and in an hour
The growth of ages shivered ; from their base
Fell regal statues, fountains changed to blood,
And in the night lights strange and quivering scudded
Across the sky."

SHELLEY.

" Then, see those million worlds which burn and roll
    Around us—their inhabitants beheld
    My sphered light wane in wide heaven ; the sea
    Was lifted by strange tempest, and new fire
    From earthquake-rifted mountains of bright snow
    Shook its portentous hair beneath Heaven's frown ;
    Lightning and Inundation vexed the plains ;
    Blue thistles bloomed in cities : foodless toads
    Within voluptuous chambers panting crawled :
    When Plague had fallen on man, and beast, and worm,
    And Famine ; and black blight on herb and tree."

These passages occur in the first division of the
" Revolutionary Epic," where Magros pleads before
Demogorgon's throne in the cause of established
institutions.   The speech of the revolutionary genius
Lyridon is naturally still more Shelley-like, but the
affinity is difficult to exhibit by any process short of
reading both poets, being rather one of sentiment
than of diction.   It may be illustrated by a passage
from Disraeli himself—the recipe for concocting
punch in "Vivian Grey," where, along with other
precepts more easy of observance by mortals, the
pupil is directed to catch the aroma of a pound
of tea.   "You perceive, my Lord," says Vivian,
"that the whole difficulty lies in catching the
aroma."   The aroma of "Queen Mab" is very
fairly caught in this portion of the "Revolutionary Epic," but when you try to analyse it, it

evaporates : it cannot, like Browning's murex, be
made into an extract—

> "flasked and fine
> And priced and saleable at last."

We come, however, to Shelleyan diction as well
as Shelleyan sentiment in passages like this :—

> "There too is seen,
> Last in that radiant host yet brightest there,
> A form that should be woman ; but methinks
> The slave hath lost her fetters.   Frank and pure—
> From Custom's cursed taint, behold her now
> Indeed the light and blessing of all life."

There are also frequent reminiscences of "Alastor." The following passage, for instance, picturesque if it had but been original, is a curious
mosaic of pieces of description from that poem :—

> "There was a spot,
> It seemed the cradle of some mighty deed :
> Tall mountains rose, with shining trees o'erspread,
> And cleft with falling rivers, with a wind
> Solemn, the solemn circus of the woods
> Filling, and flinging freshness on their boughs :
> A virgin growth, whose consecrated bark
> No axe had grazed, but on the unsullied turf
> For many a flowing age their fruit had fallen,
> Spoils of the squirrel or the fearless bird ;
> Or gentler banquet for some gentle fawn :
> And in the centre rose a natural mound,
> Verdant and soft, with many a flower bedecked,
> Beauteous and bright and strange.   With pious care
> Upon this fragrant couch I placed my charge."

"Alastor" was then a scarce poem, the first edition being exhausted, and the reprint in the Posthumous Poems having been withdrawn. It is probable that Disraeli read it in the Galignani edition, for we find proof of his acquaintance with another poem of Shelley's included in that edition, but at that time rare in England. He says :—

> "Kings and Nations
> Gaze on each other with a blended glance
> Of awe and doubt."

This is from "Hellas":—

> "Obedience and Mutiny
> Like giants in contention planet-struck
> Stand gazing at each other."

Imitation, it has been said, is the sincerest flattery. It is to be remembered that this practical appreciation of Shelley's work was manifested more than two years before Disraeli began to write "Venetia," and that, accordingly, we have every right to consider the introduction of Shelley into the novel a genuine testimony of the interest with which his character and genius have inspired the writer, and not the mere resource of a novelist in quest of a plot. So clear a deliverance from a person of Lord Beaconsfield's eminence conspicuously marks a stage in the history of public opinion respecting Shelley. If far from coming up to the claims justly advanced on Shelley's behalf by the members of his own circle, or the author of "Pauline," or the young enthusiasts who had taken him up at Cambridge, it is as great an advance on the condescension of Moore as that was on the verdict of the *Quarterly Review*. On the whole, therefore, it is an episode in English literary history to be looked back upon with satisfaction. The principal gainer by it is Lord Beaconsfield himself, whose imitation of Shelley's poetry, if not always felicitous, at least indicates discernment; and whose estimate of his character proves that he had made his way through prejudice and misrepresentation to a substantially accurate conception of the actual man. Putting Lord Beaconsfield's personal controversies aside, his dealings with men of letters as a man of letters were almost invariably to his honour; and this episode is among the most honourable. Yet it makes for the honour of Shelley himself that among the first to exhibit sensitiveness to his influence and appreciation of his character, should have been a brilliant and original person who hardly less than himself contributed to redeem our age from the imputation of commonplace.

THE STORY OF GYCIA

THE STORY OF GYCIA [1]

THE story of Gycia has been recorded by the Emperor Constantine Porphyrogenitus in his treatise *De Administrando Imperio*, and the English reader may be referred to the full abstract given by Finlay ("History of Greece," ii. 354–357). It has been made the subject of a tragedy by Sir Lewis Morris, who places or seems to place its date *circa* A.D. 970, eleven years after the death of his imperial authority in 959. This oversight inspired me with the desire of ascertaining what the date actually was, an undertaking of no difficulty in so far as the belief of the Emperor Constantine is concerned. The investigation, however, conducted me to the unforeseen and surprising conclusion that the emperor's own chronology is wrong by several centuries, and that the highly dramatic event he records took place in a much earlier and more interesting age than that to which it is attributed by him. I shall first briefly narrate the incident

---

[1] Reprinted from the *English Historical Review*, January, 1897.

itself, then elucidate the period at which Constantine supposes it to have happened, and finally state my own reasons for carrying it back for some centuries.

Constantine's extremely valuable work, *De Administrando Imperio*, was compiled by him for the instruction of his son Romanus, and may be described as a compendium of the political, historical, and geographical information most necessary for a ruler of the Byzantine empire in the tenth century. In some instances the emperor —a genuine man of letters who might have been an eminent author if he had flourished in a more auspicious era—is allured into details not entirely relevant to his subject. This is especially the case when, near the end of his work, he speaks of the Greek city of Cherson, in the Crimea, which occupied very nearly the present site of Sebastopol, and comprised within its walls the ancient temple of Artemis, renowned for the ministrations of Iphigenia. He relates at considerable length the wars of the Chersonites with the Sarmatian sovereigns of the Cimmerian Bosporus, at the eastern extremity of the Crimea, near the existing city of Kertch, and in the course of his narrative introduces the following striking story.

The people of Bosporus, we are told, having

been worsted in war by the Chersonites, and deprived of a large portion of their territory, nourished schemes of revenge. Affecting reconciliation, they proposed to the people of Cherson that Gycia, the daughter of the Chersonian chief magistrate, Lamachus, should marry the son of the Bosporian sovereign, Asander, to which the Chersonites consented on condition that the bridegroom should take up his residence among them and never return to Bosporus under pain of death. The marriage accordingly took place, but Asander's son, while ostensibly observing the conditions, only sought for an opportunity of betraying Cherson to his countrymen. After two years Lamachus died, and Gycia, who inherited his great riches, instituted an annual festival in his memory, feasting the citizens at her own expense and encouraging them to public games and sports. Her husband saw his opportunity, and under pretence of bringing gifts from Bosporus introduced from time to time a number of young Bosporians, who, coming and departing on horseback, stopped on their return under cover of the night, and, embarking in boats at the *Leimon*,¹ were clandestinely

---

¹ Λειμών, agreeing in orthography with the Greek word for meadow, but evidently here denoting a haven, perhaps the harbour of Balaklava. It must be either a dialectal variation of λιμήν, and the origin of the Tartar *liman*, which frequently occurs at this day in the sense of lake or inlet—*e.g.* Sinoi Liman (blue lake), a little

brought back to Cherson and concealed in the vaults of his palace. This went on for two years, at the end of which two hundred Bosporian youths had been collected, ready to break out and fire the city on the celebration of the Lamachian festival, when the Chersonites, it was expected, would be overcome with wine and in no condition to defend themselves. It happened, however, that on the eve of the festival a little servant girl, who for some transgression had been shut up in a room immediately over the vaults in which the Bosporians were concealed, dropped the tip of her spindle into a crevice of the floor, and, removing a brick to extract it, discovered that the apartment below was full of men. She revealed the discovery to her mistress, who, having satisfied herself of the fact, secretly convoked the principal citizens, and instructed them to celebrate the festival as usual, but to prohibit the people from drinking to excess; to pile combustibles around the walls of the palace at nightfall; and, as soon as she herself should issue thence, to set fire to these and burn the whole edifice to the ground. The festival was held accordingly, Gycia herself

to the north of Kustendji—or else this very word transplanted into Greek. This bit of local colouring proves that the narrative on which Constantine's was founded was written at Cherson, or by some one acquainted with the city.

encouraging her husband to drink freely, and apparently setting him the example by her own copious draughts from a purple cup, which in truth held merely water. When he had retired to his chamber with the intention of shortly sallying forth with his Bosporians, Gycia came out at the head of her household; the combustibles were immediately kindled, and the palace, with all its inmates, was reduced to ashes. The Chersonites wished to rebuild it at the public cost, but Gycia refused, and desired that the site where treason had been hatched should, on the contrary, be made the receptacle of the filth and rubbish of the city. Before revealing her husband's plot she had stipulated that she herself should be buried within the walls as a benefactor to the state.[1] Some years afterwards, under the archonship of Stratophilus, son of Philomusus (observe the names), desirous of testing the faith and gratitude of the Chersonites, she feigned death, and was straightway carried beyond the gates for interment in the usual place of sepulture. Upon arriving there she arose from her bier, and expressed her mind

---

[1] Intramural interment was usually forbidden by law until the prevalence of Christianity, and for a considerable time afterwards. One reason why it was coveted as an exceptional privilege was, no doubt, the more effectual protection of the remains, the robbery of graves being one of the most common and gainful branches of industry in antiquity, as archæologists know to their sorrow.

towards her countrymen with such freedom and
volubility that they unanimously besought her to
desist, and accept a tomb in any quarter of the
city that she might select, which, to prevent further
misunderstandings, was constructed in her lifetime, and provided, for additional security, with
a statue of the heroine in bronze. Two bronze
statues had already been erected in her honour
in the public square. These Constantine describes,
and adds that to his own day if any Chersonite
desired to be esteemed a person of refinement
(φιλόκαλος) he would from time to time cleanse
the pedestals and renovate the inscriptions.

At what time does Constantine himself date these
transactions? His chronology is by no means
strict, but an approximate answer may easily be
given. The first incident in the history of Cherson which he relates occurred, he tells us, in the
reign of Diocletian, before this sovereign had
taken up his residence at Nicomedia, and before
Constantius Chlorus had assumed the government
of Gaul, prior, therefore, to A.D. 292. It is a war
waged against Cherson by a Bosporian king whom
Constantine calls Sauromates, but who must certainly be identified with Thothorses, who ruled
Bosporus during the reign of Diocletian. The
next, the embassy of Diogenes, happened while
Constantine was holding his court at Byzantium,

and consequently some time between A.D. 323 and A.D. 337. The next is a war waged against Cherson by Sauromates, king of Bosporus, to avenge the captivity of his grandfather Thothorses under Diocletian, who had interposed in the affairs of the Chersonesus towards the end of the third century. This Sauromates must have been the successor of Rhescuporis VI., who is believed to have reigned to about A.D. 342. After an interval which may be conjecturally taken as about fifteen years, he, or another prince of the name, renewed the attempt, and lost his life. The attempt of the Bosporians to avenge their disaster by the plot frustrated by Gycia would no doubt be made in the succeeding generation, after which, indeed, Bosporus all but disappears from history. We may consider, therefore, that the event was supposed by Constantine to have occurred somewhere about A.D. 380.

It must have struck the attentive reader—and the impression would be strengthened if he had perused Constantine's full narrative instead of this necessarily jejune epitome—that the manners and feelings adumbrated in Gycia's history are not those of the fourth Christian century. It may not be easy to point out any particular trait as obviously anachronistic, but the general atmosphere would be far from corresponding with that of the age of

Theodosius, even if Christianity had not by that time become dominant in Cherson, as must undoubtedly have been the case. Christianity must have been the state religion by the time of Gycia if she really lived in the latter half of the fourth century, and it would be surprising to find her history without a trace of its influence. It seems doubtful whether the Christianity of the day would have permitted the festival she instituted in memory of her father, with its dancing and merry-making; certainly some kind of religious ceremony would have been demanded, and we should expect to have encountered bishops and priests, and to have heard something of hymns and thanksgivings on occasion of the deliverance of the city. Her wish to be interred within the walls must have been connected with that of reposing in some basilica— an exceptional honour much coveted at that day —and she would have had no occasion to select a special place of sepulture. A Christian Gycia would have asked to be buried not in the middle of the city, but in the middle of the church, and her interment there would have been duly recorded. These anomalies go far to convince us that the story belongs to pagan times, yet we should hesitate to rely entirely on such indications. But they are accompanied by one of much greater strength, the absolute incompatibility of the names

of the personages with their existence in the fourth
century. Lamachus, Asander, Philomusus, Stratophilus! It might be too much to assert that none
of these names was borne by any one in that age,
but they unquestionably represent types by that
time superannuated, and their simultaneous appearance in a narrative professedly belonging to the
period would alone, if it could not be shown to be
misdated, suffice to prove it a more recent fiction.
Names compounded with φίλος and στρατός, exceedingly frequent in the best ages of Greece, had
become very rare by the fourth century, and are
utterly out of keeping with the actual Chersonite
names which occur in the portion of Constantine's
narrative undoubtedly referring to this period—
Chrestus, Papias, Themistus, Byscus, Supolichus,
Pharnacus. Lamachus is an old Athenian name,
famous in the Peloponnesian war; Asander, like
Cassander, a Macedonian name which came in with
Alexander the Great. Yet both have an ancient
connection with Chersonite history, which will
assist us to determine the real date of the story.

Cherson was originally a colony from Heraclea,
in Pontus, the history of which city was written
very circumstantially by a native, Memnon. In
Photius's epitome of this work special mention is
made of one Lamachus as the most influential
citizen of Heraclea in the time of Mithridates, and

the instrument of the ruin of his country by inducing it to side with that monarch in his war with the Romans. Nothing can be more probable than that a name so distinguished in the mother city existed contemporaneously as one of repute in the daughter colony also: in the post-Christian centuries, so far as we have been able to discover, it is never heard. The existence of the name of Asander in the neighbourhood of Cherson about this time is no matter of mere conjecture; it is the name of a king of Bosporus from 47 B.C. to 16 B.C., whose history is known and whose coins are numerous. After him it disappears, unless we can believe that it crops up again suddenly near the end of the fourth century. The learned, indeed, in deference to Constantine, have inscribed a second Asander on the roll of Bosporian kings, but no coin of his has ever come to light.

The hypothesis that events ascribed to the time of an otherwise unknown Asander of the fourth century, but manifestly out of keeping with that age, really happened in the time of an Asander who unquestionably did reign over Bosporus in the first century B.C., would in any case have much to recommend it, but is very strongly confirmed by an observation made independently by the illustrious scholar Boeckh, who, in his work on Greek inscriptions, without any reference to or thought

of Constantine's narrative, points out that the
Chersonites employed a peculiar era—dating from
either 36 B.C. or 21 B.C., more probably the former
year. Both these dates fall within the reign of
Asander. Boeckh justly remarks that this era
must commence with some memorable event in
the history of Cherson, and acutely conjectures
that this was the recovery of the liberty of the
city, which had been subject to the kings of Pontus,
but is known to have regained its freedom somewhere about this time. Asander, a viceroy of the
Pontic kings in Bosporus, had made himself an
independent sovereign by murdering his master,
Pharnaces. Nothing can be more likely than that
the Chersonites would profit by the substitution
of a petty king of Bosporus for the powerful
sovereign of Pontus to throw off the yoke, or that
Asander would endeavour to subjugate them by
treachery at the first opportunity. We therefore
with some confidence refer the history of Gycia
to his reign, *i.e.* to some year between 36 and 16
B.C., a period agreeable to the manners depicted
and appropriate to the otherwise anachronistic
appellations of Asander and Lamachus. Nor is
it difficult to conjecture how the mistake may have
arisen. Asander was the brother-in-law and
successor of Pharnaces, and the history of his
plot in Constantine's work immediately follows

the exploit of the Chersonite vanquisher of the Bosporian king Sauromates — Pharna*cus*. The similarity of these names probably led to the misplacing of the story, which, unless for some heightening of the circumstances connected with Gycia's premature interment, is assuredly no fiction, as the tale is destitute of the sentimental and romantic colouring which a writer of a late period would have imparted to it. Internal evidence shows it to have been written at Cherson, or at least by some one well acquainted with the city. It is probably derived from some Chersonite historian or some record of the deeds of heroines, although the diction is Constantine's own Byzantine.[1]

---

[1] A curious illustration of the changes of signification which words may undergo is shown in τὰς θείας φιλοτιμίας, which in classical Greek would have meant *the rivalries of the gods*, but in Constantine denotes *the largesses of the emperor*.

THE LOVE-STORY OF
LUIGI TANSILLO

THE LOVE-STORY OF LUIGI TANSILLO [1]

"Now that my wings are spread to my desire,
    The more vast height withdraws the dwindling land,
    Wider to wind these pinions I expand,
And earth disdain, and higher mount and higher :
Nor of the fate of Icarus inquire,
    Or cautious droop, or sway to either hand ;
    Dead I shall fall, full well I understand ;
But who lives gloriously as I expire?
Yet hear I my own heart that pleading cries,
    Stay, madman ! Whither art thou bound? Descend !
    Ruin is ready Rashness to chastise.
But I, Fear not, though this indeed the end ;
    Cleave we the clouds, and praise our destinies,
    If noble fall on noble flight attend."

THE above sonnet, one of the finest in Italian literature, is already known to many English readers in another translation by the late Mr. J. Addington Symonds, which originally appeared in the *Cornhill Magazine,* and is prefixed to his translation of the sonnets of Michael Angelo and Campanella (London 1878), under the title of "The Philosophic Flight." In his preface Mr.

[1] Reprinted from "The Yellow Book," vol. i.

Symonds says : "The sonnet prefixed as a proem to the whole book is generally attributed to Giordano Bruno, in whose dialogue in the *Eroici Furori* it occurs. There seems, however, good reason to suppose that it was really written by Tansillo, who recites it in that dialogue. Whoever may have been its author, it expresses in noble and impassioned verse the sense of danger, the audacity, and the exultation of those pioneers of modern thought for whom philosophy was a voyage of discovery into untravelled regions." Mr. Symonds's knowledge of Italian literature was so extensive that he must have had ground for stating that the sonnet is generally attributed to Giordano Bruno; as it certainly is by De Sanctis, though it is printed as Tansillo's in all editions of his works, imperfect as these were before the appearance of Signor Fiorentino's in 1882. It is, nevertheless, remarkable that he should add : "*There seems good reason to suppose* that it was really written by Tansillo," as if there could be a shadow of doubt on the matter. *Gli Eroici Furori* is professedly a series of dialogues between Luigi Tansillo, the Neapolitan poet, who had died about twenty years before their composition, and Cicada ; but is in reality little more than a monologue, for Tansillo does nearly all the talking, and Cicada receives his instructions with singular docility.

The reason of Tansillo's selection for so great an honour was undoubtedly that, although born at Venosa, he belonged by descent to Nola, Bruno's own city. In making such free use of Tansillo's poetry as he has done throughout these dialogues, Bruno was far from the least idea of pillaging his distinguished countryman. In introducing the four sonnets he has borrowed (for there are three besides that already quoted) he is always careful to make Tansillo speak of them as his own compositions, which he never does when Bruno's own verses are put into his mouth. If a particle of doubt could remain it would be dispelled by the fact that this sonnet, with other poems by Tansillo, including the three other sonnets introduced into Bruno's dialogue, is published under his name in the *Rime di diversi illustri Signori Napoletani*, edited by Lodovico Dolce at Venice in 1555, when Bruno was about seven years old!

Mr. Symonds's interpretation of the sonnet also is erroneous—in so far at least as that the meaning assigned by him never entered into the head of the author. The poem is certainly fully susceptible of such an exposition. But Tansillo, no philosopher, but a cavalier, the active part of whose life was mainly spent in naval expeditions against the Turks, no more thought with Mr. Symonds of "the pioneers of modern philosophy"

K

than he thought with Bruno of "arising and free-
ing himself from the body and sensual cognition."
On the contrary, the sonnet is a love-sonnet, and
depicts with extraordinary grandeur the elation of
spirit, combined with a sense of peril, consequent
upon the poet having conceived a passion for a
lady greatly his superior in rank. The proof of
this is to be found in the fact that the sonnet is
one of a series unequivocally celebrating an earthly
passion; and especially so in the sonnet immediately preceding it in Dolce's collection, manifestly
written at the same time and referring to the
same circumstance, in which the poet ascribes his
Icarian flight, not to the influence of Philosophy,
but of Love :—

"Love fits me forth with wings, which so dilate,
    Sped skyward at the call of daring thought,
    I high and higher soar, with purpose fraught
Soon to lay smiting hand on heaven's gate.
Yet altitude so vast might well abate
    My confidence, if Love not succour brought,
    Pledging my fame not jeopardised in aught,
And promising renown as ruin great.
If he whom like audacity inspired,
    Falling gave name immortal to the flood,
    As sunny flame his waxen pinion fired ;
Then of thee too it shall be understood,
    No meaner prize than heaven thy soul required,
    And firmer than thy life thy courage stood."

The meaning of the two sonnets is fully recognised by Muratori, who prints them together in his treatise, *Della perfetta poesia*, and adds :— " *Volea dire costui che s'era imbarcato in un'amor troppo alto, e s'andava facendo coraggio.*"

This is surely one of the most remarkable in-ances possible to adduce of the infinite signifi-cance of true poetry, and its capacity for inspiring ideas and suggesting interpretations of which the poet never dreamed, but which are nevertheless fairly deducible from his expressions.

It is now a matter of considerable interest to ascertain the identity of this lady of rank, who could inspire a passion at once so exalted and so perilous. The point has been investigated by Tansillo's editor, Signor F. Fiorentino, who has done so much to rescue his unpublished composi-tions from oblivion, and his view must be deemed to be fully established. She was Maria d'Aragona, Marchioness del Vasto, whose husband, the Marquis del Vasto, a celebrated general of Spanish descent, famous as Charles the Fifth's right hand in his successful expedition against Tunis, and at one time governor of the Milanese, was as remarkable for his jealousy as the lady, grand-daughter of a King of Naples, was for her pride and haughtiness. Fiorentino proves his case by showing how well all personal allusions in Tansillo's poems, so far as they can be traced, agree with the circumstances of the Marchioness, and in particular that the latter is represented as at one time residing on the island of Ischia, where del Vasto was accustomed to deposit his wife for security when absent on his campaigns. He is apparently not aware that the object of Tansillo's affection had already been identified with a member of the house of Aragon by Faria e Sousa, the Portuguese editor of Camoëns, who, in his commentary on Camoëns's sixty-ninth sonnet, gives an interminable catalogue of ladies celebrated by enamoured poets, and says, "Tansillo sang Donna Isabel de Aragon." This lady, however, the niece of the Marchioness del Vasto, was a little girl in Tansillo's time, and is only mentioned by him as inconsolable for the death of a favourite dwarf.

The sentiment, therefore, of the two sonnets of Tansillo which we have quoted is sufficiently justified by the exalted station of the lady who had inspired his passion, and the risk he ran from the power and jealousy of her husband. It seems certain, however, that the Marquis had on his part no ground for apprehension. Maria d'Aragona does not seem to have had much heart to bestow upon any one, and would, in any case, have disdained to bestow what heart she had upon a poor gentleman and retainer of Don Garcia de Toledo, the son of the Viceroy of Naples. She would think that she honoured him beyond his deserts by accepting his poetical homage. Tansillo, on his part, says in one of his sonnets that his devotion is purely platonic; it might have been more ardent, he hints, but he is dazzled by the splendour of the light he contemplates, and intimidated by the richness of the band by which he is led. So it may have been at first, but as time wore on the poet naturally craved some proof that his lady was not entirely indifferent to him, and did not tolerate him merely for the sake of his verses. This, in the nature of things, could not be given; and the poet's raptures pass into doubt and suspicion, thence into despairing resignation; thence into resentment and open hostility, terminating in a cold reconciliation, leaving him free to marry a much humbler but probably a more affectionate person, to whom he addresses no impassioned sonnets, but whom he instructs in a very elegant poem ("La Balia") how to bring up her infant children. These varying affections are depicted with extreme liveliness in a series of sonnets, of which we propose to offer some translated specimens. The order will not be that of the editions of Tansillo, where the pieces are distributed at random, but the probable order of composition, as indicated by the nature of the feeling expressed. It is, of course, impossible to give more than a few examples, though

most deserve to be reproduced. Tansillo had the
advantage over most Italian poets of his time of
being in love with a real woman; hence, though
possibly inferior in style and diction to such artists
in rhyme as Bembo or Molza, he greatly surpasses
them in all the qualities that discriminate poetry
from the accomplishment of verse.

The first sonnet which we shall give is still all
fire and rapture :—

I.

" Lady, the heart that entered through your eyes
        Returneth not.   Well may he make delay,
        For if the very windows that display
Your spirit, sparkle in such wondrous wise,
Of her enthroned within this Paradise
        What shall be deemed ?   If heart for ever stay,
        Small wonder, dazzled by more radiant day
Than gazers from without can recognise.
Glory of sun and moon and silver star
        In firmament above, are these not sign
        Of things within more excellent by far ?
Rejoice then in thy kingdom, heart of mine,
        While Love and Fortune favourable are,
        Nor thou yet exiled for default of thine."

Although, however, Tansillo's heart might well
remain with its lady, Tansillo's person was neces-
sitated to join the frequent maritime expeditions
of the great nobleman to whom he was attached,
Don Garcia de Toledo, against the Turks.   The
constant freebooting of the Turkish and Barbary

rovers kept the Mediterranean in a state of com-
motion comparable to that of the Spanish Main in
the succeeding age, and these expeditions, whose
picturesque history remains to be written, were no
doubt very interesting; though from a philosophical point of view it is impossible not to sympa-
thise with the humane and generous poet when
he inquires :—

> " Che il Turco nasca turco, e'l Moro moro,
>   È giusta causa questa, ond'altri ed io
>   Dobbiam incrudelir nel sangue loro ? "

With such feelings it may well be believed that
in his enforced absence he was thinking at least
as much of love as of war, and that the following
sonnet is as truthful as it is an animated picture
of his feelings :—

II.

> " No length of banishment did e'er remove
>   My heart from you, nor if by Fortune sped
>   I roam the azure waters, or the Red,
> E'er with the body shall the spirit rove :
> If by each drop of every wave we clove,
>   Or by Sun's light or Moon's encompassèd,
>   Another Venus were engenderèd,
> And each were pregnant with another Love :
> And thus new shapes of Love where'er we went
>   Started to life at every stroke of oar,
>   And each were cradled in an amorous thought ;
> Not more than now this spirit should adore ;
>   That none the less doth constantly lament
>   It cannot worship as it would and ought."

Before long, however, the pangs of separation overcome this elation of spirit, while he is not yet afraid of being forgotten :—

III.

" Like lightning shining forth from east to west,
 Hurled are the happy hours from morn to night,
 And leave the spirit steeped in undelight
In like proportion as themselves were blest.
Slow move sad hours, by thousand curbs opprest,
 Wherewith the churlish Fates delay their flight ;
 Those, impulses of Mercury incite,
These lag at the Saturnian star's behest.
While thou wert near, ere separation's grief
 Smote me, like steeds contending in the race
 My days and nights with equal speed did run :
Now broken either wheel, not swift the pace
 Of summer's night though summer's moon be brief ;
 Or wintry day's for brevity of sun.

IV.

" Now that the Sun hath borne with him the day,
 And haled dark Night from prison subterrene,
 Come forth, fair Moon, and, robed in light serene,
With thy own loveliness the world array.
Heaven's spheres, slow wheeled on their majestic way,
 Invoke as they revolve thy orb unseen,
 And all the pageant of the starry scene,
Wronged by thy absence, chides at thy delay.
Shades even as splendours, earth and heaven both
 Smile at the apparition of thy face,
 And my own gloom no longer seems so loth ;
Yet, while my eye regards thee, thought doth trace
 Another's image ; if in vows be troth,
 I am not yet estranged from Love's embrace."

Continual separation, however, and the absence of any marked token that he is borne in memory, necessarily prey more and more on the sensitive spirit of the poet. During the first part of her husband's tenure of office as Governor of the Milanese, the Marchioness, as already mentioned, took up her residence in the island of Ischia, where she received her adorer's eloquent aspirations for her welfare—heartfelt, but so worded as to convey a reproach :—

V.

" That this fair isle with all delight abound,
  Clad be it ever in sky's smile serene,
  No thundering billow boom from deeps marine,
And calm with Neptune and his folk be found.
Fast may all winds by Æolus be bound,
  Save faintest breath of lispings Zephyrene ;
  And be the odorous earth with glowing green
Of gladsome herbs, bright flowers, quaint foliage crowned.
All ire, all tempest, all misfortune be
  Heaped on my head, lest aught thy pleasure stain,
Nor this disturbed by any thought of me,
  So scourged with ills' innumerable train,
New grief new tear begetteth not, as sea
Chafes not the more for deluge of the rain."

The "quaint foliage" is in the original "Arab leaves," *arabe frondi*, an interesting proof of the cultivation of exotic plants at the period.

The lady rejoins her husband at Milan, and Tansillo, landing on the Campanian coast, lately devastated by earthquakes and eruptions, finds everywhere the image of his own bosom, and rejoices at the opportunity which yawning rifts and chasms of earth afford for an appeal to the infernal powers :—

VI.

" Wild precipice and earthquake-riven wall ;
    Bare jagged lava naked to the sky ;
    Whence densely struggles up and slow floats by
Heaven's murky shroud of smoke funereal ;
Horror whereby the silent groves enthral ;
    Black weedy pit and rifted cavity ;
    Bleak loneliness whose drear sterility
Doth prowling creatures of the wild appal :
Like one distraught who doth his woe deplore,
    Bereft of sense by thousand miseries,
    As passion prompts, companioned or alone ;
Your desert so I rove ; if as before
    Heaven deaf continue, through these crevices,
    My cry shall pierce to the Avernian throne."

The poet's melancholy deepens, and he enters upon the stage of dismal and hopeless resignation to the inevitable :—

VII.

" As one who on uneasy couch bewails
    Besetting sickness and Time's tardy course,
    Proving if drug, or gem, or charm have force
To conquer the dire evil that assails :
But when at last no remedy prevails,
    And bankrupt Art stands empty of resource,
    Beholds Death in the face, and scorns recourse
To skill whose impotence in nought avails.

So I, who long have borne in trust unspent
    That distance, indignation, reason, strife
With Fate would heal my malady, repent,
    Frustrate all hopes wherewith my soul was rife,
And yield unto my destiny, content
    To languish for the little left of life."

A lower depth still has to be reached ere the
period of salutary and defiant reaction :—

VIII.

" So mightily abound the hosts of Pain,
    Whom sentries of my bosom Love hath made,
    No space is left to enter or evade,
And inwardly expire sighs born in vain,
If any Pleasure mingle with the train.
    By the first glimpse of my poor heart dismayed,
    Instant he dies, or else, in bondage stayed,
Pines languishing, or flies that drear domain.
Pale semblances of terror keep the keys,
    Of frowning portals they for none displace
Except for messengers of new unease :
    All thoughts they scare that wear a gladsome face ;
And, were they anything but Miseries,
    Themselves would hasten from the gloomy place."

Slighted love easily passes from dejection
into rebellion, and we shall see that such was
the case with Tansillo. The following sonnet
denotes an intermediate stage, when resignation
is almost renunciation, but has not yet become
revolt :—

IX.

" Cease thy accustomed strain, my mournful lute ;
    New music find, fit for my lot forlorn ;
      Henceforth be Wrath and Grief resounded, torn
  The strings that anciently did Love salute,
  Not on my own weak wing irresolute
      But on Love's plumes I trusted to be borne,
      Chanting him far as that remotest bourne
Whence strength Herculean reft Hesperian fruit.
  To such ambition was my spirit wrought
      By gracious guerdon Love came offering
      When free in air my thought was bold to range :
  But otherwhere now dwells another's thought,
      And Wrath has plucked Love's feather from my wing,
      And hope, style, theme, I all alike must change."

This, however, is not a point at which continu-
ance is possible, the mind must go either backward
or forward. The lover for a time persuades himself that he has broken his mistress's yoke, and
that his infatuation is entirely a thing of the past.
But the poet, like the lady, protests too much :—

X.

" If Love was miser of my liberty,
    Lo, Scorn is bounteous and benevolent,
      Such scope permitting, that, my fetter rent,
  Not lengthened by my hand, I wander free.
  The eyes that yielded tears continually
      Have now with Lethe's drops my fire besprent,
      And more behold, Illusion's glamour spent,

Than fabled Argus with his century.
The tyrant of my spirit, left forlorn
        As vassal thoughts forsake him, doth remove,
And back unto her throne is Reason borne,
        And I my metamorphosis approve,
And, old strains tuning to new keys, of Scorn
        Will sing as anciently I sang of Love."

Several solutions of this situation are conceivable. Tansillo's is that which was perhaps that most likely in the case of an emotional nature, where the feelings are more powerful than the will. He simply surrenders at discretion, retracts everything disparaging that he has said of the lady (taking care, however, not to burn the peccant verses, which are much too good to be lightly parted with), and professes himself her humble slave upon her own terms :—

XI.

" All bitter words I spoke of you while yet
        My heart was sore, and every virgin scroll
        Blackened with ire, now past from my control,
These would I now recall ; for 'tis most fit
My style should change, now Reason doth reknit
        Ties Passion sundered, and again make whole ;
        Be then Oblivion's prey, whate'er my soul
Hath wrongly of thee thought, spoke, sung, or writ.
Not, Lady, that impeachment of thy fame
        With tongue or pen I ever did design ;
But that, if unto these shall reach my name,
        Ages to come may study in my line
How year by year more streamed and towered my flame,
        And how I living was and dying thine."

There is no reason to doubt the perfect sincerity
of these lines at the period of their composition;
but Tansillo's mistress had apparently resolved
that his attachment should not henceforth have
the diet even of a chameleon; and it is small wonder
to find him shortly afterwards a tender husband
and father, lamenting the death of an infant son
in strains of extreme pathos, and instructing his
wife on certain details of domestic economy in
which she might have been supposed to be better
versed than himself.   His marriage took place in
1550, and in one of his sonnets he says that his
unhappy attachment had endured sixteen years,
which, allowing for a decent interval between
the Romeo and the Benedict, would date its commencement at 1532 or 1533.

Maria d'Aragona died on November 9, 1568, and
Tansillo, whose services had been rewarded by a
judicial appointment in the kingdom of Naples,
followed her to the tomb on December 1.   If her
death is really the subject of the two poems in
terza rima, which appear to deplore it, he certainly
lost no time in bewailing her, but the interval is
so brief, and the poems are so weak, that they may
have been composed on some other occasion.
With respect to the latter consideration, however,
it must be remembered that he was himself, in
all probability, suffering from disabling sickness,

having made his will on November 29. It is also
worthy of note that the first sonnets composed
by Petrarch upon the death of Laura are in general
much inferior in depth of tenderness to those
written years after the event. "In Memoriam" is
another proof that the adequate poetical expression
of grief, unlike that of love, requires time and
study. Tansillo, then, may not have been so completely disillusioned as his editor thinks. If the
poems do not relate to Maria d'Aragona, we have
no clue to the ultimate nature of his feelings
towards her.

A generally fair estimate of Tansillo's rank as a
poet is given in Ginguené's "History of Italian
Literature," vol. ix., pp. 340-343. It can scarcely
be admitted that his boldness and fertility of
imagination transported him beyond the limits of
lyric poetry—for this is hardly possible—but it is
true that they sometimes transcended the limits of
good taste, and that the germs may be found in him
of the extravagance which so disfigured Italian
poetry in the seventeenth century. On the other
hand, he has the inestimable advantage over most
Italian poets of his day of writing of genuine
passion from genuine experience. Hence a truth
and vigour preferable even to the exquisite elegance
of his countryman, Angelo di Costanzo, and much
more so to the mere amatory exercises of other

contemporaries.   After Michael Angelo he stands farther aloof than any contemporary from Petrarch, a merit in an age when the study of Petrarch had degenerated into slavish imitation.   His faults as a lyrist are absent from his didactic poems, which are models of taste and elegance.   His one unpardonable sin is want of patriotism; he is the dependent and panegyrist of the foreign conqueror, and seems equally unconscious of the past glories, the actual degradation, or the prospective regeneration of Italy.   Born a Spanish subject, his ideal of loyalty was entirely misplaced, and he must not be severely censured for what he could hardly avoid.   But Italy lost a Tyrtæus in him.

BECKFORD'S "VATHEK"

BECKFORD'S "VATHEK" [1]

"VATHEK" has hitherto been regarded as an exception to the maxim,

"Nil sine magno
Vita labore dedit mortalibus."

All who have written upon it since the publication of Redding's "Memoirs of Beckford," including the present editor in the "Dictionary of National Biography," have accepted the statement which Redding affirms to have been made to him by the author, and which there is no reasonable ground for doubting to have been actually made :—

"I wrote 'Vathek' when I was twenty-two years old.[2] I wrote it at one sitting and in French. It

---

[1] Introduction to the beautiful edition of "Vathek" published by Messrs. Lawrence & Bullen in 1893.

[2] He should have said twenty-one, for although the date of his birth has hitherto been given as September 29, 1759, it is proved to have been October 1, 1760, by the contemporary notices in the *Public Advertiser* and *Gentleman's Magazine.* The error as regards the day was probably occasioned by the celebration of his majority on Michaelmas Day, which fell on a Saturday, the most convenient day for a country fête. As regards the year, Redding, though he correctly gives the date of this festival as 1781, was misled by a

cost me three days and two nights of hard labour. I never took my clothes off the whole time. This severe application made me very ill " (" Memoirs of William Beckford," vol. i. p. 243).

Another illusion to be resigned ! Clear evidence is now attainable that although Beckford addressed himself to the composition of "Vathek" in an access of enthusiasm, which, when Redding conversed with him, the septuagenarian may have remembered more exactly than the actual time employed in its production, it was, nevertheless, a work of care and labour, whose production, with whatever interruptions, occupied several months, probably almost a year. This evidence exists in Beckford's contemporary correspondence with the Rev. Samuel Henley, the translator, the annotator, and, as now appears, the original inspirer of "Vathek." The letters, after being unknown for more than a century, have been recently added to the magnificent collection of autographs formed by Alfred Morrison, Esq., of Fonthill House, who has most kindly allowed the editor the free use of the as yet unissued second part of the catalogue of his treasures—no less *facile princeps* among catalogues of autograph letters than "Vathek" among the Oriental

letter from the elder Beckford to Pitt on the occasion of Beckford's christening, which is dated January 7, 1760, by an error not uncommon at the beginning of a new year.

tales of European writers. Of Henley we shall have more to say, for the moment it will suffice to state that Beckford's acquaintance with him must have been formed after the young man's return from his travels in 1781, and no doubt originated in Henley's position as tutor of his cousins on the mother's side, who seem to have lived with their preceptor at Harrow. The correspondence begins with a letter from Beckford of January 21, 1782, which shows "Vathek" not yet in being but about to be :—

"The spirit has moved me this eve, and, shut up in my apartment as you advised, I have given way to fancies and inspirations. What will be the consequence of this mood I am not bold enough to determine."

By January 29 "Vathek" is apparently in course of composition. Beckford writes :—

"I suppose, my dear sir, I am indebted to you for the capital epistle which Hamilton has written to me, and which amused me not a little, though my imagination the evening it arrived was wrapped in the thickest gloom. You are answerable for having set me to work upon a story so horrid that I tremble whilst relating it, and have not a nerve in my frame but vibrates like an aspen.

"There will be no proceeding in our work without many long consultations ; therefore I shall

trouble you with myself as soon as I can escape
the plagues of London with any decorum."

Nothing that Beckford is known or reported to
have written at all answers this description except
"Vathek." The mental excitement into which the
conception instilled into his mind by Henley had
thrown him must have impressed his memory
more powerfully than the external circumstances
connected with the composition; and half a century
afterwards he may have really persuaded himself
that this substantially took place during the first
burst of inspiration, and that all the rest was mere
literary polish. That such, nevertheless, was not
the case, is proved by the reliance on Henley's aid
expressed in this letter, and still more decisively by
the next in the series, April 25 :—

"My Arabian tale goes on prodigiously, and I
think Count Hamilton will smile upon me when
we are introduced to each other in Paradise."

"Vathek" is first expressly named in a letter
written six days afterwards, May 1, which contains
enough of family particulars, otherwise uninteresting, to show that the author's time cannot have
been exclusively devoted to his fiction : "The tale
of the Caliph Vathec goes on surprisingly."

In another letter, unfortunately undated, Beckford says, "My caliph advances on his journey
to Persepolis, but want of time, I believe, will

force me to stop his ulterior proceedings." He
went abroad in May, and "Vathek" is not again
spoken of until January 30, 1783, when it seems to
have been complete in the original French text, as
only the episodes are mentioned :—

"I go on bravely with the episodes of 'Vathek,'
and hope in a few weeks to wind up his adven-
tures."

Beckford told Redding that the episodes written
for insertion in "Vathek" were three in number :
"The histories of Alasi and Firouz, of Prince Bar-
kiarokh, of Kalilah and Zulkais, who were shut up
in the palace of subterranean fire. He had destroyed
one of the MSS. as too wild, but the others might
one day see the light." This was in 1835, but the
episodes have never appeared.[1] A fourth had been
contemplated, but probably remained unwritten.
The names and subjects of the episodes are indicated in the French text of "Vathek" but not in the
English version, which proves that Henley had not
seen them.

The remainder of the correspondence, in so far as
it relates to "Vathek," is occupied with Henley's

[1] He read them to Rogers, who thought them "extremely fine,
but very objectionable on account of their subjects."—"Table-
Talk," p. 218. Byron, answering on March 3, 1818, a letter from
Rogers of the preceding February 8, in which a visit to Fonthill
is mentioned, expresses a strong wish to borrow the episodes.—
"Letters and Journals," vol. iv. pp. 206–209.

translation and commentary, and here a few words concerning Henley himself will be appropriate. The place of his birth is not known, the year was 1740. It is uncertain what circumstances took him as a young man to America, where, in 1771, he held a professorship in William and Mary College, Williamsburg, Virginia. His return to England must undoubtedly have been occasioned by his adherence to the loyalist cause. About 1778, probably, he became a master at Harrow, and Beckford's young cousins appear to have boarded in his house. This procured him Beckford's acquaintance. His knowledge of Arabic and Persian enabled him to foster that innate love of Orientalism against which Beckford had been solemnly warned by Lord Chatham; the original impulse to "Vathek" proceeded from him; and his own admiration for the work he had inspired produced the translation without which it would have ranked among French instead of English books.[1]

On May 5, 1783, Beckford married his cousin, Lady Margaret Gordon, and immediately went abroad with her. His first letter to Henley after his departure is dated from Cologny, near Geneva, November 18, 1783 :—

---

[1] Four letters from Henley to Jefferson, all written in England in 1785-1786, will be found in the Jefferson Papers in the collections of the Massachusetts Historical Society, ser. vii. vol. i. 1900.

"You proposed likewise to translate 'Vathec,' which I left in your hands. Could I show a greater mark of confidence? You have the only copy which exists of the only production of mine which I am not ashamed of, or with which I am not disgusted. Thank God, 'Vathec' at least has produced no misunderstanding, and I may still dwell upon its recollection with pleasure; but how can I endure my book of Dreams[1] when I reflect what disagreeable waking thoughts it has occasioned us? If you have a mind to reconcile me to it, by me be assured you are not less my affectionate friend than when you silenced the

---

[1] "Dreams, Waking Thoughts, and Incidents, in a series of Letters from various parts of Europe," 1783. This was the original form of Beckford's Letters of Travel. All the copies except six are said to have been destroyed, and when Beckford republished his Travels in 1834, the passages descriptive of his dreams were entirely omitted. One of the copies preserved found its way to the British Museum, and became the subject of an article by the present writer in the *Universal Review*, which led to the restoration of the omitted passages in the edition of the Travels published in the "Minerva Library" by the late Mr. Bettany. From a passage in Moore's Diary it appears that Beckford even then proposed to reprint his Travels, and that Rogers thought he would gladly enlist, and munificently remunerate Moore's services in preparing them for the press. Moore, however, on grounds easily intelligible, declined to have anything to do with them. Neither he nor Rogers, notwithstanding, felt any scruple in stealing from the copy to which Beckford allowed them access. See Lockhart in the *Quarterly Review*, vol. li. ; *Notes and Queries*, 2nd series, vol. iv. p. 14, and Beckford's own sarcastic allusion in the preface to the edition of 1834.

hiss of serpents at Fonthill. Neither Orlando
nor Brandimarte was ever more tormented by
dæmons and spectres in an enchanted castle than
William Beckford in his own hall by his nearest
relations. . . . Our abode, a strange antiquated
mansion, with the lake fretting and tormenting
itself amongst loose fragments below, and a steep
bank jaundiced with fallen leaves above, is not
formed to inspire the most cheerful ideas. However, my spirits are tolerably lively, my health
good, and my mind serene. I shall bring you
some caliphs not unworthy to succeed your beloved
Vathec."

By a letter dated January 25, 1784, it would
appear that Henley is reading " Vathek," but has
not yet begun to translate it. At the date of the
next letter, May 19, 1784, Beckford is again in
London, and Henley has obtained the living of
Rendlesham, in Suffolk, where he is apparently
about to receive as pupil a young friend of Beckford's concerning whom the latter writes with
interest, and adds:—

" Pray introduce him to ' Vathec,' whom at present
he hardly knows by name. I suppose you are deep
in the [letter torn] Halls of Damnation, hearing the
melancholy voice of Eblis in the dead of night, and
catch moonlight glimpses of Nouronihar. I long
eagerly to read your translation, and feel more

grateful for the pains you must have taken with it than I 'can express."

By the next letter, written from Fonthill on October 19, 1784, it would appear that the episodes of "Vathek" were not yet completed, but that the translation was :—

"Mr. Lane is *rockifying*, not on the high places, but in a snug copse by the river side, where I spend many an hour dreaming about my unfortunate princes, and contriving reasonable ways and means of sending them to the devil. What are you about now? Have you got a fair copy of your translation?"

The fair copy cannot have been ready, for it is not until February 26, 1785, that Beckford acknowledges the arrival of a portion of it :—

"Your translation has all the spirit of the caliphs and their dæmons. I long for the continuation, and hope you will soon gratify my impatience."

"*March* 21, 1785.

"You make me proud of 'Vathek.'[1] The blaze

---

[1] It will be observed that Beckford here, for the first time, spells "Vathek" in the accepted manner. It must be remembered that the original text of the romance was French, in which language the letter *k* is but a naturalised foreigner. Henley in his version had evidently substituted *k* for *c*, as more agreeable to the genius of the Oriental languages, and Beckford followed his example both in he Paris and the Lausanne edition of the French original.

just at present is so overpowering that I can see
no faults; but you may depend upon my hunting
diligently after them.   Pray send the continuation.
I know not how it happens, but the original when
first born scarce gave me so much rapture as your
translation.   Were I well and in spirits, I should
run wild among my rocks and forests telling
stones, trees, and labourers, how gloriously you
have succeeded.   My imagination is again on fire.
I have been giving the last trimmings to one
episode, and sown the seeds of another, which I
trust will bring forth fruit in due season.   I
eagerly hope you will one day or other introduce
these plants to their English soil.   We have had
a dismal winter, ground cracked and shrubs
pinched, &c., workmen numbed, but I have gone
on sinking my princes to hell with active perseverance."

"*April* 9.

"I shall sit down immediately to revise 'Vathek,'
and much approve of your idea of prefacing the tale
with some explanation of its costume."

"*April* 23.

"I have given my attention for several days
past to 'Vathek,' and have made several little
alterations which you will not perhaps disapprove.
The 'Arabian Nights' will furnish some illus-

trations, particularly as to goules, &c.; but much more may be learned from Herbelot's *Bibliothèque Orientale* and Richardson's 'Dissertations.' I know not how to make the damnations you advise. I have always thought Nouronihar too severely punished,[1] and if I knew how, conveniently, would add a crime or two to her share. What say you? Let me know."

It would seem by the next letter, June 11, 1785, that the original French manuscript from which the translation was made had been returned in the interval:—

"The Caliph Vathek is safe in my possession, and had I not been engaged in the very manner you conjecture, notice would have been long since sent to Rendlesham of his arrival.

"As I have some things of importance to say to you, I must beg the favour of seeing you here immediately, as the preparations for our journey are in great forwardness. I suppose you can easily come in a couple of days, and I will detain you no longer than is absolutely necessary for the revisal of 'Vathek,' the selection of notes, and the explanation of doubtful passages."

The visit did not take place, for, on July 22, Beckford writes on the eve of departure:—

"I am surprisingly sorry at not having had an

[1] Every reader must have thought so too.

opportunity of seeing you. . . . I would send the
episodes, but have not a second copy. 'Vathec'
I have delivered to the care of Mr. Thornton. . . .
Leave the description of the evening scene as it
was originally—we have already more description
than we know what to do with."

The next epistle, dated from Vevay, February 9,
1786, strikes the first note of disagreement, and
indicates the rock on which Beckford's friendship
with Henley was to split:—

"The publication of 'Vathek' must be suspended
at least another year. I would not on any account
have him precede the French edition. . . . The
episodes are nearly finished, and the whole work
will be completed within a twelvemonth. You
must be sensible that notwithstanding my eagerness to see 'Vathek' in print, I cannot sacrifice
the French edition to my impatience. The antici-
pation of so principal a tale as that of the Caliph
would be tearing the proudest feather from my
turban. I must repeat, therefore, my desire that
you will not give your translation to the world
till the original has made its appearance, and
we have talked more on the subject. You may
imagine how I long for the moment of enjoying
your notes and the preliminary dissertation, which
I doubt not will be received with the honours due
to so valuable a morsel of Orientalism."

By April 13, 1786, Beckford, now returned to England, had received Henley's preliminary dissertation, and had discovered that the writer laboured under the general infirmity of commentators: "they study rather to display themselves than to explain their author." His remarks evince much good sense:—

"Upon my word, you pay 'Vathek' much more attention than he deserves; and do you not think we shall usher him too pompously into the world with a dissertation on his fable and machinery? Notes are necessary, and the dissertation I myself should very much approve, but fear the world might imagine I fancied myself the author, not of an Arabian tale, but an epic poem. Supposing you limit your preface and preliminary discourse, I make no doubt your good taste will suggest to you a light, easy style. Misses, &c., may not be scared, for, after all, a poor Arabian storyteller can only pretend to say *Virginibus puerisque canto.* As for the rhapsody, it deserves to be pushed, not only into the margin of the book, but quite out of it. Though you have given it some pointed touches, it still limps in a manner to excite compassion; and as for instruction, don't fancy it contains any. The river Kalismer never flowed but in my brain. The nine pillars are entirely my own erection, &c., &c. After this confession you will not wish, I should think, to insert the poetical whine to Thelminar. I believe in most respects I have been discreet in my costume. The domes of Shadukiam and Amberabad you will find explained in Richardson.[1] The Cocknos is a bird whose bill is much esteemed in Persia for its beautiful polish. See ' Persian Tales,' ' History of the Sorrowful Vizir and Zelica Begum.' The butterflies of Cachemire are celebrated in a poem of Meschi I slaved at with Zemir, the old Mahometan who assisted me in translating Wortley Montagu's MS. ; but they are hardly worth a note.[2] I suppose you will prepare a tolerably long comment on the Simorgue, and that most respectable bird deserves all you can say of her. Soliman Daki and Soliman Gian-ben-Gian will furnish ample field for a display of Oriental erudition. The miscellany of Eastern learning and the history of Bababaloukism may partly help to enlighten your researches.

[1] "Oh ! am I not happy ? I am, I am,
　　To thee, sweet Eden, how dark and sad
　Are the diamond turrets of Shadukiam,
　　And the fragrant bowers of Amberabad ! "
　　　　　　　　　　—Paradise and the Peri.

[2] This shows that part of the Oriental lore in Henley's notes was supplied by Beckford himself. According to an article by Mr. Parsons, in the *Scots Observer* for 1892, Henley insinuated to Douce that Beckford derived the plot of " Vathek " from his Oriental teacher. It must be hoped that there was some misunderstanding, for the statement would have been mendacious.

"The catastrophe of Carathis had better remain as you first intended. I am perfectly at a loss how to deepen Vathek's damnation; and as for the end where mention is made of Gulchenrouz, be assured we cannot improve it. The period runs admirably, and for my part, I think the contrast between the boisterous caliph and the peaceable Gulchenrouz not ill imagined."

The introductory dissertation never appeared, and its merits or demerits must remain food for conjecture. Respecting the annotations, the reader of "Vathek" in this edition will be able to judge for himself. It may be remarked here that a few hitherto unnoticed misprints in Henley's text and notes have been silently corrected, but that no endeavour has been made to reduce his Oriental orthography to the modern standard.

Beckford's wife, Lady Margaret Beckford, died at Vevay on May 26, 1786, of miliary fever, twelve days after giving birth to a daughter. On June 12 Henley wrote him a letter of condolence, to which Beckford replied from some unnamed part of Switzerland on August 1 :—

"I thank you for your letter of the 12th June, and the sentiments so feelingly expressed in it. My spirits and rest is broken, and it is with difficulty that I hold my pen. The slow fever which has been preying upon me almost without

M

interruption since the latter end of May, has most disagreeably diverted my mind from 'Vathec'; but upon reading over your letter, it appears you had sent the MS. for my inspection. If you have, Heaven knows its fate; certainly it has not reached my hands, any more than a letter to which you allude as immediately preceding your last. I beg you will clear up these doubts, being anxious to receive your notes and illustrations.

"I fear the dejection of mind into which I am plunged will prevent my finishing the other stories, and of course 'Vathek's' making his appearance in any language this winter. I would not have him upon any account come forth without his companions."

Everything that Beckford here pronounces impossible or undesirable was to happen. "Vathek" did appear in both languages, and his companions never appeared at all. Late in 1786,[1] J. Johnson, of St. Paul's Churchyard, published "The History of the Caliph Vathek, an Arabian tale from an unpublished manuscript, with notes critical and explanatory."[2] We can only conjecture Henley's motives for so unpardonable a breach of confidence.

[1] And, as the above correspondence alone would establish, not in 1784, as asserted by all recent writers, who have been misled by Cyrus Redding.

[2] We take this title from the half-title, for the title-page has only "An Arabian Tale," &c.

Cupidity was probably among the least, as the emolument must have been small, and he might have been deprived even of this by legal proceedings. Vanity was most likely a more powerful agent, combined with impatience to see his labours in print, and a perhaps not ill-grounded apprehension that Beckford's caprice might prevent the English version from ever seeing the light. Had this indeed happened, England would have lost a classic without France gaining one, for the place of the original text in French literature has always been that of a literary curiosity. Henley's translation, on the other hand, though not without traces of its Gallic extraction, such as the employment of "superb" instead of "proud," and mistakes such as the rendering of *figure* by "figure," where "countenance" is evidently intended, and of *clous* by "grape-shot" centuries before the invention of artillery, is sufficiently idiomatic to have ranked from the first as an English book. It does, indeed, profess itself a translation, but from the Arabic. "Nothing," says Henley very coolly in one of his notes, "can impress a greater awe upon the mind than does this passage *in the original.*" This denial of Beckford's originality must have angered him even more than the breach of trust, and he protested against it when publishing the French text. It probably obtained little credence. Stephen

Weston, an intrepid meddler with Arabic, Chinese, Etruscan, and other such simple and familiar languages, propounded the theory in the *Gentleman's Magazine* that the tale had been written for the sake of the notes, which he evidently deemed much the more valuable. Henley,[1] who may not have widely dissented from this view, nevertheless rejected the apparent implication that the tale and the notes were by the same writer, and assured Weston that the former was really and truly translated from a foreign language, diplomatically avoiding the acknowledgment that this was neither more nor less than French. His connection with it must soon have transpired. In the British Museum copy, the book is attributed to him in a manuscript note, imperfectly erased by a later librarian, who has substituted Beckford's name.

In what manner Henley may have sought to excuse his breach of confidence to Beckford never will be known. Beckford's reply, if he vouchsafed any, was too withering for Henley to retain; it does not appear in the correspondence. The impression produced on Beckford is best indicated by the haste with which he proceeded to publish the French text of his romance, both in Lausanne and Paris.

---

[1] In the catalogue of Beckford's library appears a copy of "Vathek," with manuscript notes by Weston, "correcting Mr. Henley's ignorance of Arabic."

In issuing these he spoke in measured terms of the "indiscretion" which had occasioned the premature publication of the English version, and flatly contradicted the assertion of its Arabic origin. His anger eventually subsided into contemptuous indifference. When questioned by Redding he affected not to know who the translator was, but admitted that "it was tolerably well done," and afterwards that "on the whole it did him justice." One more trace of his relations with Henley exists in the correspondence. In 1797 the latter, who had fallen into embarrassed circumstances, mustered up resolution to apply to Beckford for assistance, and has preserved his negative reply. It is couched in very cold terms, but magnanimously abstains from allusion to the applicant's unfaithfulness, and grounds the refusal on Beckford's obligations to his immediate connections and dependants. Our own obligations to Henley as suggester, translator, and possibly preserver of "Vathek," are after all so considerable that it is satisfactory to find reason for believing that he ultimately escaped from his embarrassments. In 1805 he obtained the highly important and responsible post of Principal of the East India Company's College at Haileybury, which he held until within a short time of his death in 1815.

Beckford's first care was now to vindicate his

claim to originality by bringing out the French version of his work. He obtained the approbation of the Paris censor on January 26, 1787; and in the course of the year two editions were published, one at Paris and the other at Lausanne. It has hitherto been impossible to determine the priority of these editions, nor is the point yet perfectly clear, notwithstanding the light thrown upon it by the following extremely interesting manuscript note, first published by Mr. Julian Marshall in *Notes and Queries*, April 20, 1880, written by M. Chavannes, to whom the publication of the Lausanne edition had been entrusted by Beckford, upon the title of a copy of this extremely rare book, sold on March 29, 1889, in a London auction room :—

"À la demande de M. Beckford je me suis chargé de corriger son manuscrit et de le faire imprimer à Lausanne. Je me suis repenti d'avoir cédé à sa solicitation, l'ouvrage ne me paraissant ni moral ni interessant. J'ai de plus des desagrémens. M. Beckford en quittant Lausanne se hâta de le faire imprimer à Paris au prejudice de l'imprimeur de Lausanne, et je dus menacer M. Beckford de mettre dans les papiers son infidelitè,[1] qui fit qu'on

---

[1] Mr. Marshall remarks on the oddity of this phrase, which alone seems sufficient to establish that M. Chavannes' correction of "Vathek" was confined to the correction of the press.

arrêta à la douane de France l'envoy de l'imprimeur Hignon, les trois exemplaires qu'il envoyait à Paris, et M. B. se hâta de dedommager l'imprimeur pour éviter la publicitè."

At first sight this seems to establish the priority of the Lausanne edition, which certainly was the first commissioned by Beckford. But the three copies sent to Paris would in all probability be despatched as soon as printed, and it appears that they found the Paris edition already in possession of the field. They could not have been seized as contraband if the French edition had not existed; it is, nevertheless, possible that, although protected by royal privilege, it had not actually left the press. The privilege bears date August 22, and the registration September 4.[1] It may also be the case that, prior to the registration of the Paris privilege, the Lausanne edition had circulated freely in France; though this seems hardly reconcilable with M. Chavannes' "se hâta," "les trois exemplaires." It scarcely seems possible to determine the question of priority with absolute certainty, unless it could be exactly ascertained when the Swiss edition reached France. That it ought to have been the *editio princeps* is unquestionable, and Beckford's

---

[1] These documents are given in M. Mallarmé's reprint of the Paris edition. The British Museum copy of the latter, to which alone we have access, does not contain them, but no doubt wants a preliminary leaf.

conduct doubtless appeared very shocking in the
eyes of the worthy Genevese. We, better acquainted with "England's wealthiest son," may
feel certain that the sublunary question of copyright never entered his mind, and that he did not
need the threat of exposure in the newspapers to
incline him to remedy the wrong he had inadver-
tently committed. It is further to be remarked
that the publication of the Paris edition took place
when Beckford was far away, he having sailed
for Portugal in the March preceding.

An extraordinary fact respecting these French
editions remains to be pointed out; the texts do not
always correspond. So far as can be ascertained,
this has not hitherto been noticed, save by a
casual remark of the late Rev. W. E. Buckley in
Notes and Queries, doubtless because no editor
till now has had both the rare Paris and the even
rarer Lausanne edition[1] before him at the same
time. The discrepancies are not always important,[2]
but they are numerous, and extend entirely through
the book. Their general character will be sufficiently indicated by a brief comparative table.

[1] No copy of the Lausanne edition appears in the sale catalogue
of Beckford's own library.

[2] The most important is perhaps the alteration of "le quatrième
prince," near the end, into "le troisième," showing that Beckford
had intended to write four episodes, but that the fourth was not
begun when publication was forced upon him.

LAUSANNE EDITION.

P. 2, l. 6. Il n'étoit nullement scrupuleux.

P. 2, l. 21. À mesure qu'ils étoient consumés.

P. 6, l. 12. Pour éviter d'être noyé.

P. 9, l. 20. Ce que celui-ci fit assez modérément.

P. 11, l. 6. Quoiq'il eut les yeux fixès sur l'œil terrible et meurtrier.

P. 16, l. 19. Ou lui brûlera jusqu'au moindre poil de la barbe.

P. 23, l. 2. Là.

PARIS EDITION.

P. 4, l. 2. These words are omitted.

P. 4, l. 15. À mesure qu'ils se refroidissoient.

P. 7, l. 7. Pour se sauver d'un nouveau deluge.

P. 9, l. 22. Celui-ci prit peu de chose.

P. 11. l. 1. L'œil terrible et meurtrier ne fit aucun effet sur lui.

P. 15, l. 12. Ou lui brûlera la barbe jusqu'au moindre poil.

P. 20, l. 2. Sur leurs bords verdoyants.

It will be seen that no alteration is made without a reason, and the same is the case with the hundreds of others which might be adduced. All are preserved in the definitive edition of 1815, which adds a few more, evidently the result of careful revision. The eleven thousand steps of Vathek's tower, for example, have become fifteen hundred, Beckford having doubtless reflected that at a height so far surpassing the clouds, cities would not have been visible even as shells, or, as the new edition has it, mole-hills.[1] Unfortunately this handsome volume is inaccurately printed, and not all the misprints are corrected in the list of errata.

[1] Perhaps the double meaning of *coquilles* had occurred to him.

The question now arises, which of these versions is to be regarded as the more authentic text? Internal and external evidence combine to decide the point in favour of the Paris edition. Its variations are almost always improvements, and such as could have been introduced by no one but the author. They are also, as we have seen, maintained in the London edition of 1815, stated by Beckford himself to reproduce "*ce petit ouvrage tel que je l'ai composé.*" "With my final revisions and corrections" would have been more accurate, for the Paris edition, and still more the London, certainly fails to represent the book as originally written. This original can only be identified with the text which Henley had had in his hands three years before the appearance of the French editions, and upon comparison of these with his version it will be found to agree far more closely with the Lausanne than with the French impression. Some conclusions of considerable literary interest result.

1. The Lausanne text substantially represents "Vathek" as originally written.

2. Beckford gave his book a thorough revision some time between placing it in the hands of M. Chavannes to bring out in Switzerland, probably late in 1786, and his departure for Portugal in 1787. This may have been before or after his

obtaining the licence of the French censor on January 26, 1787, but was probably before.

3. When Henley's translation is compared with the French original, it must be remembered that he had not the latter before him in the form in which alone it is now generally accessible. The only fair comparison is with the Lausanne text.

4. Though M. Chavannes says, "Je me suis chargé de corriger son manuscrit," the almost exact agreement of his text with that which Henley had in his possession three years earlier proves that his corrections, if any, must have been of the slightest.

The pretensions of "Vathek" as a French literary composition are thus estimated by M. Mallarmé. After remarking that although Voltaire is evidently the model, Beckford frequently appears a precursor of Chateaubriand, he adds :—

"Tout coule de source, avec une limpidité vive avec un ondoiement large de périodes; et l'éclat tend à se fondre dans la pureté totale du cours, qui charrie maintes richesses de diction inaperçues d'abord; cas naturel avec un étranger inquiet que quelque expression trop audacieuse ne le trahisse en arrêtant le regard."

It only remains to be added that the Lausanne edition has no notes, but that the Paris edition is accompanied by a selection from Henley's. Did Beckford translate these himself?

Not much need be or can be said about the
literary qualities of " Vathek."   Alive with un-
diminished vitality after a century's existence, it
has proved its claim to a permanent place in
literature by obtaining it; nor, at any period of
its history, has it been a book which criticism
could greatly help or hinder, or which allowed
sound criticism much scope for controversy.   Its
beauties are by no means of the recondite order;
and inability to appreciate them is one of those
innate distastes, not for the book but its *genre*,
against which expostulation is impotent.   A man
may be reasoned into admiring Wordsworth, but
not into liking the " Arabian Nights."   Criticism
can only be usefully exercised in analysing the
psychology of the author, a curious and attractive study.   The most remarkable feature is perhaps the singular doubleness of character evinced
throughout the book.   As has been elsewhere said,
the peculiar distinction of " Vathek" is its alliance of the fantastic and the sublime.   The former
attains an unsurpassed pinnacle in the early scenes
between Vathek and the Indian; the latter almost
challenges comparison with Milton in the description of the hall of Eblis.   Between these summits
lies a deep depression; for a time the story flags,
seems almost in peril of becoming tedious.   The
same doubleness pervades the whole; the book is

at once very French and very English, very Oriental and very European, very frivolous and very tragic, very shallow and very profound. In this it represents its author, a child of the eighteenth century unconsciously inspired with the emotions of the nineteenth, who, as M. Mallarmé very justly says, in imitating Voltaire, announces Chateaubriand. While few books display more either of the lucidity of the eighteenth century or of its sarcastic persiflage, it is equally animated by the spirit of vague unrest and yearning melancholy which were to attain such proportions in "René" and "Childe Harold." The same is true of Beckford's Travels, that remarkable picture of a society on the eve of transformation. There are brighter stars in the literary firmament than Beckford, but few which can with equal propriety be likened to the evening star and to the morning star. Nor is there, probably, any modern Oriental story except "Vathek" which might appear without disadvantage in the "Arabian Nights," with Aladdin on its right hand and Ali Baba on its left. Its Gallicisms, as it happens, rather help the illusion, for, after modern translators have done their best, it is through the English rendering of Galland's French version that these tales will always be popularly known.

It seems hardly possible that it should be left

to us to point out the derivation of one of the most striking passages in modern English poetry from " Vathek"; but we have not met with this observation as respects the catastrophe of Southey's " Curse of Kehama," a noble poem at present so unjustly neglected that it may be expedient to cite the entire passage :—

> " He did not know the holy mystery
> Of that divinest cup, that as the lips,
> Which touch it, even such its quality,
> Good or malignant : Madman ! and he thinks
> The blessed prize is won, and joyfully he drinks.

> " Then Seeva opened upon the Accursed One
> His Eye of Anger : upon him alone
> The wrath-beam fell.   He shudders—but too late
> The deed is done,
> The dreadful liquor works the will of Fate.
> Immortal he would be,
> Immortal he is made, but through his veins,
> Torture at once and immortality,
> A stream of poison doth the Amreeta run,
> And while within the burning anguish flows,
> His outward body glows
> Like molten ore, beneath the avenging Eye,
> Doomed thus to live and burn eternally.

> " The fiery Three,
> Beholding him, set up a fiendish cry,
> A song of jubilee ;
> Come, Brother, come ! they sung : too long
> Have we expected thee.
> Henceforth we bear no more
> The unequal weight ; Come, Brother, we are Four.

" Vain his almightiness, for mightier pain
Subdued all power ; pain ruled supreme alone ;
And yielding to the bony hand
The unemptied cup, he moved toward the Throne,
And at the vacant corner took his stand.
Behold the golden Throne at length complete,
And Yamen silently ascends the judgment seat."

Part of Kehama's penalty is perpetual immo-
bility, part of Vathek's perpetual unrest, but the
thought is the same—the fruition of the sinner's
desire is the sinner's punishment—and the virtual
identity of the catastrophes is obvious. Southey
claims originality for his story, but if he did not
unearth this particular incident from some nook
of the myriad-chambered Hindu Pantheon, he
must have found it in " Vathek," with which his
correspondence proves him to have been acquainted
at least as early as 1804. The three upholders of
Yamen's throne, moreover, are manifest though far
from servile copies of Soliman ben Daoud and the
pre-Adamite sultans.

" After the Bastile was destroyed he came home ;
and in 1791 visited Paris again. *He was there
at the death of the king.*" Louis XVI. was executed in January 1793, thus this cursory remark
of Redding's is an independent confirmation of
the following remarkable anecdote of Beckford's
life, which has not hitherto appeared in an English

book, but will be found in the preface to the
catalogue of M. Brunet's library, sold at Paris in
1868. The writer is probably M. Potier :—

"En 1793, l'amour des livres rares et précieux
avait retenu à Paris un Anglais de distinction et
riche, William Beckford, de Fonthill Abbey, qui
poursuivait avec ardeur les depouilles opimes que
la Revolution jetait dans les rues. Chardin entre-
nait de frequents rapports avec le riche amateur,
auquel il revendait les curiosités tombeès entre
ses mains et dont il ne voulait pas. Chardin, me
dit M. Brunet, ne tarda pas a savoir que les jours
de l'honorable sir Beckford étaient ménacés ; il
courut chez lui et l'en informa, lui fit, séance
tenante, changer ses vêtements contre ceux d'un
commis libraire, le conduisit chez Merigot, bou-
quiniste célèbre de cette époque, et l'y installa à
titre de commis. Après quelques semaines, Chardin
trouva le moyen de faire delivrer un passe-port sous
un nom d'emprunt à sir Beckford qui put retourner
en Angleterre. Celui-ci temoigna généreusement
sa reconnoissance à son sauveur, il lui fit passer
tous les ans une rente de deux mille quatre cents
francs, qui lui fut payée jusque vers 1820, époque
à laquelle mourut Chardin."

If M. Brunet related this story as true, he certainly believed it, and there seems no sufficient
reason for rejecting it. Its truth is indirectly

confirmed by the amount of the pension stated to
have been bestowed upon Chardin, which seems
curious at this day, but would have been perfectly
natural in 1793, when the gold piece contained
twenty-four francs instead of twenty as at present.
A pension of 2400 francs, therefore, would have
been equivalent to one of a hundred louis.

THOMAS MOORE

THOMAS MOORE [1]

IT was the maxim of a great Chinese philosopher, "Always be in sympathy with your age." The advice, admirable in most cases, fails in that of men of genius, save only in those exceptional instances, such as the Italian Renaissance, or the Elizabethan era, when an entire generation is as it were lifted off its feet, elevated above its level, and pushed forward it knows not how, by the influence of an invisible power. A Michael Angelo and a Shakespeare can thus be in fullest sympathy with an age which they far transcend. But, as a rule, the men of letters and artists, especially the former, in whom a period discerns the fullest response to its own requirements, and whom it consequently crowns with the amplest meed of popularity, fall after a while into the second or even an inferior rank; and others previously neglected or contemned as unsympathetic with their contemporaries, are advanced to fill the vacant thrones. It is also to be observed that as regards these latter, the world's revised

[1] Prefixed to the "Thomas Moore Anecdotes." Jarrold & Sons: 1899.

verdict is generally final. Seldom indeed has one thus promoted been remitted to the ranks; his gold has been tried in the fire, and its worth is henceforth unquestionable. But as regards the slighted favourite, there is more room for vacillation and oscillation of judgment. Never, or hardly ever does such a one regain the place which he originally held in the world's esteem; but depreciation is not unfrequently adjudged to have gone too far, and a wholesome reaction restores him to a position not too remote from his former altitude. It often appears that the error lay after all not so much in an exorbitant estimate of the man himself as in a misapprehension of his rank in relation to his contemporaries.

Stronger examples of this twofold reaction could hardly be found than in what was once deemed by far the most conspicuous light of the glorious poetical constellation of the earlier decades of this century—Byron; and his brilliant satellite, Thomas Moore. Byron expressed the spirit of his age so perfectly that few contemporaries doubted or could doubt that he was its chief as well as its chosen poet. At present it would be hard to find a critic with any just claim to the character who did not perceive and admit the great superiority of Wordsworth and Coleridge, Shelley and Keats, in everything that discriminates

the inspired poet from the writer of effective
prose; and the reaction has proceeded so far
that many have even denied Byron the title of
poet. This absurd injustice has in its turn begotten another reaction which will doubtless end
by putting Byron in his proper place, "below
the great" (using this adjective in its very
highest sense), "but far above the good." The
same reaction ought in its degree to have bene-
fited his acolyte and biographer, Thomas Moore,
but this scarcely seems to have yet come to pass.
There is perhaps no conspicuous poet of that time
at present so decidedly at a discount as Moore,
once second in popularity to Scott and Byron
alone. This is most unjust. Moore is not only
an excellent poet and a consummate man of letters,
but he is a representative man in several departments. It happens unfortunately that none of these
is at present particularly in favour. It takes a
Swinburne or a Morris to make the metrical
romance palatable just now. Moore's graceful wit
and satire, though they can never miss admiration, were of necessity mainly expended upon
themes of temporary interest. The music which
contributed so largely to the success of his "Irish
Melodies" is now unfashionable, as the music of a
past generation, whatever its merits, invariably
seems to become. Worst of all, he has lost his

rank as the national poet of Ireland, partly from the emergence of new ideals among his countrymen, but chiefly, it must be owned, from the discovery that there is little specifically Celtic in his genius except his wit and animation; and, in particular, that he is totally devoid of that priceless quality, "Celtic magic." It cannot be, however, that oblivion will in the long run be allowed to overtake so interesting a literary figure. As the poet of the Ireland of his day, and not less of English parliamentary liberalism, Moore ought always to remain a conspicuous figure in national as well as literary history. It is impossible to replace him in anything near his old position. An age that has fed upon Wordsworth and Shelley, Tennyson and Browning, will not be deeply moved by Moore. But apart from the poets who mould opinion, and are, as one of them said, "the unacknowledged legislators of the world," an honourable place remains for poets of the library, who embalm the spirit of their own age, and hand its volatile essence down to posterity in a compact and clarified form. Such a poet was Moore, the best method of perpetuating whose fame, apart from the actual reimpression of his writings, is to show by a clear account of his life and literary activity the important position which he held in the worlds of letters and politics of his own day.

Thomas Moore was born in Aungier Street,
Dublin, May 28, 1779, and was the son of a
grocer, who gradually developed into a wine merchant, and declined into a barrack master. Both
his parents were Roman Catholics, victims of the
unjust legislation and the still more pernicious
social exclusion which had come down as the ugly
but inevitable legacy of troubled times. Trinity
College, however, was open to all as a place of
education, though not at that period as a field of
honour and emolument; and Moore, who was a
remarkably clever and precocious boy, acquired
sufficient Latin at private schools, partly by extra
lessons from a friendly usher named Donovan, to
justify his matriculation there in 1794, at what
would now be thought the early age of fifteen.
Roman Catholic disabilities had been so far removed in the preceding year as to allow Romanists
to practise as barristers, and it was the dearest
wish of Moore's mother—much the more interesting of his parents—to see her son a counsellor.
Nothing, probably, would have made Moore a
lawyer, but he would have gained distinction as a
speaker notwithstanding his short figure and un-
heroic physiognomy; he would have been a useful
adjutant to O'Connell, and his career might very
well have ended in an Irish judgeship. But,
though far from idle or dissipated, he could no

more than Petrarch, Boccaccio, or Ariosto, addict himself to the study of the law. His college reputation was that of a wit and an elegant scholar. He translated into English verse the most difficult Greek author, perhaps, with whom he was as yet competent to grapple, namely Anacreon; and the appellation of Anacreon Moore, the more appropriate from his cheerful and festive cast of countenance, adhered to him for the remainder of his life. The Provost would willingly have distinguished the translator by a special reward, but doubted whether the college could officially countenance anything "so amatory and convivial." That nothing might be wanting to his character as a representative Irishman, Moore struck up a friendship with Robert Emmet, and would probably have been drawn into the plots of the United Irishmen had not Emmet scrupulously abstained from soliciting him. Moore came exceedingly well out of the investigation which resulted, both as regarded his own behaviour and his loyalty towards more compromised persons. In 1799 he proceeded to England to study for the bar at the Middle Temple, taking with him his translation of Anacreon, which his University honoured by subscribing for to the extent of two copies, when he had succeeded in making an arrangement with the London publishers. It is shocking to our sense of congruity to hear of an Anacreon in quarto, but such was the form of publication adopted, and there were erudite notes, probably cribbed, into the bargain. The success of this publication opened the way for Moore's appearance as an English Anacreon under the pseudonym of Thomas Little. This otherwise insignificant publication is noteworthy as a warning to young men of genius to be careful what they publish at the beginning of their career. Twenty years later it would have excited no attention, but as the work of a clever young man just beginning to be productive, it was taken as a sample of the entire crop, and fixed a reputation for immorality upon Moore entirely unsupported by his subsequent writings. The same thing, *mutatis mutandis*, was happening at the same time to Wordsworth, who was making for himself a reputation with the mass of the public as a childish and prosaic writer by publishing a few poems where simplicity was exaggerated into triviality in illustration of his theory of poetic diction, but which critics and readers insisted on taking as the standard of his taste and the measure of his powers.

Moore's great success in English society, nevertheless, was but slightly attributable to his poetry, and still less to his law. He was a musical virtuoso, and, by the admission of the inimical Croker, who had known him as a young man in Dublin, could not only play but sing, or rather warble, bewitchingly, "set off by an expression of countenance and charm of manner the most graceful, the most natural, and the most touching that we have ever witnessed." He had brought over a high reputation in this department from Ireland, and had in particular gained the admiration of Lord Moira, through whom, in all probability, he obtained presentation to the Prince of Wales, then very liberal, very pro-Catholic, and very ready to patronise promising Irishmen. And now was witnessed a curious phenomenon—a return to primitive practice on the part of one of the most artificial of modern poets. The great objection to Moore's poetry is its want of nature; there is no getting over that. Yet this conventional and theatrical writer was doing what Wordsworth and Coleridge could not do—he was reciting his own compositions with musical accompaniment, just like a Scandinavian skald or a Homeric rhapsodist, and would probably have been considered by Homer himself as supporting the character of a sacred bard better than any of the Lakers. Thus did primitive customs for a season revive in London drawing-rooms; and as it was probably true even then that

"Silent rows the songless gondolier,"

these drawing-rooms perhaps then exhibited what

could not have been found elsewhere in the civilised world.

Of one of the ancient minstrels whom Moore thus emulated it is recorded that "he could harp a fish out of the water." Moore surpassed this feat by harping, not only fishes, but loaves and fishes out of the Admiralty. In 1803, through the influence of Lord Moira, he was appointed to the Admiralty Registrarship in the Bermudas, one of those places which one fills, when one can, by deputy. He was obliged, however, to go out and take possession, which having accomplished, and having installed, as subsequently appeared, the greatest rogue in the islands as his *locum tenens*, he returned by way of the United States and Canada. The poems which he published upon his return (1806), contained some illiberal attacks upon America, of which Jeffrey properly took notice in the *Edinburgh Review*, but in assailing Moore's amatory poetry he travelled beyond the record, and according to the code of the time justified the challenge which Moore addressed to him. The incidents which grew out of this cartel, as detailed by Moore himself, resemble those of a comic opera, and their ludicrousness was increased by the diminutive stature of the pair of combatants. The *dénouement*, however, was what it ought to have been, a firm friendship. It is remarkable that the two most important literary intimacies of Moore's life should have arisen out of abortive duels. The second—which, especially as it grew out of the quarrel with Jeffrey, may be mentioned a little out of chronological order for convenience' sake—was Moore's misunderstanding with Byron, who had sneered (1811) at the incident of the absence of the bullet from Jeffrey's pistol in a manner too clearly evincing his scepticism as to the presence of bullets in either weapon. Moore proceeded with more temper and discretion on this occasion, and the general conduct of the affair does honour both to him and to Byron. Byron never made a real friend after his native pride had been fostered into egotism by immoderate success, but his fidelity to his early intimacies shows that he was not naturally incapable of friendship. His intimacy with Moore came in the middle period, when he was beginning to be flattered and idolised, but was not yet a golden image with feet of clay. His regard for Moore, if not amounting to affection, was frank and cordial, and assuredly disinterested. The latter attribute was as difficult for Moore to sustain as it was easy for Byron. But he was, in a greater degree than has been generally recognised, a gentleman and a man of spirit. No unworthy compliance can be alleged against him; no slur

ever rested upon his independence towards any
man, or any body of men. His attitude towards
Byron could not in the nature of things be comfortable or altogether dignified; he could not love
him, and he could not help being horribly afraid
of him. The satellites of Jupiter may revolve in
peace, but it is an awful thing to be the satellite
of a comet which may at any moment rush off
into space. That Moore should have incurred
disfavour with advanced Liberals by seeking to
restrain Byron from quarrelling too openly with
the established order of things was natural, was
inevitable, but was still inequitable. It may be
granted that he was wrong. As a poet and an
intellectual force Byron was a revolutionist, or was
nothing. But from Moore's own point of view he
was right, and there is no reason to believe that
his conduct was dictated by any other motive than
a regard for Byron's most visible interests. It
was much to have preserved to the last both
Byron's respect and his own.

When Moore presumed to demand explanations
from Byron the position of the two poets in popular esteem approximated more closely than was
ever afterwards the case. Byron was only known
by "English Bards and Scotch Reviewers," which
had indeed produced a considerable sensation, but
was just the kind of performance frequently

achieved by a clever man who soon recognises that his sphere is rather politics than poetry. Moore's attempts in heroic verse, " Corruption," a satire, and " The Sceptic," which might be and perhaps was designed as a reply to some passages in Campbell's " Pleasures of Hope," had not been remarkably successful, but he was already known as the author of " The Irish Melodies," and although the publication continued until 1834, enough had already been done to give him a leading rank among the lyrists of his day. Alone among them all he wrote for music which he found ready to his hand, and thus insured that his pieces should be real songs. This great quality, which far more sweet and subtle lyrists do not always attain, has been made a ground of unfavourable criticism. Moore's songs are said to be of little value when divorced from their music. But, rejoins Professor Minto, they were never intended to be divorced from their music. The melody is an integral part of the poem, and in fact this very modern poet has made a long step back towards the practice of the ancients. Others no doubt have done the same in isolated instances, but no one has given such a *corpus* of song adapted to music, and so completely wedded the two arts. It inevitably follows that the Irish Melodies cannot convey the same pleasure when merely read as when performed to their natural accompaniment. Much that seems trivial has its full musical justification, but this the reader cannot be expected to consider. Their merits as a body of national minstrelsy have been variously estimated. Many, undoubtedly, are only national in so far as the tunes to which they are adapted are Irish. Others breathe a truly patriotic feeling, which may appear somewhat out of date now that Roman Catholic grievances have been redressed, but was perfectly legitimate in its own day. The conceits, prettinesses, and tricks of diction which undoubtedly marred the "Irish Melodies" considered merely as literary compositions, do not affect this feeling, which is never insincere, though the note is not that of "Who Fears to Talk of Ninety-eight?" or "The Shan Van Vocht." If it is said that under the then circumstances of his country Moore ought to have been a rebel, such was not his own view. He was a good Irishman, but also a good Briton. He expected the redress of Irish grievances by peaceful means, and lived to see the fulfilment of most of his anticipations. The political verse of Davis and others has great merit in many respects, but only a small portion of it has obtained acceptance as classical English poetry. The proportion of Moore's melodies, on the other hand, which have become household

O

words, is very considerable. It will suffice to
name, "Go where glory waits thee," "The harp
that once through Tara's hall," "When he who
adores thee has left but the name," "Rich and
rare were the gems she wore," "As a beam o'er
the face of the waters may glow," "At the mid
hour of night," "Come o'er the sea," "When first
I met thee," and "Come rest in this bosom, my
own stricken deer." It cannot be affirmed that
there are many which owe their popularity to
meretricious glitter, false sentiment, or anything
except the felicitous marriage of good words to
good music. They cannot be said to be masterpieces. The songs of Goethe, Heine, and Béranger
possess all their recommendations, along with much
higher ones which lay entirely beyond Moore's
sphere. But these are not equally national. They
express the national character to perfection, they
are not equally expressive of the national aspirations. The competition of Burns, no doubt, crushes
Moore; but one may be far behind Burns, Goethe,
Heine, and Béranger, and still be an excellent poet.

There is another class of literature in which
Moore began to distinguish himself about this
time in which he has little competition to fear,
that of light epigrammatic satire. The incentive
to this new departure was the conduct of the
Prince Regent when, on coming nominally to the

head of affairs through the insanity of his father (1811), he broke with his old political associates, and continued to govern by the aid of his father's Ministers, espousing a system which he and his friends had continually denounced as pernicious, and repudiating all his former political convictions, or what had been supposed to be such. The situation was a painful one, and the Regent's chief fault was that he did not sufficiently feel it to be so. Had it been possible to believe him actuated by principle, his conduct might have been defended as wise and patriotic. Any Liberal administration that could have been formed must of necessity have been a very weak one, and weak government at home must have paralysed the nation in its tremendous struggle with Napoleon. If the Prince had really subordinated private attachments to public duty his conduct would have deserved applause. Unfortunately it was not possible to believe that he was in truth actuated by such motives, or that estrangement from his old associates cost him anything. It was evidently the more comfortable course for him to pursue, and, neither his political nor his personal character entitled him to credit for higher motives. Yet, whatever the motive, the action was in itself right, and did not merit the obloquy with which it was visited by the Whigs, infuriated by the disappointment of all their expectations, and the apparent prospect of another quarter of a century's exclusion from office. Moore had his own peculiar disappointment; he had long looked for a provision at the hands of Lord Moira, shortly to be Marquis of Hastings and Governor-General of India, the only one of the Regent's old friends who had not broken with him, but who could now only offer Moore a dubious provision in India, whither of course he was disinclined to proceed. He was now a husband and father, having married the charming actress, Bessie Dyke, in 1811; India, therefore, was more out of the question than ever, and he resigned himself to accept Lord Moira's valedictory gift of fifteen dozen of wine. All his social affections and intimacies, moreover, drew him to take an active part against the Prince; his talents had long recommended him to the brilliant society of Holland House, and he was becoming the associate of Lords Lansdowne and Holland, of Rogers, Sydney Smith, Mackintosh, and the rest. But the chief justification for the acrimonious hostility he evinced towards a Prince who had always personally treated him with kindness, was undoubtedly his strong resentment at the Prince's desertion of the Roman Catholic claims, which not unnaturally overbalanced imperial considerations in the mind of an oppressed

Irish Catholic. Moore's patriotism was ardent, and on this point was reinforced by horror of bigotry and enthusiasm for toleration. Ere long it was discovered that English literature had acquired such a satirist as it had never had before, whose prototype among classical writers was not Juvenal or Horace, but Martial. Martial, for excellent reasons, never meddled with politics, but the same mordant wit which he expended upon men's folly and frivolity was now found effective as a political weapon. English literature had not wanted something of the kind before, but the airy malice of "The Twopenny Post Bag" is a great advance upon the elaborate pleasantry of the "Rolliad." It has more affinity to the *esprit* of Voltaire, while at the same time the manner, no less than the matter, is distinctively Moore's own, and is substantially the same as that employed on quite a different class of subject in the "Irish Melodies" and their companion amatory lyrics. The merit of the songs, apart from the melody of the verse, is quite as much intellectual as poetical, consisting usually in the development of some exquisitely graceful or pathetic idea. In the satires there is a perfect shower of ideas, an incessant bombardment of the enemy with pungent sarcasm ; but here, as in the songs, the pleasure received arises in great measure from the poet's intellectual force, intimated by the felicity of the thoughts themselves and the rare polish imparted to them by an intellectual process. Pope would probably have left us much poetry like Moore's if he had been endowed with Moore's lyrical faculty.

The sale of "The Twopenny Post Bag" was prodigious, but there could be no very great profit upon so small a book, and the "Irish Melodies," though appearing regularly and largely circulated, would not keep a family whose head, under pain of extinction, was obliged to appear continually in the best society. Moore was compelled to undertake some more extensive work; his industry and independence did him honour; but it is some shock to high ideas of poetical imagination to find him contracting with Longmans to give them the best metrical romance that had yet been written upon condition of receiving the highest price that had yet been paid. This was not the way in which Wordsworth or Shelley would have gone to work, though Scott had followed it. So high was the estimate of Moore's talent, which implies an equally high estimate of his conscientiousness, that Longmans agreed to pay three thousand pounds for any poem he might produce without having seen a line of it. Such was the origin of "Lalla Rookh," generally regarded on its publication as a work of the most ethereal fancy. In 1815 Moore had made such progress with it as to offer the publishers a sight of the manuscript, of which they declined to avail themselves. In 1816 the unsatisfactory state of business prompted a noble offer from him to cancel the agreement, which the publishers, with equal magnanimity, refused. In 1817 the poem was published, and everybody was satisfied, the publishers with the sale, the poet with his honorarium, and the public with the important addition which seemed to have been made to English literature. Earl Russell repeats the verdict of his generation when, with a touching confidence that his views cannot be out of fashion, he writes in his preface to Moore's Diary: "'Lalla Rookh' is the work next to the Melodies and Sacred Songs in proof of Moore's title as a poet. It is a poem rich with the most brilliant creations; a work such as Pope always wished to write; such as Tasso might have written." On the other hand, the greatest of English critics—who also, unluckily for Moore, was a great and unjustly neglected poet —wrote on the appearance of the poem: "I have read two pages of 'Lalla Rookh,' or whatever it is called. Merciful Heaven! I dare read no more, that I may be able to answer at once to any questions 'I have but just looked at the work.' O Robinson! if I could, or if I dared, act and feel as Moore and his set do, what havoc could I not make amongst their crockery-ware! Why, there are not three lines together without some adulteration of common English." The truth lies between these extremes. The comparison of Moore with Tasso does seem somewhat ludicrous, while, on the other hand, the soured and splenetic feelings which impelled Coleridge to so severe a judgment are fully revealed by his admission that he had not read more than two pages of the poem he vituperates. "Lalla Rookh" should be read as a whole, not because it is a work of consummate art, or that it really matters very much where it is opened, as because it is an assemblage of small brilliancies individually ineffective, but resplendent in the mass. It is not a great poem, but is a great literary feat; it has no creative imagination, but much radiant fancy; if the author read up Oriental lore for it, and went out of his way to make niches for picturesque circumstances, Southey had done the same in "Thalaba" and "Kehama." The undercurrent of political allegory, with constant reference to the woes of Ireland, if out of place in an Oriental romance, served at all events to deepen the human interest. Great praise is due to the beautiful invention of "Paradise and the Peri," which has added a new and very attractive figure to the gallery of fairy mythology.

In 1817, the year of the publication of "Lalla

Rookh," Moore seemed at the pinnacle of good
fortune. He had scarcely taken Sloperton Cottage,
a delightful retreat in Wiltshire, near his friend
Lord Lansdowne, when a terrible blow fell upon
him by the defalcation of his deputy at Bermuda,
which rendered him liable for six thousand pounds.
His correspondence proves the fortitude with which
he bore the disaster, which elicited the most generous offers of help from Jeffrey, Lord Lansdowne,
and others. It was found advisable, however, that
he should for a time be out of the way, and he re-
treated to the Continent in 1819. In 1818 he had
begun to keep a diary, which renders the materials for
his life more copious and satisfactory from this date.

Moore's absence, with a brief interval in 1821,
lasted until April 1822. It had been partly spent
in Italy, where he renewed acquaintance with
Byron, "grown fat, which spoils the picturesque-
ness of his head," partly in Paris, where he stayed
too long. He found himself able to arrange his
Bermuda difficulties without recourse to Jeffrey
or Lord Lansdowne, by anticipating a legacy from
Byron, who bequeathed him his own autobiographic
memoirs. On these Moore, as was no doubt intended that he should, raised sufficient money from
Murray to put himself straight with the world; but
he was far from foreseeing the complications which
this unlucky autobiography was to occasion. Upon

Byron's death in 1824 his friends and Lady Byron's friends were nearly unanimous in protesting against the publication. It was of course admitted that Moore must be compensated for the loss to himself, but this he absolutely refused to hear of, and repaid the money borrowed from Murray by effecting another loan from Longman. So far the transaction was most honourable to him, but it is a serious question, usually answered in the negative, whether he could be justified in disappointing the trust reposed in him by Byron, who undoubtedly wished and designed the publication of the Memoirs, and relied upon Moore to realise his intention. Moore himself does not appear to have seen any reason for withholding them until pressure was brought to bear upon him, and it is probable that the fear of giving offence and creating scandal had more weight with him than he acknowledged to himself. On the other hand, the property in the Memoirs had become so intricate that it was not clear that it did not vest in Murray, who desired their destruction, and had the advantage of actual possession. The right course would have been that which Moore himself proposed, to consult all parties interested, and then publish the diary with erasures and omissions. He ought not, perhaps, to have allowed himself to be overborne; but in judging his conduct one point must always be kept

in mind, that publication would have been much
to his own pecuniary interest, and suppression the
reverse, a consideration which would have great,
even undue influence upon one so nervously sensitive and delicately honourable in all pecuniary
matters. After all, the chief cause of the unto-
ward fate of the manuscript was Byron's own want
of precision. If he had bequeathed it to Moore with
an absolute injunction to publish it, and the proviso
that in the event of his failing to do so it should go
to some such person as William Cobbett, the objections would have quickly disappeared. According
to Earl Russell, who had read most of it, it contained little that could do Byron's memory, or
English literature, either credit or the reverse.
This may well be believed, for great men who
write their autobiographies have a trick of leaving
off just as these are beginning to be interesting.
We should probably have heard much about the
rake of the early Regency; something about the
crazes of Lady Caroline Lamb, and the insufferable
virtues of Lady Byron; but little of the Byron of
" Manfred " and " Sardanapalus," of the " Vision of
Judgment " and " Don Juan."

Instead of being Byron's editor, Moore was fated
to be his biographer. Byron's bequest had manifestly marked him out for the office, and he was on
the point of giving evidence of his qualifications

for biography by his "Life of Sheridan," which had lingered long in his hands, but eventually made its appearance in 1825. If Moore was marked out as the ideal author for such a book, Murray was no less distinctly indicated as the only possible publisher, as Moore himself had admitted by depositing the Memoirs with him. The two were at open variance, but mutual interest spoke more strongly than resentment; a negotiation was successfully conducted through Hobhouse, and Murray enabled Moore to acquit his obligation to Longman by returning the two thousand guineas repaid to himself, and adding two thousand pounds for literary labour. The result was Moore's "Life of Byron," published in 1831, his principal achievement as a prose writer, and which will never be forgotten, even should it be superseded. An exhaustive and accurate book it certainly is not, such a performance would have been absolutely impossible at that period. But neither is it deceptive. It is reticent, but not insincere. It is exactly such a book as it became a man of Moore's high standing to write of a generous, though erring, friend and benefactor, at the time reputed the first poet of his age; and if Byron himself is spared, so are his adversaries. On the whole it is exactly the biography which the age and the circumstances required; and when the time arrives for Byron's

career to be dealt with in a more fearless and
searching manner, and with fuller access to materials, it is much to be hoped that the task may be
performed with equal tact, delicacy, and soundness
of judgment. Byron's career offers great tempta-
tions to a realistic biographer, but although a work
of this class may supplement Moore, it will not
supersede him. As a literary performance the
book is entitled to high praise; it is one to take
down at any time, open anywhere, and always
read with pleasure. It is quite true that much of
the charm resides in the copious use of Byron's
correspondence, nor could it be expected that
Byron at one remove should be as attractive as
Byron himself. An edition of Byron's works succeeded, able and adequate.

We must now return to Moore's literary activity
between the first commencement of "Lalla Rookh"
and the publication of the "Life of Byron." It
included many interesting productions, but nothing
of first-rate importance. In 1815 and 1816 had
appeared "National Airs" and "Sacred Songs,"
including pieces so universally popular as "Flow
on, thou shining river," "Oft in the stilly night,"
and "Sound the loud timbrel." "The Fudge
Family in Paris," "The Fudges in England,"
"Rhymes on the Road," and "Fables for the Holy
Alliance," were satirical verses in the style of

"The Twopenny Post Bag," and evincing the same capacity for light pungent satire. The last appeared in 1823, shortly after which time Moore began to be a regular contributor of satirical verses to the *Times*, receiving an annual retainer. The number and the topics of his communications were left to himself, and the connection continued to the mutual advantage of paper and poet for many years. His position as laureate of Liberalism was thus not unlike that subsequently assumed by Heine, and his pieces do not yield to Heine's in wit, although not like Heine's spiced with poetry. During his exile in Paris he had written "The Loves of the Angels," a romantic poem in the style of "Lalla Rookh," the subject of which was apparently suggested by Byron's "Heaven and Earth." It cannot be considered a very successful performance, manifesting more of the extravagance and false taste chargeable upon "Lalla Rookh," with less of pathos and fancy, and much less felicity of invention. It brought the author, however, a thousand pounds, and thus freed him from obligation to Lord Lansdowne. "Alciphron," a metrical Egyptian romance of the Roman period, began well, but the writer tired of it as a poem, and turned it into prose as "The Epicurean," a striking tale, but whose unfaithfulness to ancient manners drew upon Moore an annihilating criticism in the *Westminster Review* from a real scholar, Thomas Love Peacock. It is probably now best known by the highly imaginative illustrations of Turner. "Memoirs of Captain Rock" (1824), and "Travels of an Irish Gentleman in search of a Religion" (1834), were books of a partly polemical tendency, the former satirising the Irish Church Establishment in its legal and social aspects; the latter vindicating the Roman Catholic religion, to which Moore always adhered, though he brought his children up as Protestants. The "Life of Lord Edward Fitzgerald" appeared in 1831.

Moore's latter years were full of care and sorrow. The deaths of all his children, and of his two sisters, tried his affectionate spirit to the utmost, and in the case of the eldest son the trouble was aggravated by the youth's wildness and extravagance. He was also bent beneath the burden of a work which, with his usual industry and loyal determination to exert himself to the utmost for his family, he had undertaken without duly estimating its wearisomeness and difficulty, or the incipient decline of his own powers. This was the "History of Ireland," which he had engaged to write for Lardner's "Cabinet Cyclopædia." "The few entertaining volumes in this compilation," wrote a contemporary critic, "are but like lumps of sugar thrown in to sweeten the mess"; and Moore's four volumes, no sugar to anybody, were to him exceedingly bitter pills. In truth, it was no disgrace to him to have failed with a hopeless subject. The legendary history of Ireland is poetical and attractive, but taboo to the serious historian; the mediæval period illustrates Milton's observation touching the wars of the kites and the crows; the later history resembles the scenery of the country, very fine isolated portions only attainable by journeying across tedious morasses. History has few more brilliant pages than Macaulay's narrative of the suppression of the Irish revolt of 1688–90; but he had lighted upon an oasis; all before and all after is uninviting for many a long year. Moore, who was highly competent to narrate a single straightforward episode, was utterly unqualified to reduce the chaos of conflicting statements and contemporary transactions to order, and the effort so entirely wore him out that when at length (1846) the toil of ten years was completed, he could not sum up sufficient energy to write the preface, which was added by another hand. It is to this period that Earl Russell's remark applies :—" The brilliant hues of his varied conversation had faded, and the strong powers of his intellect had manifestly sunk." His mind, like Southey's, was worn out, and from the same causes, domestic sorrow and excessive literary toil. The wreck, nevertheless, was much less complete in his case than in Southey's. He continued his diary until 1847, and up to 1849 was frequently able to converse with freedom and gaiety; but after a fit which visited him on December 20th of that year his memory almost entirely failed, although his intelligence was never totally extinguished. "To the last day of his life," says Lord John Russell, " he would inquire with anxiety about the health of his friends, and would sing, or ask his wife to sing to him, the favourite airs of his past days. Even the day before his death, he 'warbled,' as Mrs. Moore expressed it, and a fond love of music never left him but with life." He died on February 26, 1852, and was buried at Bromham, a village adjoining his Wiltshire residence. A pension of three hundred pounds a year had been most properly conferred upon him in 1835, through the good offices of Lord John Russell. To this a civil list pension of one hundred pounds a year was subsequently added. This was continued to his widow, who also obtained an annuity from the investment of the sum of three thousand pounds, paid by Longmans for the copyright of his "Memoirs, Journals, and Correspondence," edited in eight volumes by Lord John Russell from 1853 to 1856.

The Memoirs consist of an autobiographic fragment by Moore himself, extending from his birth

P

to his introduction to Lord Moira in 1799. In a note written in 1833 they are stated as having been commenced some years before that date, but as unlikely to be completed. They are agreeably written, and it is not Moore's fault if most of the incidents recorded would have appeared of little interest but for his subsequent celebrity. Apart from this personal significance, their importance chiefly consists in the illustration they afford of the feelings of Roman Catholics of superior education under the unjust disabilities from which they then suffered, and their testimony to the considerable mitigation of this injustice through the liberality of Trinity College, Dublin. They further suggest that, desirable as an endowed Roman Catholic university may be in many points of view, it was fortunate for Moore that no such institution existed in his days.

Moore's letters, with the supplement, extend from 1793 to 1847. After 1818 they become very scanty, and throughout many of the best are not from him, but from his correspondents. His own letters in various hands must be exceedingly numerous, but no pains seems to have been taken to collect them except by an application from Lord John Russell to Rogers, who himself selected those which he deemed worthy of publication. A new and more diligent biographer could probably add

largely to their number, and retrieve many particulars worthy of preservation, but he would not be
likely to add to Moore's fame as a letter-writer. In
this department of literature he is mediocre, neither
bad nor good, but nearer to good than bad. He
certainly did not, as Wordsworth affected to do,
make his letters dull on purpose to prevent publication, for he did not mind publication, and he is not
dull. Neither did he polish them like Pope and
Gray, but wrote simply and naturally like Byron;
and the measure of the difference is the power of
their minds. Byron, though incapable of severe
continuous thought, had a most piercing insight,
and almost every literary gift which a good letter-
writer requires—perspicuity, vehemence, playful-
ness, narrative and descriptive power—had been
vouchsafed to him in profusion. Moore possesses
an average stock of these endowments, but no
more; hence his letters are not interesting as
letters, but as records of feelings and circumstances, thus their merit is not epistolary, but
biographical, and varies with the occasion which
called each forth. You can never say of any of
Moore's letters that in it you have Moore, but in
any of Byron's letters you find Byron.

The character, nevertheless, which fails to come
to light in a letter may be fully revealed in a diary
extending over a long period. The impression

derived from the first entries is continually reiter-
ated, and after a while the person depicted becomes
a reality.   No self-portraiture anywhere can match
the vividness of Pepys's, who did not aim at self-
portraiture in the smallest degree.   Every diarist
but Mr. Pepys has had some reticence, and in proportion as he has thus embellished his character for
himself he has obscured it for posterity.   Moore had
neither more nor less reticence than the generality
of men ; we gradually come to know him, and the
impression deepens until our estimate of his character is probably not less accurate than that which
we have formed of Pepys's, notwithstanding Moore's
immeasurable inferiority in graphic force.   It is a
pleasing and amiable picture.   Moore has many
little foibles, but no fault inconsistent with the character of an intellectual and high-minded man.   The
besetting sin, as to be expected, is vanity, not immoderate, nor ungraceful, nor wholly unjustifiable,
and most commonly exhibited in the amiable form
of recording the handsome things which others have
said of him.   There is no fatuity about his self-
complacency ; he is aware that he actually is entitled
to a prominent place among the distinguished men
of letters of his day, and hopes that it may be really
as high as people seem to think it.   Scott and
Byron he understands, and owns for his superiors.
Wordsworth and Coleridge he does not understand,

yet is able to admire. Keats is only once mentioned throughout the Diary, and that in a quotation. If Moore thought himself the third poet of his age (and he nowhere says so), he had the full assent of his editor, Lord John Russell, who deliberately declares, " When these two great men " (Scott and Byron) " have been enumerated, I know not any writer of his time who can be put in competition with Moore." Preposterous as this judgment now appears, Lord John only repeated what Moore had been hearing all his life from his own circle. It says much for his heart that the self-appreciation which such praise could not fail to engender should have been so gracious and sociable, so entirely free from all taint of arrogance. Of the tenderness of his affections it is needless to speak, almost every page bears witness to it.

The chief interest of Moore's Diary, however, is not its delineation of himself, but the intimacy into which it admits us with the most refined society of his day. Undoubtedly Moore's record would have gained much in literary and historical value if he had possessed more graphic power. It was not necessary that he should paint elaborate portraits of the men he knew, but a more vivid gift of representation would have enabled him to make these more real to us. It would be unreasonable to compare him with artists of such unique power

as Carlyle or Borrow, but put even Emerson's
account of his interviews with Coleridge and
Wordsworth side by side with Moore's, and the
latter's inferiority is immediately apparent. Emerson has shown us the men, Moore has talked
agreeably about them. Regarding the Diary, however, not as a gallery of portraits, but as an
assemblage of notes and observations upon the
most intellectual society of Moore's time, its value
is very considerable. If it does not portray personages, it reproduces the general atmosphere.
We feel as if we were living in the period, and
well content to do so. It is a most entertaining
book, full of anecdotes and *bon mots* which have
lost nothing of their freshness. It has a general
air of politeness and urbanity, and exhibits human
nature to advantage, displaying a man of humble
birth and comparatively narrow means, with nothing
but his accomplishments to recommend him, enjoying the intimate society of the great, without
servility on his part or condescension on theirs.
Its freedom from sensational scandal of any sort
is the more creditable when it is considered that,
commencing it as he did under the pressure of
his Bermuda difficulty, Moore in all probability
entertained from the first the idea of making it
serve as a provision for his family. He must
have heard every day stories which would have

greatly enhanced its value as "copy," but there is little which it would have been better to omit on grounds of discretion or delicacy, and there is no reason to suppose that this immunity from scandal is due to the editor rather than to the diarist.

The editing of the Diary, indeed, is the least satisfactory circumstance connected with it. The years of its publication, 1853–56, were the most unfortunate in Earl Russell's life. During part of the time he was a discontented Minister, dissatisfied with the proceedings of his colleagues, and chafing at his own subordinate position; during the remainder he was exiled from office, deserted except by his closest intimates, and the object of popular dislike and disapproval. It was unlikely that under the circumstances he should give much attention to his editorial duties, and he would have done far better to have entrusted them to some competent man of letters, reserving merely the prestige of his name for the title-page. As it is, the original edition of the "Memoirs, Journals, and Correspondence," is a monumental example of slovenly editing. Earl Russell has given us both too much and too little. He has allowed numerous trivialities to stand which should never have been printed, while he has done little or nothing to retrieve the correspondence which might have added so much to the interest of the book.

He has made no endeavour to supply the connecting narrative upon which the light discursive details of the Diary should have rested; and the few insignificant notes he has added to a book standing in special need of annotation are the merest *obiter dicta*. It is a great testimony to the intrinsic merits of Moore's work that it should, nevertheless, have established itself as one of the most generally appreciated English examples of the invaluable class of literature to which it belongs. This is not solely or even mainly owing to its well-merited character as a store of good things, or the degree into which it admits us to the intimacy of so many respecting whom the world is curious. It is rather from a pervading aroma of geniality and urbanity which editorial shortcomings cannot affect. It may be said of it in Moore's own words—

"You may break, you may shatter the vase if you will :
But the scent of the roses will cling to it still."

Earl Russell nevertheless deserves praise, in literature as in politics, for the gallantry with which he espouses a good cause, and the spirit with which he vindicates it. This was exemplified in his treatment of Croker, who, exasperated at a remark in the Diary which seemed to show that Moore had not rated his talents very highly, retaliated by a review of the first four volumes in the *Quarterly* of unmatched malignity and offensiveness, but after all not so characteristic of the perversion of the writer's heart as of the narrowness of his mind. The extent to which the pettiest points are laboured would seem incredible if the article were not before us. The worst of the matter was that the review was unquestionably, and to all appearance deliberately adapted to inflict severe pain on Mrs. Moore, whose innocence and bereavement should have shielded her from the most envenomed vindictiveness. Lord John Russell replied by a contemptuous note in a subsequent volume, which drew a remonstrance from Croker, who made his case ten times worse by insisting that Moore had been his friend, whence it followed that he had also been Moore's. Such episodes explain the general aversion for a man whose own memoirs prove him to have been by no means incapable of kind thoughts and kind actions, and whose offences are perhaps sufficiently accounted for as the offspring of excessive vanity and excessive censoriousness.

We began by intimating that it has been Moore's great misfortune to be overpraised, and thus to have a character forced upon him which he was incapable of supporting. The truth, however, is perhaps not so much that he was personally overrated as that his greater contemporaries were unduly disparaged. If Wordsworth, Keats, and the rest had been allowed their proper places, Moore would have fallen naturally into his own. His reputation has appeared unduly inflated when it has become known that he was once esteemed the third poet of his day; if, however, we discard comparisons, and look merely at performances, it is undeniable that English literature has been greatly enriched by him. His fame rests principally upon his songs, and if not one of them is quite in the first-class, it is certain that he has written more deserving of a secondary rank than any other English poet. By restoring the old association between poetry and music he did much for both; and he is not to be judged solely by the impression of his words as read from the printed page—

> "Ach! wie traurig sieht in Lettern,
> Schwarz auf weiss, das Lied mich an,
> Das aus deinem Mund vergöttern,
> Das ein Herz zerreissen kann!"

As a satirist Moore stands at the head of his class, and as a constructor and embellisher of metrical romances he is the cleverest of the poets. It is, in truth, a reproach to him to have been too clever, to have been too little of an inspired bard, and too much of a man of letters. He could have

excelled in anything demanded by the taste of his
day; the one distinctively poetical endowment
which he really possessed was an inexhaustible
fount of melody. In his employment of this he
evinced more talent than genius; yet he never
expressed a sentiment discordant with his own
nature, and he recognised the existence of a realm
of inspiration into which he was but rarely permitted to enter—

> " Many a time, on summer eves,
>   Just at that closing hour of light,
>   When, like an Eastern Prince, who leaves
>   For distant war his harem bowers,
>   The Sun bids farewell to the flowers
>   Whose heads are sunk, whose tears are flowing
>   Mid all the glory of his going :
>   Even I have felt beneath those beams
>   When wandering through the fields alone,
>   Thoughts, fancies, intellectual gleams,
>   Which, far too bright to be my own,
>   Seemed lent me by the Sunny Power
>   That was abroad at that still hour."

These beautiful lines occur very unexpectedly
near the beginning of " Rhymes on the Road." It
is also noteworthy that, in enumerating some passages of Wordsworth which have become household
words, he selects the deeply impressive " Whose
dwelling is the light of setting suns."

If overvalued as a poet, Moore has been underrated as a man.   Foibles he had in abundance, but compensated by captivating virtues.   Chief among these was a manly independence almost attaining the heroic, and the more striking because Moore's character is not in general one of heroic lineaments. Independence is expected from a haughty Wordsworth or a surly Schopenhauer; its absence would have been easily excused in a butterfly poet, the ornament of the drawing-room.   To spend a lifetime in the intimacy of his social superiors without a single mortification required rare qualities, the more remarkable inasmuch as his destiny compelled him to be continually incurring obligations. These he was as continually redeeming, and no transaction of this nature ever involved the slightest diminution of his self-respect.   In truth he gave the society which caressed him much more than he received from it.   His enjoyment of its gaieties has been made a reproach to him, but most unjustly. Society was his element, intercourse with the world his stock-in-trade; he and his family could not have subsisted without it.   He has been accused of neglecting his charming wife, for whom in fact he made the greatest sacrifice possible to one of his tastes and habits by fixing his habitation in the country, knowing that residence in London would expose her to continual mortification.   This entailed frequent absences from her—he could not neglect

society without grave injury to his and her interests
—but no impartial reader of his Diary can doubt
that London gaieties would have been more enjoyed
by him if his Bessy could have participated in
them.

Intellectually, Moore's defect is a certain small-
ness. He has excellent sense and spirit, but when
measured, even by himself, against any contemporary of much distinction, he invariably appears the
shorter. He is a sound but by no means a penetrating or illuminating critic, and his observations
on politics and manners reveal but moderate insight.
He could nevertheless execute a difficult piece of
work like the " Life of Byron " with consummate tact
and skill, and until worn out by labour and sorrow
he rarely failed in any undertaking. If he was less
distinctively a poet than a man of letters, the same
may be said of his contemporary, adversary, and
yet in many respects counterpart, Robert Southey.
The poetry of both survives and will survive, yet
their better title to fame is their brilliant versatility
in many and various fields of literature.

THOMAS LOVE PEACOCK

THOMAS LOVE PEACOCK [1]

FEW modern authors, whose works have survived them, and whose lives have been prolonged beyond the ordinary span, have so well complied with the ancient precept λάθε βιώσας—live by stealth—as Thomas Love Peacock. The early poems which bore his name attracted little attention, the novels which might have made a known author famous were anonymous, and their writer could not have been easily identified with the Examiner of East India Correspondence, a situation, its importance considered, itself one of the most unostentatious and impersonal in the world. The life thus screened from observation offered, indeed, but little to observe. Genius and the friendship of a greater genius, however, have made it interesting to a wider circle than the personage himself expected or perhaps desired. Without violence to his known wishes and preferences, a brief memoir, mainly founded on what his attached grand-

[1] Introduction prefixed to the writer's edition of his works, published by Messrs. Dent & Co., 1891.

daughter and the editor of his collected works have thought it right to relate, and supplemented by a few letters and particulars in the possession of the present writer, may not inappropriately minister to the curiosity respecting a man of exceptional character, which an edition of his choicer writings, destined, as is hoped, to a wider popularity than its predecessors, should not fail to create.

Thomas Love Peacock was born at Weymouth, October 18, 1785. His father was a glass merchant in London, partner of a Mr. Pellatt, presumably founder of the celebrated firm ; his mother was the daughter of Thomas Love, formerly master of a man-of-war, and whom Lord Rodney's great victory had deprived of a leg. Another Love, the eccentric and corpulent bookseller of Weymouth, must have been a relation : so that Peacock's tastes for good literature, good living, navigation, and shipbuilding, seem all distinctly traceable to his mother's side of the family. Of the father we know nothing but his calling, and that he left his son an orphan at the age of three. Mrs. Peacock went to live with her father at Chertsey, and from eight to thirteen Peacock was at a school at Englefield Green, kept by a Mr. Wicks, of whom he wrote later in life, "The master was not much of a scholar ; but he had the art of inspiring his pupils with a love of learning." Mr. Wicks is said to have prognosticated his pupil's future eminence, and indeed Peacock's juvenile compositions, some of which have been privately printed by Sir Henry Cole, exhibit just the sort of formal precocity which a schoolmaster would appreciate, and are by no means unworthy forerunners of "The Genius of the Thames" department of his writings, while displaying nothing of the peculiar fancy and humour which have given him his abiding place in literature. More interesting is a prize contribution to "The Juvenile Library," a magazine for youth whose competitions excited the emulation of several other boys destined to celebrity, among them Leigh Hunt, De Quincey, and W. J. Fox. Peacock, in 1800, gained the eleventh prize for an essay in verse on the comparative advantages of history and biography as themes of study, Leigh Hunt winning the fourth. The number of the magazine announcing the competition contains a coloured plate of an ourangoutang, attired, in defiance of reason and nature, in an apron, which may have had its influence on the production of "Melincourt."

Peacock is described as at this period a remarkably handsome boy; his copious flaxen curls, afterwards brown, attracted the notice of Queen Charlotte, who stopped her carriage to kiss him. His recollections of the royal family were kindly; in his charming paper, "The Last Day of Windsor

Forest," he simply mentions George the Fourth's exclusiveness without other than implied censure, and dwells with delight on the reverse trait in the character of William the Fourth. Of his other family or friendly connections, apart from his grandfather's house, nothing seems to be known except what may be gleaned from his paper, "Recollections of Childhood," contributed to "Bentley's Miscellany," and reprinted in "Tales from Bentley." Here we have pleasing reminiscences of an old-fashioned country-house and a family life placid, uneventful, and, it must be added, uninteresting to a degree impossible since the world has been waked up by railways and the French Revolution.

At the age of fourteen Peacock removed with his mother to London, and was for a time a clerk in the mercantile house of Messrs. Ludlow, Fraser, and Co., Angel Court, Throgmorton Street. Indefatigable in bodily exercise and the acquisition of congenial knowledge, he was throughout his life indolent in every other particular, and probably lost little time in exchanging the counting-house for the Reading-Room of the British Museum, which he frequented for many years, a diligent student of the best literature in Greek, Latin, French, and Italian, becoming in time one of the best classical scholars of his day, who gained in breadth what he lost in verbal accuracy.   His circumstances, though narrow, must have been independent, for in 1804 and 1806 he published two volumes of poetry, "The Monks of St. Mark" and "Palmyra," from which profit could hardly have been expected, and in 1807 he is found engaged to a young lady not named, whom in the summer of that year he used to meet in the ruins of Newark Abbey, about eight miles from Chertsey.   The interviews were apparently clandestine, else it is difficult to imagine how "the underhand interference of a third person," probably exercised in intercepting letters, could have led the young lady to suppose herself deserted, and bestow her hand elsewhere with a precipitancy only to be paralleled by her exit from this mortal scene in the following year.   Something probably remains untold.   Whatever reason for reproach Peacock may have had, her memory remained as a tender possession with him to the last hour of his life.   "He always," says his granddaughter, "wore a locket with her hair in it, and only a few days before his death he spoke of her to me, saying that he had been dreaming of dear Fanny, that she had come to him in the night in his sleep, and he expressed himself as greatly pleased with the dream, remarking that it had for some weeks frequently recurred."

Thirty-five years after his loss, Peacock's feelings

in connexion with the scene of his early attachment found expression in some most beautiful
verses, especially admired by Tennyson, which,
as his poetry, outside his novels, will not be reprinted in this edition, may find a place in the
memoir :—

NEWARK ABBEY.

" I gaze where August's sunbeam falls
Along these gray and lonely walls,
Till in its light absorbed appears
The lapse of five-and-thirty years.
  If change there be, I trace it not
In all this consecrated spot :
No new imprint of Ruin's march
On roofless wall and frameless arch :
The woods, the hills, the fields, the stream,
Are basking in the selfsame beam ;
The fall, that turns the unseen mill,
As then it murmured, murmurs still.
  It seems as if in one were cast
The present and the imaged past,
Spanning, as with a bridge sublime,
That fearful lapse of human time,—
That gulf unfathomably spread
Between the living and the dead.
  For all too well my spirit feels
The only change that time reveals.
The sunbeams play, the breezes stir,
Unseen, unfelt, unheard by her,
Who, on that long-past August day,
Beheld with me these ruins gray.
  Whatever span the fates allow
Ere I shall be as she is now,

Still in my bosom's inmost cell
Shall that long-treasured memory dwell,
That, more than language can express,
Pure miracle of loveliness,
Whose voice so sweet, whose eyes so bright,
Were my soul's music and its light ;
In those blest days when life was new,
And hope was false, but love was true."

Disappointment and bereavement may have disposed Peacock to try a change of life, and his friends, as he hints, thought it wrong that so clever a man should be earning so little money. In the autumn of 1808 he became private secretary to Sir Home Popham, commanding the fleet before Flushing. His preconceived affection for the sea did not reconcile him to nautical realities. "Writing poetry," he says, "or doing anything else that is rational, in this floating inferno, is next to a moral impossibility. I would give the world to be at home and devote the winter to the composition of a comedy." He did write prologues and addresses for dramatic performances on board the *Venerable :* his dramatic taste then and for nine years subsequently found expression in attempts at comedies and pieces of a still lighter class, all of which fail from lack of ease of dialogue and the over-elaboration of incident and humour. He left the *Venerable* in March 1809, and is shortly afterwards found engaged in a pedestrian expedition to discover the source of the Thames, which probably supplied inspiration sufficient for the completion of the most elaborate, after "Rhododaphne," of his longer poems, "The Genius of the Thames," which he had meditated in 1807. It was published in 1810. There is a surprising contrast between these more ambitious undertakings and the lyrics scattered through his novels, on which his reputation as a poet entirely rests. The latter are so graceful, simple, and naturally melodious, that they might seem to have come into being of their own accord. The former are works of labour and reflection; they compel admiration of the author's powers of mind, and in "Rhododaphne" his sympathy for the vanished beauty of Hellas occasionally exalts vigorous writing into poetry. Otherwise they are best described by the passage from Plato, so admirably translated by himself in illustration of Shelley, with entire unsuspiciousness of any personal application :—

"There are several kinds of divine madness. That which proceeds from the Muses, taking possession of a tender and unoccupied soul, awakening and bacchically inspiring it towards songs and other poetry, adorning myriads of ancient deeds, instructs succeeding generations; but he who, without this madness from the Muses, approaches the poetical gates, having persuaded himself that by art alone he may become sufficiently a poet, will find in the end his own imperfection, and see the poetry of his cold prudence vanish into nothing before the light of that which has sprung from divine insanity."

In January 1810 Peacock made his first expedition into North Wales. He was there as late as August, as appears from the last of several letters given in Sir Henry Cole's privately printed "Biographical Notes." In April 1811 he was on the point of returning to London, as shown by the following hitherto unpublished letter. We do not know whether he had spent the whole intervening period in the country, or had made a second visit. The letter, like the others, is addressed to his friend and publisher—Hookham :—

"MACHYNLLETH, *April* 9, 1811.

"Your letter arrived on Sunday morning. I then gave my landlord the bill and walked up to the parson's, as I could not leave the vale without taking leave of Jane Gryffydh—the most innocent, the most amiable, the most beautiful girl in existence. The old lady being in the way, I could not speak to her there, and asked her to walk with me to the lodge. She was obliged to dress for church immediately, but promised to call on the way. She did so. I told her my intention of departing that day, and gave her my last remaining copy of the

"Genius." She advised me to tell my host. I did so, and arranged matters with him in a very satisfactory manner. He will send my remaining bills under cover to you. As I told him my design of walking home through South Wales, he will probably not send them for three weeks. If they arrive before me, which I do not think they will, have the goodness to lay them quietly by. This is coming off with flying colours. I then waited my lovely friend's return from church, took a final leave of her, started at three in the afternoon, and reached Dolgelly—eighteen miles—at eight. Yesterday morning I walked through a succession of most sublime scenery to the pretty little lake, Tal-y-llyn, where is a small public-house, kept by a most original character, who in the triple capacity of publican, schoolmaster, and guide to Cadair Idris, manages to keep the particles of his carcase in contact. I ascended the mountain with him, seated myself in the Giant's Chair, and "looked from my throne of clouds o'er half the world." The view from the summit of this mountain baffles description. It is the very sublimity of Nature's wildest magnificence. Beneath, the whole extent of Cardigan Bay; to the right, the immense chain of the Snowdonian mountains, partly smiling in sunshine, partly muffled in flying storm: to the left, the wide expanse of the southern principality, with all its mountain summits below us. This excursion occupied five hours. I then returned to Minffordd Inn, as he calls it, took some tea, and walked hither through a romantic and beautiful vale. The full moon in a cloudless sky illumined the latter part of my march. I shall proceed to Towyn this morning, having promised Miss Scott to call at her uncle's seat on my way to England. From Towyn I shall proceed to Aberystwith, and from thence to the Devil's Bridge at Hafod. From one of these places I will write to you again.

"I have a clean shirt with me, and Luath, and Tacitus. I am in high health and spirits. On the top of Cadair Idris I felt how happy a man may be with a little money and a sane intellect, and reflected with astonishment and pity on the madness of the multitude.

"T. L. PEACOCK."

In 1812 Peacock published another elaborate poem, "The Philosophy of Melancholy," and in the same year made the acquaintance of Shelley: according to his grand-daughter and Sir Henry Cole at Nant Gwillt, near Rhayader, in Radnorshire. But this is a mistake. Peacock tells us himself, in his memoir of Shelley, that he did not behold this romantic spot [1] until after Shelley had

---

[1] Now (1901) on the point of submersion in connection with the Birmingham water supply.

quitted it, when he went on purpose to view it: he also says that he "saw Shelley for the first time just before he went to Tanyrallt," whither Shelley proceeded from London in November 1812 (Hogg's "Life of Shelley," vol. ii., pp. 174, 175). The medium of introduction was no doubt Mr. Thomas Hookham, the publisher of all Peacock's early writings, whose circulating library ministered to Shelley's intellectual hunger for many years. He had sent "The Genius of the Thames" to Shelley, and in the "Shelley Memorials," pp. 38–40, will be found a letter from the poet, under date of August 18, 1812, extolling the poetical merits of the performance, and with equal exaggeration censuring what he thought the author's misguided patriotism. Personal acquaintance almost necessarily ensued, and hence arose an intimacy not devoid of influence upon Shelley's fortunes both before and after his death, and which has made Peacock interesting to many who would not otherwise have heard of his name. At the risk of some digression, it will be most convenient to treat the subject in this place.

Though neither sufficiently ardent nor sufficiently productive to rank among famous literary friendships, the friendship of Shelley and Peacock was yet interesting both in itself and its results. Without it we should not have perused Shelley's matchless descriptive letters from Italy, almost rivalling his poetry in beauty, yet genuine letters, not rhapsodies. As authors, the two men remained almost entirely unaffected by each other's writings. Not a trace of direct influence can be found in the style of either: but the superiority of "Rhododaphne," written during the period of their intimacy, to Peacock's other elaborate poems, justifies the inference that Shelley was performing his usual office for his friends of impregnating their brains; while on his own part he took from Peacock the idea of a poem on the suicide of Otho, which proved abortive. He justly censured Peacock's style in poetry as framed by the canons of the "exact and superficial school," but fully appreciated the merit of his prose. "I know not," he says, speaking of "Nightmare Abbey," "how to praise sufficiently the lightness, chastity, and strength of the language of the whole." He naturally desiderated more moral earnestness. "Is not the misdirected enthusiasm of Scythrop what Jesus Christ calls the salt of the earth?" This craving for definiteness of purpose made him prefer "Melincourt" among Peacock's novels, in which few will agree with him. Peacock, on his part, gave, during Shelley's life, no indication of a just perception of the latter's place among poets, unless it was such to inform him, on occasion of the publication of

"Adonais," that "*if* he would consider who and what the readers of poetry are, and adapt his compositions to the depth of their understandings and the current of their sympathies, he would attain the highest degree of poetical fame." Afterwards, however, he wrote of Shelley's genius as "unsurpassed in the description and imagination of scenes of beauty and grandeur; in the expression of impassioned love of ideal beauty; in the illustration of deep feeling by congenial imagery; and in the infinite variety of harmonious versification." He will command the assent of most readers, though not ours, when he adds, "What was, in my opinion, deficient in his poetry, was the want of reality in the characters with which he peopled his splendid scenes." These passages occur in the contribution to Shelley's biography which he published at an advanced period of his life, and which must be alluded to here if only to give the present writer an opportunity of retracting criticism from his own pen which he now feels to have been unjust and uncharitable, but which he cannot feel to have been inexcusable. That Peacock totally mis-stated the matter of Shelley's separation from Harriet is as clear to him as ever; but any suspicion of wrong motives has been dispelled by more intimate acquaintance with his character, and in particular with the moral impossibility under which he laboured of relinquishing any opinion which had once become a conviction. In fact, the real point at issue continues to be misapprehended by almost every one who writes upon the question. It is exceedingly simple. If Shelley forsook Harriet for Mary merely because he liked Mary better, he cannot be justified by any code of morality. If, after an insanable breach with Harriet, he transferred his affections elsewhere, his conduct, right or wrong, would have had the approbation of Milton. It is certain that such a breach had occurred before Shelley had seen Mary; and it is equally certain, without any groundless aspersion of Harriet's conjugal fidelity, that the fault was not Shelley's.

For some years, except for an anecdote in the auto-biography of J. A. Roebuck, the course of Peacock's life is only known from its connection with his illustrious friend. In the winter of 1813 he accompanies Shelley and Harriet to Edinburgh: throughout the winter of 1814–15 he is an almost daily visitor of Shelley and Mary at their London lodgings. In 1815 he shares their voyage to the source of the Thames. "He seems," writes Charles Clairmont, a member of the party, "an idly-inclined man; indeed, he is professedly so in the summer; he owns he cannot apply himself to study, and thinks it more beneficial to him as a human being entirely to devote himself to the beauties of the season while they last; he was only happy while out from morning till night." During the winter of 1815–16 Peacock was continually walking over from Marlow, where he had established himself sometime in this year, to visit Shelley at Bishopgate. There he met Hogg, and "the winter was a mere Atticism. Our studies were exclusively Greek." The benefit which Shelley derived from such a course of study cannot be overrated. Its influence is seen more and more in everything he wrote to the end of his life. The morbid, the fantastic, the polemical, fade gradually out of his mind; and the writer who had begun as the imitator of the wildest extravagances of German romance would, had not his genius transcended the limits of any school, have ended as scarcely less of a Hellene than Keats and Landor.

In 1815 "Headlong Hall" was written, and it was published in the following year. With this book Peacock definitively takes the place in literature which he was to maintain throughout his life, without substantial alteration or development beyond the mellowing which wider experience and increasing prosperity would naturally bring. The wine was to be the same, but improved by keeping. Of Peacock's general characteristics as an author we shall have to speak hereafter. It need only be said here that "Headlong Hall" signalises his literary emancipation as decisively as another and far more important book written in the same year indicates the emancipation of a far greater genius. "Alastor" proclaimed Shelley's discovery that the bent of his genius was not to the didactic; and "Headlong Hall" showed no less decisively Peacock's final recognition of his deficient appreciation of form, and the futility of his endeavours to construct a comedy. What he had to do was to give plot and accurate delineation of character to the winds, make his personages typical rather than individual; throw them together pell-mell and let dialogue and incident evolve themselves from the juxtaposition, and the result would be that original creation the Peacockian novel, which may be described as the spirit of comedy diffused in exemption from the restraints of the stage, like gas liberated by the disintegration of a solid.

In 1816 Shelley went abroad, and Peacock was the recipient of his beautiful descriptive letters from Switzerland. He would appear to have been entrusted with the commission of providing the Shelleys with a new residence, and it is not surprising that he should have fixed them near his own abode at Great Marlow. They settled there in December. The climate was more congenial to Peacock's constitution than to Shelley's; but

R

the choice cannot be considered wholly unfortunate, for the beautiful river scenery reappears
transfigured in some of the most splendid passages
of the " Revolt of Islam," which Shelley composed
during his residence, partly, as he himself says,
where

> " With sound like many voices sweet,
> Waterfalls leapt among wild islands green,"

partly, as Peacock tells us, " on a high prominence
in Bisham wood, where he passed whole mornings
with a blank book and a pencil." His note-books
show that Peacock at this time received an annuity
of £50 from him, which, if gossip in Miss Mitford's
correspondence may be trusted, he repaid by driv-
ing away uninvited guests who would have eaten
Shelley out of house and home. " Melincourt "
was published at this time; and " Nightmare
Abbey " and " Rhododaphne " written. The former
book, constructed on the same lines as " Headlong
Hall," but a great advance upon it, is supposed to
contain a portrait of Shelley, but the resemblance,
if any, is most superficial. " Rhododaphne," by
far the best of Peacock's more ambitious poems,
enjoyed the signal but barren honour of a review
from Shelley's pen. Shelley is said to have assured
the author that Byron professed himself willing
to have fathered it, but we have not found the

passage in his letters. Before these works were published in 1818 Shelley was again on the wing, and Peacock and he were never to meet again. Restlessness and embarrassment, says Peacock, were the causes of the emigration, but there were others, personified in Godwin and Byron. Peacock's fidelity as a correspondent ("this is the third letter," he says on June 14, "that I have written since I received one from you") was repaid by the magnificent series of letters from Shelley descriptive of Italy, which only ceased when, in the summer of 1819, he found himself settled in the comparatively uninteresting city of Leghorn. Peacock's own letters to Shelley are the principal authority for his life at this time. On May 30, 1818, he says, not speaking by the spirit of prophecy :—

"I have no idea and no wish remaining to leave Marlow at all, and when you return to England you will find me still here, though not perhaps in the same house. I have almost finished 'Nightmare Abbey.' I think it necessary to make a stand against the encroachments of black bile. The fourth canto of 'Childe Harold' is really too bad. I cannot consent to be *auditor tantum* of this systematical poisoning of the mind of the reading public."

On July 19 he reports :—

"I have changed my habitation, having been literally besieged out of the other by horses and children. I propose to remain in the one I am in now till death, fortune, or my landlord turns me out. It is cheap, and exceedingly comfortable. It is the one which Major Kelley lived in when you were here, facing the Coiting Place, in West Street. [This "coiting place" still exists.] The weather continues dry and sultry. I have been very late on the river for several evenings, under the beams of the summer moon, and the air has been as warm as the shade by day, and so still that the tops of the poplars have stood, black in the moonlight, as motionless as spires of stone. If the summer of last year had been like this, you would not, I think, be now in Italy; but who could have foreseen it? Do not think I wish to play the tempter. If you return to England, I would most earnestly advise you to stay the winter in a milder climate. Still I do speculate on your return within two years as a strong probability, and I think where you are likely to take up your abode. Were I to choose the spot I would fix you on one of the hills that border this valley. The Hunts would plant you at Paddington. Your own taste, and Mary's, would perhaps point to the Forest. If you ever speculate on these points among yourselves, I should be glad to understand the view you take of them. It is pleasant to plant cuttings of futurity, if only one in ten takes root. But I deem it a moral impossibility that an Englishman who is not encrusted either with natural apathy or superinduced Giaourism, can live many years among such animals as the modern Italians. There is nothing new under the political sun, except that the forgery of bank-notes increases in a compound ratio of progression, and that the silver disappears rapidly; both symptoms of inextricable disarrangement in the machinery of the omnipotent paper-mill."

"*August* 30, 1818.

"I do not find this brilliant summer very favourable to intellectual exertion. The mere pleasure of existence in the open air is too absorbing for the energies of active thought, and too attractive for that resolute perseverance in sedentary study to which I find the long and dreary winter so propitious. To one who has never been out of England, the effect of this season is like removal to a new world. It is the climate of Italy transmitted to us by special favour of the gods; and I cannot help thinking that our incipient restoration of true piety has propitiated the deities, and especially *hoc sublime candens quod vocamus omnes Jovem.* For the most part, my division of time is this: I devote the forenoon to writing; the afternoon to the river, the woods, and classical poetry; the evening to philosophy —at present the *Novum Organon* and the *Histoire Naturelle*, which is a treasury of inexhaustible delight. My reading is, as usual at this season, somewhat desultory. I open to myself many vistas in the great forest of mind, and reconnoitre the tracts of territory which in the winter I propose to acquire."

There is enough evidence of studying and sailing at all hours of the day in a little diary kept at this time, and privately printed by Sir Henry Cole, but not much of writing in the forenoon, though literary projects were not laid aside. "Could not read or write for scheming my romance—rivers, castles, forests, abbeys, monks, maids, kings, and banditti dancing before me like a masked ball." This was "Maid Marian," "a comic romance of the twelfth century," he tells Shelley on November 29, "which I shall make the vehicle of much oblique satire on all the oppressions that are done under the sun." As, excepting three chapters, it was entirely composed in 1818, it must have made very rapid progress. A great change in Peacock's life was impending. In the above quoted letter he says, "I have heard no more of the affair which took me to London last month. I adhere to my resolution of not going there at all, unless particular business should call me, and I do not at present foresee any that is likely to do so." On December 15, he describes himself as "rooted like a tree on the banks of one bright river." But on January 13, 1819, he writes from 5 York Street, Covent Garden : "I now pass every morning at the India House, from half-past ten to half-past four, studying Indian affairs. My object is not yet attained, though I have little doubt but that it will be. It was not in the first instance of my own seeking, but was proposed to me. It will lead to a very sufficing provision for me in two or three years. It is not in the common routine of office, but is an employment of a very interesting and intellectual kind, connected with finance and legislation, in which it is possible to be of great service not only to the Company, but to the millions under their dominion." It would appear that the East India Company had become aware that their home staff was too merely clerical, and had determined to reinforce it by the appointment of four men of exceptional ability to the Examiner's office, including Peacock and James Mill. The circumstances of the appointment of Mill, who did apply, and who experienced many obstacles on account of the censure of the Company in his

"History of British India," are narrated in Professor Bain's biography, pp. 184, 185. His salary is said to have been £800 a year; we do not know whether Peacock received as much. The latter's appointment is said by Sir Henry Cole to have been owing to the influence of Peter Auber, the Company's secretary and historian, whom he had known at school, though probably not as a schoolfellow. Mill appears to have undergone no probation; Peacock did, but the test papers which he drafted were returned to him with the high commendation, "Nothing superfluous, and nothing wanting"—another proof that a poet and a novelist may be a man of business. Peacock's name does not appear in the official list until 1821, when his position was improved: but already, by March 9, Leigh Hunt tells Shelley: "You have heard, of course, of Peacock's appointment in the India House; we joke him upon his new Oriental grandeur, his Brahminical learning, and his inevitable tendencies to be one of the corrupt, upon which he seems to apprehend Shelleian objurgation. It is an honour to him that prosperity sits on him well. He is very pleasant and hospitable." These hospitalities must have been exercised in lodgings: for we learn from Hogg that it was on July 1, 1819, that Peacock slept for the first time in "a house in Stamford Street (No. 18) which, as you might expect from a Republican, he has furnished very handsomely." His mother continued to reside with him, and the household soon received an addition in the person of Jane Gryffydh, henceforth Peacock, the Cambrian παρ- θένος ὀυρεσίφοιτος, ἐρῆμαδι σύντροφος ὑλῃ, whom, as we have seen, he had pronounced, so long ago as 1811, "the most innocent, the most amiable, the most beautiful girl in existence." He had never seen or communicated with her since, and it says much for the depth of the impression he had received and his own constancy that on November 29 he should have addressed her as follows :—

"It is more than eight years since I had the happiness of seeing you : I can scarcely hope that you have remembered me as I have remembered you : yet I feel confident that the simplicity and ingenuousness of your disposition will prompt you to answer me with the same candour with which I write to you. I long entertained the hope of returning to Merionethshire under better auspices than those under which I left it ; but fortune always disappointed me, continually offering me prospects which receded as I approached them. Recently she has made amends for her past un- kindness, and has given me much present good, and much promise of progressive prosperity, which leaves me nothing to desire in worldly advantage, but to participate it with you. The greatest blessing this world could bestow on me would be to make you my wife : consider if your own feelings would allow you to constitute my happiness. I desire only to promote yours; and I desire only you, for your value is beyond fortune, of which I want no more than I have. The same circumstances which have given me prosperity confine me to London, and to the duties of the department with which the East India Company has entrusted me; yet I can absent myself once in every year for a few days; if you sanction my wishes, with what delight should I employ them in bringing you to my home! If this be but a baseless dream, if I am even no more in your estimation than the sands of the sea-shore—yet I am sure, as I have already said, that you will answer me with the same candour with which I have written. Whatever may be your sentiments, the feelings with which I now write to you, and which more than eight years of absence and silence have neither obliterated nor diminished, will convince you that I never can be otherwise than most sincerely and affectionately your friend."

Sir Henry Cole thinks this "the model of a reasonable offer of marriage." Romantic would seem a more appropriate term, unless Peacock had entirely satisfied himself that Miss Gryffydh had not in the interim acquired a wooden leg, like the young lady wooed under similar circumstances in one of Theodore Hook's tales. Shelley observed with more justice: "The affair is extremely like the denouement of one of your own novels, and as such serves to a theory I once imagined, that in everything any man ever wrote, spoke, acted, or imagined, is contained, as it were, an allegorical idea of his own future life, as the acorn contains the oak." Jane Gryffydh's acceptance of the proposal may also be thought to have evinced courage, but there was probably no more choice of wooers at Maentwrog than of wigs on Munrimmon Moor. She might also have been convinced of his constancy if she could have seen the MS. of an unfinished and unpublished romance, "Sir Calidore," written in 1816 or 1817, and to be included, it is hoped, in this edition; in which she is depicted with loving partiality amid a highly genial but at the same time highly uncongenial environment— a fairy islet in an ocean of strong ale. The marriage took place on March 20, 1820. "Mrs. Peacock," says Mrs. Gisborne, "seems to be a very good-natured, simple, unaffected, untaught, prettyish Welsh girl."

The following years were not eventful. In 1820 Peacock published in Ollier's "Literary Pocket

Book" the "Four Ages of Poetry," a clever para-
dox, inspired by disappointment at his own failure
to command attention as a poet, but memorable
for having provoked Shelley's "Defence." On
June 3, 1821, he tells Shelley, "I have paid
Grayhurst and Harvey for the plate which you
had in 1813, and which finally remained in Harriet's
possession, £45, including interest." In October
he acknowledges the repayment of this sum by
Shelley, and mentions the birth of "a charming
little girl (now eleven weeks old), who grows and
flourishes delightfully in this fumose and cinereous
atmosphere." In the same letter he says, "I
should not like your Indian project" (Shelley's
letter respecting this is lost, it must have been
suggested to him by Medwin), "which I think
would agree neither with your mind nor body, if
it were practicable. But it is altogether impossible.
The whole of the Civil Service of India is sealed
against all but the Company's covenanted servants,
who are inducted into it through established grada-
tions, beginning at an early period of life. There
is nothing that would give me so much pleasure
(because I think there is nothing that would be
more beneficial to you), than to see you following
some scheme of flesh and blood—some interesting
matter connected with the business of life, in the
tangible shape of a practical man : and I shall

make it a point of sedulous inquiry to discover if there be anything attainable of this nature that would be likely to please and suit you." Excellent advice, if Shelley had not been a great poet! Shelley's death in the ensuing July put an end to all projects of this nature, and in the absence of the co-executor, Lord Byron, the duties of the executorship devolved upon Peacock. One vexatious circumstance gave Mary Shelley intense annoyance, and became the occasion of much mischief—the loss of a box of papers deposited in Peacock's care when the Shelleys quitted Marlow, and very improperly left by him in the keeping of Shelley's landlord Maddocks on his own removal to London. Maddocks, who was now in desperate circumstances, refused to restore them, pretending that they were collateral security for a debt, and while Peacock hesitated about taking legal proceedings they disappeared, and have been the source of most of the Shelley forgeries which for a long time infested the autograph market.

In 1822 "Maid Marian," begun in 1818, was completed and published. " A beautiful little thing," says Mrs. Gisborne on April 28, " but it has not taken yet. Ollier says the reason is that no work can sell which turns priests into ridicule." It was, however, soon dramatised with great success by Planché, and enjoyed the honour of translation into French and German. Peacock's salary was now £1000 a year, and in 1823 he acquired the residence at Lower Halliford, which continued his predilection to the end of his life. It was formed by throwing two cottages together. In March 1823 another daughter was born, whose death in January 1826 called forth these affecting lines, still to be read upon the gravestone in Shepperton Churchyard :—

> " Long night succeeds thy little day ;
>   O blighted blossom ! Can it be
>   That this gray stone and grassy clay
>   Have closed our anxious care of thee ?
>
> The half-formed speech of artless thought
>   That spoke a mind beyond thy years ;
>   The song, the dance, by nature taught ;
>   The sunny smiles, the transient tears ;
>
> The symmetry of face and form,
>   The eye with light and life replete ;
>   The little heart so fondly warm ;
>   The voice so musically sweet :
>
> These, lost to hope, in memory yet
>   Around the hearts that loved thee cling,
>   Shadowing with long and vain regret
>   The too fair promise of thy spring."

" My grandmother," writes Peacock's granddaughter, " was inconsolable for the loss of this little child, Margaret ; she fell into bad health, and

until her death in 1852 she was a complete invalid.
Very soon after Margaret's death my grandmother
noticed a little girl in its mother's arms, at the door
of a cottage on Halliford Green; she was much
taken with the child, seeing in it a strong likeness
to the little one she was so sorely grieving after;
she coaxed the little girl, Mary Rosewell, into her
own house by a promise of some cake, and dressed
it in her lost child's clothes. My grandfather, on
his return from town, looked in through the dining-
room window as he passed round to the door of his
house, and seeing the child standing on the hearth-
rug in the room, he was so struck by its likeness to
Margaret that he afterwards declared that he felt
quite stunned, for the moment believing that he
really saw her again before him. My grandparents
finally adopted the child, Mary Rosewell, whose
family had lived for generations much respected in
the neighbourhood, and a most devoted and un-
selfish adopted daughter she always proved to be."

Peacock's life was protracted forty years longer,
but the incidents in it worthy of record are but few.
"Paper Money Lyrics," and the inimitable satire
on Sabbatarianism beginning, " The poor man's sins
are glaring," were written about this time. In 1829
came " The Misfortunes of Elphin," and in 1831
" Crotchet Castle," the most mature and thoroughly
characteristic of all his works. More might have

followed, but in 1833 he was visited by the heaviest
sorrow of his life, the death of his mother.   It
should have been foreseen, as Mrs. Peacock was
born in 1754, and the effect upon Peacock showed
the weak side of his philosophy of life, the obstinate
refusal to look beyond the present day.   " He often
said that after his mother's death he wrote nothing
of value, as his heart was not in the work."   A
severe illness followed in 1835, but in 1836 his
official career was crowned by his appointment as
Chief Examiner of Indian Correspondence, in succession to James Mill.   The post was one which
could only be filled by one of sound business
capacity and exceptional ability in drafting official
documents: and Peacock's discharge of its duties,
it is believed, suffered nothing by comparison either
with his distinguished predecessor or his still more
celebrated successor, Stuart Mill.   It is much to be
regretted that so little is known of the old India
House, or of its eminent occupants in their official
capacity.   It does not seem to have afforded an
employment of predilection to any of them.   When
Peacock's books came to be sold, it was observed
that hundreds of volumes relating to India, presents
or perquisites of office, were left religiously uncut,
and the same is said to have been the case with
those of MacCulloch, James Mill's predecessor.
Stuart Mill's autobiography avoids the subject

entirely, except for one memorable passage acknowledging the invaluable benefit he derived from the official collar, and the necessity of running in team and harness. Nearly all our insight is derived from Professor Bain's most interesting account of his visit to Stuart Mill at the India House, for the little way it goes altogether illuminative, as Carlyle would have said. Peacock has let in a little light in another direction :—

"A DAY AT THE INDIA HOUSE.

"From ten to eleven, have breakfast for seven ;
From eleven to noon, think you've come too soon ;
From twelve to one, think what's to be done ;
From one to two, find nothing to do ;
From two to three, think it will be
A very great bore to stay till four."

But if there were intervals of idleness, owing chiefly to the long interruptions of the mails while yet the Red Sea route was not, there were also serious duties and emergencies calling for the display of practical statesmanship. Peacock's occupation seems to have principally lain with finance, commerce, and public works. The first clear glimpse we obtain of its nature is the memorandum prepared by him at the request of a Director respecting General Chesney's projected Euphrates expedition, and reprinted in the preface to the

S

General's narrative as a tribute to its sagacity.[1] The line of inquiry thus prescribed was followed up, and, after the production of an article in the *Edinburgh Review* for 1835, and much valuable evidence before Parliamentary Committees, resulted in the construction under his superintendence of iron steamboats designed to demonstrate his view of the feasibility of steam navigation round the Cape, a view propounded and steadfastly adhered to when Dr. Lardner was denying the possibility of a steam voyage even to America. Not only was the voyage successfully made, but the boats, arriving at the time of the Chinese war, rendered valuable service in naval operations. It is noteworthy, nevertheless, that he opposed the no less practicable undertaking of navigating the Red Sea by steam, whether from conviction or from deference to the supposed interests of his employers. It fell to his lot in 1834 and 1836 to advocate these interests in two very unpopular cases before the committees respectively appointed to inquire into the grievances of Mr. Silk Buckingham and the Company's salt monopoly. In neither instance, however, had he to do any violence to

[1] " Read the memorandum the Chairs gave me respecting the application of steam navigation to the internal and external communications of India. It has been prepared carefully and ably, and is very interesting."—" Lord Ellenborough's Diary," December 21, 1829.

his sense of justice : he knew that Mr. Buckingham
was an adventurer; that the people of Liverpool
merely wanted to appropriate the Company's
monopoly to themselves; and that, odious as a
tax upon a prime necessary of life may appear,
it is preferable to financial derangement.   His
evidence on both these occasions is most interesting reading ; it reveals powers and accomplishments which could not otherwise have been
suspected, insomuch that it may be truly said
that he who does not know it does not know
Peacock.   No barrister could have surpassed the
lucidity and cogency with which he establishes his
case against Mr. Buckingham ; and the evidence
before the Salt Committee evinces an equally
remarkable ability for mastering intricate details
and rendering them intelligible to others.   The
Company were always generous masters, and it is
not surprising that in the case of so useful a servant,
a salary, handsome in itself, but inadequate to his
free habits of expenditure, should have been frequently supplemented by extraordinary gifts.

For many years after his appointment as Chief
Examiner Peacock's authorship was in abeyance,
with the exception of operatic criticisms contributed to the *Examiner*, and an occasional article
in the *Westminster Review* or *Bentley's Miscellany*.
To the former he had, so long previously as 1827,

contributed a review of Moore's "Epicurean," by
far the best criticism he ever wrote, utterly anni-
hilative of the book as a delineation of antique
manners, while leaving it the credit to which it is
justly entitled on the score of fancy and pictu-
resqueness.   Subsequent contributions, including
a review of the biographies of Jefferson, and the
plea of *laudator temporis acti* for old London
Bridge, though characteristic, were much less
remarkable.   In 1837 "Headlong Hall," "Nightmare Abbey," "Maid Marian," and "Crotchet
Castle" appeared together as vol. lvii. of Bentley's
Standard Novels.   In 1852 he lost his wife, whose
memory he honoured with an affecting Latin
epitaph.   About the same time, taste or leisure
for authorship returned, and he commenced a
series of contributions to *Fraser's Magazine* with
the first, and most interesting, paper of his
"Horae Dramaticae," a delightful restoration of
the "Querolus," a Roman comedy, probably of
the fourth century.   Many other papers followed,
of which the three on Shelley were by far the
most important ; but the review of Müller and
Donaldson's "History of Greek Literature" was the
ablest and most characteristic.   One little essay
of singular charm, "The Last Day of Windsor
Forest," written out fairly for the press but never
printed, was rescued from oblivion by the present

writer, and published in the *National Review*. Peacock had in the interim retired from the India House on an ample pension (March 29, 1856). Throughout 1860 his last novel, "Gryll Grange," continued to appear in *Fraser's Magazine*. Though not so nearly on a par with his other works as has been sometimes asserted, it is still a surprisingly vigorous performance for a man of his years. The volatile spirit of humour has indeed mainly evaporated, but the residuum is anything but a *caput mortuum*. The principal note of senility is, as in the second part of "Wilhelm Meister," the serious respect paid to ceremonial mummeries which previously would only have been introduced to be laughed at.

Peacock died at Lower Halliford, January 23, 1866, and is buried in the new cemetery at Shepperton. In penning this memoir, we seem to have unconsciously depicted much of his character, and his writings will do the rest. It will, nevertheless, be well to record some traits, which might not readily be collected from either, in the simple and affectionate words of his grand-daughter :—

" In society my grandfather was ever a welcome guest, his genial manner, hearty appreciation of wit and humour in others, and the amusing way in which he told stories, made him a very delightful acquaintance ; he was always so agreeable and so very witty that he was called by his most intimate friends the 'Laughing Philosopher,' and it seems to me that the term 'Epicurean Philosopher,' which I have often heard applied to him, describes him accurately and briefly. In public business my grandfather was upright and honourable; but as he advanced in years his detestation of anything disagreeable made him simply avoid whatever fretted him, laughing off all sorts of ordinary calls upon his leisure time. His love of ease and kindness of heart made it impossible that he could be actively unkind to any one, but he would not be worried, and just got away from anything that annoyed him. He was very fond of his children, and was an indulgent father to them, and he was a kind and affectionate grandfather; he could not bear any one to be unhappy or uncomfortable about him, and this feeling he carried down to the animal creation; his pet cats and dogs were especially cared for by himself, the birds in the garden were carefully watched over and fed, and no gun was ever allowed to be fired about the place. After he retired from the India House he seldom left Halliford; his life was spent among his books, and in the garden, in which he took great pleasure, and on the river. May-day he always kept in true old English fashion; all the children of the village came round with their garlands of flowers, and each child was presented with a new

penny, or silver threepenny or fourpenny piece,
according to the beauty of their garlands ; the
money was given by the Queen of the May, always
one of his grand-daughters, who sat beside him,
dressed in white and crowned with flowers, and
holding a sceptre of flowers in her hand."

Peacock's position in the intellectual world was
intended by him to have been expressed by the
motto on his seal : " Nec tardum opperior, nec
præcedentibus insto " ; but the first half of the
precept was insufficiently observed by him. Injustice, however, is done to him by those who call
him a mere Pagan ; he allowed. English, French,
and Italian a place among the great literatures
of the world, and his unreasonable prejudice
against German at all events prevented his taking
trouble to acquire what would not after all have
suited him. His knowledge of the literature he
did relish was exceedingly accurate, but his re-
productions of antique models have neither the
antique form nor the antique spirit, and he cannot
escape the reproach, common with exact scholars,
of anathematising in a modern what he admired in
an ancient. Tennyson he could never appreciate,
and of Keats he says in a letter to Shelley, " I
should never read 'Hyperion' if I lived to the age
of Methuselah." His tepidity towards Byron and
Shelley arose rather from antipathy in the strict

etymological sense than from insensibility: we have seen his deliberate verdict on Shelley, and he says in a letter to him, "'Cain' is fine, 'Sardanapalus' finer, 'Don Juan' best of all." But the milder beauties of Wordsworth and Coleridge were fairly recognised by him. His own strongest predilections were naturally for the humourists, and rather for the genial extravagance of Aristophanes and Rabelais, or the polished wit of Voltaire and Petronius, than the moody bitterness of writers like Swift. Urbane philosophers like Cicero, or romantic narrators like Boiardo, held, however, an almost equal place in his esteem. He made a particular study of Tacitus, from whom he learned the pregnant brevity that renders both writers such valuable models to an age whose worst literary fault is diffuseness.

Peacock's own place in literature is pre-eminently that of a satirist. This character is not always a passport to goodwill. Satirists have met with much ignorant and invidious depreciation, as though a talent for ridicule was necessarily the index of an unkindly nature. The truth is just the reverse: as the sources of laughter and tears lie near together, so is the geniality of an intellectual man usually accompanied with a keen perception of the ridiculous. Both exist in ample measure in Peacock, whose hearty and sometimes misplaced

laughter at what he deemed absurd is usually
accompanied with a kindly feeling towards the
exemplars of the absurdity.·· The only very notice-
able instance of the contrary is the undoubtedly
illiberal ridicule of the Lake poets in his earlier
writings; still there is sufficient evidence elsewhere
of his sincere admiration of their works. Brougham
he certainly abhorred, and yet the denunciation of
him in "Crotchet Castle" has hardly more of in-
vective than the gibes at the "modern Athenians."
Add to this geniality a bright fancy, a lively
sense of the ludicrous, a passion for natural beauty,
strong sense, occasionally warped by prejudice,
genuine tenderness on occasion, diction of singular purity, and a style of singular elegance, and
it will be allowed that, *prima facie*, Peacock should
be popular. That he has nevertheless been only
the favourite of the few is owing in a measure
to the highly intellectual quality of his work, but
chiefly to his lack of the ordinary qualifications
of the novelist, all pretension to which he entirely
disclaims. He has no plot, little human interest,
and no consistent delineation of character. His
personages are mere puppets, or, at best, incarna-
tions of abstract qualities, or idealisations of dis-
embodied grace or beauty. He affected to prefer
—perhaps really did prefer—the pantomimes of
"the enchanter of the south" to the novels of

" the enchanter of the north"; and, by a whimsical retribution, his own novels have passed for pantomimes. "A queer mixture!" pronounced the *Saturday Review*, criticising "Gryll Grange," and such has been the judgment of most. It will not be the judgment of any capable of appreciating the Aristophanic comedy of which, restricted as their scale is in comparison, Peacock's fiction is, perhaps, the best modern representative. Nearly everything that can be urged against him can be urged against Aristophanes too; and save that his invention is far less daring and opulent, his Muse can allege most of " the apologies of Aristophanes." When he is depreciated, comparison with another novelist usually seems to be implied, but it would be as unfair to test him by the standard of Miss Austen or Miss Edgeworth, as to try Aristophanes by the rules of the New Comedy. A master of fiction he is not, and he never claimed to be; a satirist, a humourist, a poet he is most undoubtedly. Were these qualities less eminent than they are, he would still live by the truth of his natural description and the grace and finish of his style: were even these in default, the literary historian would still have to note in him the first appearance of a new type, destined to be frequently imitated, but seldom approached, and never exactly reproduced.

MATTHEW ARNOLD

MATTHEW ARNOLD [1]

THE incontestable importance of Matthew Arnold's place in English poetical literature arises not merely from the beauty of much of his poetry, but from his peculiar distinction as one of the few eminent English poets who are enrolled among the legislators of their art, not more by the indirect influence of their metrical compositions, than by the authority universally accorded to their critical utterances. Coleridge, the most penetrating critic Britain ever possessed, is too casual and desultory to rank among legislators, and the two poets who admit of most profitable comparison with Arnold in this respect are Dryden and Wordsworth. Each of the three had definite convictions on the subject of poetry which he exemplified in his own practice; and each, along with error and exaggerated truth, contributed elements to the formation of a poetical ideal which can never be ignored. To a certain extent Arnold's work was a corrective of that of

[1] Introduction to "Alaric at Rome, and other Poems," by Matthew Arnold, published by Messrs. Ward, Lock, & Bowden : 1896.

Wordsworth, the great emancipator of English poetry. In overthrowing a merely conventional orthodoxy, Wordsworth had inevitably given somewhat of a shock to those great models and eternal principles by whose corrupt following this conventionalism had been engendered. It was Arnold's mission to restore the balance, inculcating alike by example and precept the cardinal doctrines of antiquity, that form is of equal importance with matter, and that the value of a poem consists more in the force and truth of the total impression than in isolated fine thoughts sparkling forth in the heat of composition. This, substantially, was Matthew Arnold's critical gospel, a deliverance interesting as an episode in the eternal strife between Classic and Romantic, and valuable as a corrective of tendencies inherent in the English genius. This is not generally architectonic, it overwhelms with affluence of thought and imagery, but the shaping hand is too often absent. Arnold thought that much of the characteristic English indifference to form arose from indiscriminate admiration of Shakespeare; but the truth is that while fancy, passion, and reflection come to gifted Englishmen by nature, the sense of symmetry usually has to be engrafted upon them. We are a nation of colourists, and great colourists, except by determined efforts, rarely became good draughtsmen. Arnold's admonition, therefore, was most serviceable, it may be ranked with Wordsworth's protest against the conventionalities of his day, and was perhaps even more valuable; for while Wordsworth assailed an aberration which in course of time would have corrected itself, Arnold denounced ingrained vice and besetting sin. It was, moreover, eminently seasonable, appearing in 1853, when there did seem a real danger of English poetry becoming an assemblage of purple patches upon a core of perishable wood, the very definition of a scarecrow. This did not, however, arise, as Arnold thought, from a special infirmity in the age, whose imperfections he greatly exaggerated, but from the abuse of what was best in it. The infinite significance of even the humblest human life was beginning to be recognised as it had never been before, but a discovery invaluable in the social sphere had not unnaturally generated the dangerous artistic heresy that what is good enough for a novel is also good enough for a poem. The year 1853, the date of Arnold's memorable preface, was also the period, not indeed of the culminating, but of the too exclusive influence of Shelley and Keats, who were receiving their long withheld recompense with usury. These great poets, in their more mature productions, rather surpass than fall short of the ordinary English standard of symmetrical construction, but their architecture is obscured by the splendour of their painting, and too many had come to confound the art of poetry with the art of phrasing. To such Matthew Arnold's remonstrance came like an exorcism, and its weight was greatly enhanced by the method of its delivery; not poured as from a vase into the turbid torrent of periodical criticism, but prefixed as a confession of faith to a volume of poetry designed for and destined to endurance.

It is a great reinforcement to the weight of poetical criticism when the critic is himself a recognised poet. The Goddess of Wisdom herself is not recorded to have lectured to the Muses, and the precepts of mere prose writers, however excellent, have something of the air of instructions to Hannibal in the art of war. Even Aristotle qualified for his Poetics by writing a song, and a very good one. Arnold, when he came forward in 1853 to discourse on poetry, could produce sufficient credentials as the author of two poetical volumes of great though unequal merit, "The Strayed Reveller, and other Poems" (1849); and "Empedocles on Etna, and other Poems" (1852). Neither of these, however, as we shall see presently, sufficiently exemplified the particular principles which he chiefly desired to enforce. His argument would have wanted the weight which theory derives from conformity to practice, if, upon the republication in 1853 of such of these poems as he then cared to preserve, they had not been accompanied by another so completely exemplifying his views respecting the supreme necessity of perfection of form, dignity of subject, unity of action, and sobriety of treatment that it might have been written to illustrate them. Great poems, nevertheless, cannot be composed to order, and it is much more probable that the preface grew out of the poem than the reverse.

No subject could better than "Sohrab and Rustum" have enabled Arnold to exemplify his own precepts :—"Choose a fitting action, penetrate yourself with the feeling of its situations; this done everything else will follow." This exhortation, indeed, is insufficiently limited and defined. The action must be not only abstractedly fitting for a poet to undertake, but the poet must fit the action. Coleridge, perhaps, would have made no more of "Sohrab and Rustum" than Arnold would have made of "The Ancient Mariner"; and when at a later period Arnold endeavoured to dramatise the story of Merope, the unanimous voice of criticism informed him that although the subject was undeniably fitting, and the poet adequately

T

penetrated by it, "everything else" had not
followed. But "Sohrab and Rustum" suited him
to perfection, for it is an heroic action whose
greatness consists not in its grandeur, but in its
pathos. Pathos is the note of all his best poems,
there is hardly one of them which is not more
or less an appeal for compassion on account of
the character of the incident described, or some
human or spiritual sorrow, or some real or imaginary distress of the age. No more affecting incident than the involuntary death of a son by his
father's hand can be found in history or fiction,
and it especially impressed Arnold, from that
strength in him of the parental instinct revealed
by his recently published correspondence. What
he received intimately he reproduced vividly, and
the conduct of his story and the tissue of his
diction are masterpieces of judgment. Nothing,
he rightly perceived, can be more essential to the
impressiveness of a story of profound pathos than
that it should be told in the simplest language,
yet unrelieved simplicity throughout a long narrative must wear an aspect of poverty, perhaps even
of affectation. The general homeliness of the exposition, therefore, is occasionally interrupted by
elaborate similes, little poems in themselves, and
involving close and accurate word-painting. These
for a moment suspend, but do not divert, the

reader's attention to the main action, whose pathos goes on deepening with every line, until there is no modern poem, with perhaps the exception of Tennyson's "Edward Gray," that it is so difficult to read without tears. Arnold, nevertheless, saw that, although the impression of unrelieved tragedy created by such poems as "Edward Gray" may be right in a lyric, it would be amiss in an epic, and, since the situation itself could not be modified, he has mitigated it by the majestic concluding passage describing the course of the Oxus, emblematic of the greatness of Nature in comparison with the accidents of man's brief career, and, at its termination, of the sea in which human joys and sorrows are finally swallowed up.

Besides "Sohrab and Rustum," the volume of 1853 contained another poem of length and importance, of an earlier date of composition, whose unlikeness to "Sohrab" adds to the probability that the writer's high and just estimate of the latter poem had much to do with moulding the doctrine of his memorable preface. "Tristram and Iseult" is exceedingly unlike "Sohrab" in everything but poetical beauty, and entirely fails to produce that total impression which Arnold propounds as the chief object of the poet. While the action of "Sohrab" is transparently clear, that of "Tristram and Iseult" is so confused that it would be difficult to make out the subject of the poem if this were not already known. The merits are entirely of detail, and these are most conspicuous in the third part, an appendage to the poem which would never have been missed if it had never existed, but with which no one would now consent to part, so many and exquisite are its beauties. The strength of parental feeling is again visible in the description of the children at play, to be matched only by that of the sleeping children in Part I. The story of Vivien's enchantment of Merlin is admirably told, but, unlike the similar episode of the river in "Sohrab and Rustum," is a mere ornament with no vital relation to the poem.

"Tristram and Iseult" had been published in 1852 along with "Empedocles on Etna," which failed to reappear in the 1853 volume. Arnold explains its withdrawal by saying that he had come to look upon this powerful representation of the discouragement of a philosopher compelled to surrender the healthy objectivity of the early Greeks as over-morbid and monotonously painful. "Everything is to be endured, nothing is to be done." There is truth in the self-criticism, but after all there seems no reason why a poet may not paint a dejected mood in a long soliloquy, especially when this is broken by such exquisite lyrics as the songs of Callicles, which are among the loveliest examples in our language of description blent with lyrical emotion. The poem was ultimately restored to a place in the author's works at the intercession of Robert Browning.

Arnold's poems of later date than 1853, having no place in this edition, do not, strictly speaking, concern us; but the two most important cannot well be omitted from any general review of his work, especially as the principal, "Balder Dead," has received much less praise than it deserves. It is astonishing to find so competent a critic as Mr. T. H. Ward, and one who might so easily have been forgiven for a partial judgment, apparently doubting whether "Balder Dead" "has a distinct value of its own." It seems to us impossible to allow any considerable interval between this poem and "Sohrab and Rustum"; the style is very similar, the action of each equally noble and affecting; the conduct of either story equally admirable; the interspersed similes equally happy and carefully worked out; the pathos of the respective situations much on a level, and affording almost equal scope for the tenderness which, even more than depth of thought, is Arnold's strong point as a poet. It may, indeed, be said that the manner and diction of "Balder" are even more Homeric than those of "Sohrab and Rustum," while, considering the peculiarity of the locality and the action, they might with propriety have been less so; it is also true that there are more lapses into the prosaic, and more lines deficient in metrical effect. These defects, however, are very inconsiderable in comparison with the general impression of godlike grandeur and human pathos. "Thyrsis," after "Balder" the most important of Arnold's later poems, is an elegy on his friend Arthur Clough, not, certainly, a "Lycidas," or an "Adonais," but rich in beauties both of thought and description. It is somewhat marred for the general reader by a circumstance which probably enhances its charm for Oxonians, the numerous local allusions which endear the poem to those familiar with the scenery, but fall flat when not understood. The note of personal affection is unmistakable, and it may be from over-jealousy for his friend's repute and his own that Arnold's poem smells somewhat of the lamp, and hardly produces so much effect as a simpler composition, the exquisite poem on the deaths of his brother and his sister-in-law, full of rich local colouring, and not too local.

With these exceptions, and his dignified but frigid tragedy of "Merope," the chief part of Arnold's poetical work was composed by 1853, and is comprehended in three volumes, one mainly a reprint. There is nothing extraordinary in the gradual impoverishment of his poetical vein, which had never been remarkable for affluence. His criticisms and private letters betray a limited sympathy with his poetical predecessors and immediate contemporaries, which, since it assuredly was not in the slightest degree inspired by envy or unworthy jealousy, can only be interpreted as betokening an undue preponderance of the critical instinct, fatal to the enthusiasm required for continuous productiveness in poetry. The teeming soul is enthusiastic and lavish of admiration, for only so can it sufficiently respond to the innumerable impressions, physical and spiritual, through which alone it is possible to sustain incessant poetical activity. Arnold's intellectual force and intellectual interests never waned, but were diverted more and more from the sphere of creation to the sphere of criticism ; in which, however, so novel and striking were his views and so original his method of developing them, that he almost became a creator. He laid English literature, in particular, under the greatest obligation by his two golden little books, "On Translating Homer," and "On the Study of Celtic Literature." His own attempts at Homeric translation, indeed, were by no means fortunate, but this in no respect detracts from the value of his criticism. His more ambitious prose writings have permeated modern English thought, and furnished it with a new and most beneficial element; it may be added, that in effecting this they have parted with their own individuality, and will soon exist rather as a tint than as a substance. This is merely to say that they were admirably suited for their time, of which his poems are comparatively independent. We entirely agree with Mr. Frederic Harrison, that Arnold's fame will mainly rest upon his poetry, and that it will be durable, pure, and high. We have mentioned his most conspicuous productions, but those which we have not mentioned, or even a few of them, would suffice for an enviable poetical reputation. The development of his mind, nevertheless, as shown in the chronological sequence of his poems (obscured by the classified arrangement adopted in his own edition) is not in the direction of poetry. In the finest productions in his first volume ("The Strayed Reveller," "The Forsaken Merman," "Mycerinus") the poetical impulse is dominant, the treatment is healthy- and objective, spiritual strivings and questionings, though the pieces are really inspired by them, are kept in the background. The finest poems in the second volume, on the other hand ("Memorial Verses," "The Buried Life," "The Youth of Nature," "The Youth of Man," above all "A Summer Night"), come from within. They are not less admirable than their predecessors, but they indicate the waning of that joy in external things without which it is most difficult to keep the flame of poetry alight, especially when, like Arnold, one is tried by the demands of a responsible and harassing official position.

If we were called upon to indicate Arnold's place upon the roll of English poets by comparison with one of accepted fame, we should seek his nearest parallel in Gray. Both are academic poets, the dominant note of each is a tender and appealing pathos, each possessed a refinement of taste which in some measure degenerated into fastidiousness, and tended to limit a productiveness not originally exuberant. If they are to be judged by their strongest performances, the palm must indisputably be given to Gray, for Arnold has nothing that can be equalled with the immortal " Elegy." If, on the other hand, diversity of excellence is to be the criterion, he infinitely surpasses his prototype : who would, however, have written much more, and even better, if he had enjoyed Arnold's unspeakable advantage of living after the second great age of English poetry instead of before it. It may not be unreasonable to predict that posterity will place them nearly on a level. In venturing this prophecy, full allowance has been made for the inevitable deduction from Arnold's charm when, in the general mutation of things, he shall have ceased to represent contemporary thought and feeling. He is perhaps the most characteristic representative that the blended religion and scepticism of our exceptional epoch have had, and he will be invaluable as a document for the literary and philosophical historian of the future. But for this very reason he must some day cease to be a vital force in the present, and must rely upon his strictly poetical merits, independent of any reference to the spiritual conflicts of his day. That these merits will preserve his name, we have no doubt whatever. His first charm, to our mind, is depth of pathos; and in the next place beauty of description, exquisite but not obtrusive. An analysis of his best poems will show that pathos is hardly ever absent; he is almost invariably representing some sorrow, actual or ideal, but always most tenderly felt and deeply realised. Sohrab, Rustum, Balder, Hoder, Iseult, Mycerinus, Empedocles, the Forsaken Merman, the Sick King of Bokhara, the Modern Sappho—what a gallery of pathetic figures! The note of sorrow, whether for himself or for mankind, rings equally from nearly all the personal poems; it is his unique distinction to have been at the same time so elegiac and so manly. His descriptive passages are delightful for their grace and accuracy, but not brilliant, like Tennyson's glowing canvas; or forcible, like Browning's intense etching; their charm is rather that of delicate water-colour. His fondness for unrhymed lyric, arising probably from defect of musical volume in his poetical constitution, sometimes, as Froude remarks, renders his "fine imaginative painting" merely "the poetry of well-written, elegant prose." It is hardly necessary to add that Arnold is before all things the poet of culture, and that, though his pathos usually appeals to the universal feelings of the human heart, the appeal will seldom find an echo in uncultivated or semi-educated readers. For example, the beautiful final stanza of that beautiful poem "On the Rhine":

> "Ah, Quiet, all things feel thy balm !
> Those blue hills too, this river's flow,
> Were restless once, but long ago
> Tamed is their turbulent youthful glow :
> Their joy is in their calm,"

will be lost upon him who does not know that the hills which border the Rhine were at one time volcanoes.

RALPH WALDO EMERSON

RALPH WALDO EMERSON

"NOTEWORTHY also," says Carlyle, "and serviceable for the progress of this same individual,
wilt thou find his subdivision into generations."
It is indeed the fact that the course of human
history admits of being marked off into periods,
which, from their average duration and the impulse
communicated to them by those who enter upon
adolescence along with them, may be fitly deno-
minated generations, especially when their opening
and closing are signalised by great events which
serve as historical landmarks. No such event indeed, short of the Day of Judgment or a universal
deluge, can serve as an absolute line of demarcation ;
nothing can be more certain than that history and
human life are a perpetual Becoming; and that
although the progress of development is frequently
so startling and unforeseen as to evoke the poet's
exclamation—

> "New endless growth surrounds on every side,
> Such as we deemed not earth could ever bear ;"

this growth is but development after all. The

association of historical periods with stages in the
mental development of man is nevertheless too convenient to be surrendered; the vision is cleared and
the grasp strengthened by the perception of a well-
defined era in American history, commencing with
the election of Andrew Jackson to the Presidency
in 1828 and closing with the death of Abraham
Lincoln in 1865, a period exactly corresponding
with one in English history measured from the
death of Lord Liverpool, the typical representative
of a bygone political era, in the former year, to
that of Lord Palmerston, another such representative, in the latter. The epoch thus bounded
almost precisely corresponds to the productive
period of the two great men who, more than any
of their contemporaries, have stood in the conscious
attitude of teachers of their age. With such men
as Tennyson and Browning, vast as their influence
has been, the primary impulse has not been
didactic, but artistic ; Herbert Spencer, George
Eliot, Matthew Arnold, and others, have been
chiefly operative upon the succeeding generation ;
Mill and the elder Newman rather address special
classes than the people at large ; and Ruskin and
Kingsley would have willingly admitted that, however eloquent the expression of their teaching,
its originality mainly consisted in the application
of Carlyle's ideas to subjects beyond Carlyle's

range.   Carlyle and Emerson, therefore, stand
forth like Goethe and Schiller as the Dioscuri of
their period; the two men to whom beyond others
its better minds looked for guidance, and who had
the largest share in forming the minds from which
the succeeding generation was to take its com-
plexion.   Faults and errors they had; but on the
whole it may be said that nations have rarely
been more fortunate in their instructors than the
two great English-speaking peoples during the
age of Carlyle and Emerson.   Of Carlyle this
is not the place to speak further; but writing on
Emerson, it will be necessary to exhibit what we
conceive to have been the special value of his
teaching; and to attempt some description of
the man himself in vindication of the high place
claimed for him.

It has been said of some great man of marked
originality that his was the sole voice among many
echoes.   This cannot be said of Emerson's; his age
was by no means deficient in original voices.   But
it may be said with truth to have been the chief
vocal utterance in an age of authorship.   It is a
trite remark that many of the men of thought
whose ideas have most influenced the world have
shown little inclination for literary composition.
The president of a London freethinking club
in Goldsmith's time supposed himself to be in

U

possession of the works of Socrates, no less than those of Tully and Cicero, but no other trace of their existence has come to light. Had Emerson lived in any age but his own it is doubtful whether, any more than Socrates, he would have figured as an author. " I write," he tells Carlyle, " with very little system, and, as far as regards composition, with most fragmentary result—paragraphs incomprehensible, each sentence an infinitely repellent particle." We also hear of his going forth into the woods to hunt a thought as a boy might hunt a butterfly, except that the thought had flown with him from home, and that his business was not so much to capture it as to materialise it and make it tangible. This peculiarity serves to classify Emerson among the ancient sages, men like Socrates and Buddha, whose instructions were not merely oral but unmethodical and unsystematic; who spoke as the casual emergency of the day dictated, and left their observations to be collected by their disciples. An excellent plan in so far as it insures the endowment of the sage's word with his own individuality; exceptionable when a doubt arises whether the utterance belongs to the master or the disciple, and, in the case of diametrically opposite versions, whether Socrates has been represented more truly by the prose of Xenophon or the poetry of Plato. We may be thankful that

the spirit of Emerson's age, and the exigencies of
his own affairs, irresistibly impelled him to write ;
nevertheless the fact remains that with him Man
Thinking is not so much Man Writing as Man Speaking, and that although the omnipotent machinery
of the modern social system caught him too, and
forced him into line with the rest, we have in him
a nearer approach to the voice, apart from the dis-
turbing and modifying effect of literary composition,
than in any other eminent modern thinker. This
annuls one of the most weighty criticisms upon
Emerson, so long as he is regarded merely as an
author—his want of continuity and consequent
want of logic. Had he attempted to establish a
philosophical system, this would have been fatal.
But such an undertaking is of all things furthest
from his thoughts. He does not seek to demonstrate: he announces. Ideas have come to him
which, as viewed by the inward light, appear important and profitable. He brings these forward
to be tested by the light of other men. He does
not seek to connect these ideas together, except in
so far as their common physiognomy bespeaks their
common parentage. Nor does he seek to fortify
them by reasoning, or subject them to any test save
the faculty by which the unprejudiced soul discerns
good from evil. If his jewel will scratch glass, it is
sufficiently evinced a diamond.

It follows that although Emerson did not write most frequently or best in verse, he is, as regards the general constitution of the intellect, rather to be classed with poets than with philosophers. Poetry cannot indeed dispense with the accurate observation of nature and mankind, but poetic genius essentially depends on intuition and inspiration. There is no gulf between the philosopher and the poet; some of the greatest of poets have also been among the most powerful of reasoners; but their claim to poetical rank would not have been impaired if their ratiocination had been ever so illogical. Similarly, a great thinker may have no more taste for poetry than was vouchsafed to Darwin or the elder Mill without any impeachment of his power of intellect. The two spheres of action are fundamentally distinct, though the very highest geniuses, such as Shakespeare and Goethe, have sometimes almost succeeded in making them appear as one. To determine to which of them a man actually belongs, we must look beyond the externalities of literary form, and inquire whether he obtains his ideas by intuition, or by observation and reflection. No mind will be either entirely intuitive or entirely reflective, but there will usually be a decided inclination to one or other of the processes; and in the comparatively few cases in which thoughts and feelings seem to come to it

unconsciously, as leaves to a tree, we may consider
that we have a poet, though perhaps not a writer of
poetry. If indeed the man writes at all he will
very probably write prose, but this prose will be
impregnated with poetic quality. From this point
of view we are able to set Emerson much higher
than if we regarded him simply as a teacher. He
is greater as the American Wordsworth than the
American Carlyle. We shall understand his position best by comparing him with other men of
genius who are poets too, but not pre-eminently
so. In beauty of language and power of imagination, John Henry Newman and James Martineau,
though they have written little in verse, yield to
few poets. But throughout all their writings the
didactic impulse is plainly the preponderating one,
their poetry merely auxiliary and ornamental;
hence they are not reckoned among poets. With
Emerson the case is reversed: the revealer is first
in him, the reasoner second; oral speech is his
most congenial form of expression, and he submits
to appear in print because the circumstances of his
age render print the most effectual medium for the
dissemination of his thought. It will be observed
that whenever possible he resorts to the medium
of oration or lecture; it may be further remarked
that his essays, often originally delivered as
lectures, are very like his discourses, and his

discourses very like his essays. In neither, so far
as regards the literary form of the entire composition, distinguished from the force and felicity of
individual sentences, can he be considered as a
classic model. The essay need not be too severely
logical, yet a just conception of its nature requires
a more harmonious proportion and more symmetrical construction, as well as a more consistent
and intelligent direction towards a single definite
end, than we usually find in Emerson. The orator
is less easy to criticise than the essayist, for oratory
involves an element of personal magnetism which
resists all critical analysis. Hence posterity frequently reverses (or rather seems to reverse, for
the decision upon a speech mutilated of voice and
action cannot be really conclusive) the verdicts of
contemporaries upon oratory. "What will our
descendants think of the Parliamentary oratory of
our age?" asked a contemporary of Burke's, "when
they are told that in his own time this man was
accounted neither the first nor the second nor even
the third speaker?" Transferred to the tribunal of
the library, Burke's oratory bears away the palm
from Pitt and Fox and Sheridan; yet, unless we
had heard the living voices of them all, it would be
unsafe for us to challenge the contemporary verdict.
We cannot say, with the lover in Goethe, that the
word printed appears dull and soulless, but it

certainly wants much which conduced to the
efficacy of the word spoken :—

> "Ach ! wie traurig sieht in Lettern,
> Schwarz auf weiss, das Lied mich an,
> Das aus deinem Mund vergöttern
> Das ein Herz zerreissen kann !"

Emerson's orations are no less delightful and
profitable reading than his essays, so long as they
can be treated as his essays were intended to be
treated when they came into print; that is, read
deliberately, with travellings backward when needed,
and frequent pauses of thought. But if we consider them as discourses to be listened to, we shall
find some difficulty in reconciling their popularity and
influence with their apparent disconnectedness, and
some reason to apprehend that, occasional flashes of
epigram excepted, they must speedily have passed
from the minds of the hearers. The apparent
defect was probably remedied in delivery by the
magnetic power of the speaker; not that sort of
power which "wields at will the fierce democracy,"
but that which convinces the hearer that he is
listening to a message from a region not as yet
accessible to himself. The impassioned orator
usually provokes the suspicion that he is speaking
from a brief. Not so Emerson: above all other
speakers, he inspires the confidence that he declares

a thing to be, not because he wishes, but because he perceives it to be so. His quiet, unpretending, but perfectly unembarrassed manner, as of a man with a message which he simply delivers and goes away, must have greatly aided to supply the absence of vigorous reasoning and skilful oratorical construction. We could not expect a spirit commissioned to teach us to condescend to such methods; and Emerson's discourse, whether in oration or essay, though by no means deficient in human feeling or of the "blessed Glendoveer" order, frequently does sound like that of a being from another sphere, simply because he derived his ideas from a higher world; as must always be the case with the man of spiritual, not of course with the man of practical genius. It matters nothing whether this is really so, or whether what wears the aspect of imparted revelation is but a fortifying of the natural eye, qualifying it to look a little deeper than neighbouring eyes into things around. In either case the person so endowed stands a degree nearer to the essential truth of things than his fellows; and the consciousness of the fact, transpiring through his personality, gives him a weight which might otherwise seem inexplicable. Nothing can be more surprising than the deference with which the learned and intelligent contemporaries of the humble and obscure Spinoza resort to his judgment before he has so much as written a book.

This estimate of Emerson as an American Wordsworth, one who like Wordsworth not merely enforced but practically demonstrated the proposition that—

> " One impulse from a vernal wood
> May teach you more of man,
> Of moral evil and of good,
> Than all the sages can,"

is controverted by many who can see in him nothing but a polisher and stringer of epigrammatic sayings. It is impossible to argue with any who cannot recognise the deep vitality of "Nature," of the two series of essays first published, and of the most of the early orations and discourses ; but it may be conceded that Emerson's fountain of inspiration was no more perennial than Wordsworth's, and that in his latter years it was mainly his gift of epigrammatic statement that enabled him to avoid both the Scylla and the Charybdis of men of genius whose fount of inspiration has run low. In some such cases, such as Wordsworth's, the author simply goes on producing, with less and less geniality at every successive effort. In others, such as Browning's, he escapes inanity by violent exaggeration of his characteristic mannerisms. Neither of these remarks applies to Emerson : he does not, in ceasing to be original, become insipid, nor can it be said that he is any more mannered at the last than at the first. This is a clear proof that his peculiarity of speech is not mannerism but manner; that consequently he is not an artificial writer, and that, since the treatment of his themes as he has chosen to treat them admits of no compromise between nature and rhetoric, he has the especial distinction of simplicity where simplicity is difficult and rare. That such is the case will appear from an examination of his earlier and more truly prophetic writings.

Of these, the first in importance as in time is the tract "Nature," commenced in 1833, rewritten, completed, and published in 1836. Of all Emerson's writings this is the most individual, and the most adapted for a general introduction to his ideas. These ideas are not in fact peculiar to him; and yet the little book is one of the most original ever written, and one of those most likely to effect an intellectual revolution in the mind capable of apprehending it. The reason is mainly the intense vitality of the manner, and the translation of abstract arguments into concrete shapes of witchery and beauty. It contains scarcely a sentence that is not beautiful—not with the cold beauty of art, but with the radiance and warmth of feeling. Its dominant note is rapture, like the

joy of one who has found an enchanted realm, or
who has convinced himself that old stories deemed
too beautiful to be true are true indeed.   Yet it
is exempt from extravagance, the splendour of the
language is chastened by taste, and the gladness
and significance of the author's announcements
would justify an even more ardent enthusiasm.
They may be briefly summed up as the statements
that Nature is not mechanical but vital; that the
Universe is not dead but alive; that God is not
remote but omnipresent.   There was of course
no novelty in these assertions,   or can Emerson
bring them by a hair's-breadth nearer demonstration than they have always been.   He simply re-
states them in a manner entirely his own, and
with a charm not perhaps surpassing that with
which others had previously invested them, but
peculiar and dissimilar.   Everything really Emersonian in Emerson's teaching may be said to
spring out of this little book : so copious, however, were the corollaries deducible from principles
apparently so simple, that the flowers veiled
the tree; and precious as the tract is, as the
first and purest draught of the new wine, it
is not the most practically efficient of his
works, and might have missed its aim if it had
not been reinforced by a number of auxiliary
compositions, some produced under circumstances

which could not fail to provoke wide discussion and consequent notoriety. The principles unfolded in "Nature" might probably have passed with civil acquiescence if Emerson had been content with the mere statement; but he insisted on carrying them logically out, and this could not be done without unsettling every school of thought at the time prevalent in America. The Divine omnipresence, for example, was admitted in words by all except materialists and anti-theists; but if, as Emerson maintained, this involved the conception of the Universe as a Divine incarnation, this in its turn involved an optimistic view of the universal scheme totally inconsistent with the Calvinism still dominant in American theology. If all existence was a Divine emanation, no part of it could be more sacred than another part—which at once abolished the mystic significance of religious ceremonies so dear to the Episcopalians; while the immediate contact of the universe with the Deity was no less incompatible with the miraculous interferences on which Unitarianism reposed its faith. Such were some of the most important negative results of Emerson's doctrines; in their positive aspect, by asserting the identity of natural and spiritual laws, they invested the former with the reverence hitherto accorded only to the latter, and restored to a mechanical and prosaic society

the piety with which men in the infancy of history
had contemplated the forces of Nature. Substantially, except for the absence of any definite relation to literary art, Emerson's mission was very
similar to Wordsworth's; but by natural temperament and actual situation he wanted the thousand
links which bound Wordsworth to the past, and
eventually made the sometime innovator the patron
of a return towards the Middle Ages. Emerson
had no wish to regress, and, almost alone among
thinkers who have reached an advanced age,
betrays no symptom of reaction throughout the
whole of his career. The reason may be that
his scrupulous fairness and frank concessions
to the conservative cast of thought had left him
nothing to retract or atone for. He seems to have
started on his journey through life with his con-
servatism and liberalism ready made up, taking
with him just as much of each as he wanted.
This is especially manifest in the discourse "The
Conservative" (1841), in which he deliberately
weighs conservative against progressive tendencies,
impersonates each in an imaginary interlocutor,
and endeavours to display their respective justification and shortcomings. Nothing can be more
rigidly equitable or more thoroughly sane than
his estimate; and as the issues between conser-
vatism and reform have broadened and deepened,

time has only added to its value. It is a perfect
manual for thoughtful citizens desirous of understanding the questions that underlie party issues,
and is especially to be commended to young and
generous minds, liable to misguidance in proportion
to their generosity.

This celebrated discourse is one of a group
including one still more celebrated—the address
to the graduating class of Divinity College, Cambridge, published as "The Christian Teacher"
(1838). This, says Mr. Cabot, seems to have
been struck off at a heat, which perhaps accounts
for its nearer approach than any of Emerson's
other addresses to the standard of what is usually
recognised as eloquence. Eloquent in a sense
Emerson usually was, but here is something which
could transport a fit audience with enthusiasm.
It also possessed the power of awakening the
keenest antagonism; but censure has long since
died away, and nothing that Emerson wrote has
been more thoroughly adopted into the creed of
those with whom external observances and material
symbols find no place. Equally epoch-making in a
different way was the oration on "Man Thinking,"
or "The American Scholar" (1837), entitled by
Dr. Holmes "our intellectual declaration of independence," and of which Mr. Lowell says, "We
were socially and intellectually moored to English

thought till Emerson cut the cable and gave us a chance at the dangers and glories of blue water." In these three great discourses, and in a less measure in "The Transcendentalist" and "Man the Reformer" (both in 1841), America may boast of possessing works of the first class, which could have been produced in no other country, and which —even though, in Emerson's own phrase, wider circles should come to be drawn around them— will remain permanent landmarks in intellectual history.

These discourses may be regarded as Emerson's public proclamations of his opinions; but he is probably more generally known and more intimately beloved by the two unobtrusive volumes of Essays originally prefaced for England by Carlyle. Most of these indeed were originally delivered as lectures, but to small audiences, and with little challenge to public attention. It may be doubted whether they would have succeeded as lectures but for the personal magnetism of the speaker; but their very defects aid them with the reader, who, once fascinated by their beauty of phrase and depth of spiritual insight, imbibes their spirit all the more fully for his ceaseless effort to mend their deficient logic with his own. Like Love in Dante's sonnet, Emerson enters into and blends with the reader, and his influence will often

be found most potent where it is least acknowledged. Each of the twenty may be regarded as
a fuller working-out of some subject merely hinted
at in "Nature"—statues, as it were, for niches left
vacant in the original edifice. The most important
and pregnant with thought are "History," where
the same claim is preferred for history as for the
material world, that it is not dead but alive; "Self-
reliance," a most vigorous assertion of a truth
which Emerson was apt to carry to extremes—
the majesty of the individual soul; "Compensation," an exposition of the Universe as the incarnation of unerring truth and absolute justice;
"Love," full of beauty and rapture, yet almost
chilling to the young by its assertion of what is
nevertheless true — that even love in its human
semblance only subserves ulterior ends; "Circles,"
the demonstration that this circumstance is in no
way peculiar to Love—that there can be nothing
ultimate, final, or unrelated to ulterior purpose,
nothing around which, in Emersonian phrase, you
cannot draw a circle; "The Over-Soul," a prose
hymn dedicated to an absolutely spiritual religion;
"The Poet," a celebration of poetry as co-extensive
with imagination, and in the highest sense with
Reason also; "Experience" and "Character,"
valuable essays, but evincing that the poetical
impulse was becoming spent, and that Emerson's

mind was more and more tending to questions of conduct. The least satisfactory of the essays is that on "Art," where he is only great on the negative side, Art's inevitable limitations. The æsthetical faculty which contemplates beauty under the restraints of Form was evidently weak in him.

"Representative Men," Emerson's next work of importance (delivered as lectures in 1845, published in 1850), shows that his parachute was descending; but he makes a highly successful compromise by taking up original ideas as reflected in the actions and thoughts of great typical men, one remove only from originality of exposition on his own part. The treatment is necessarily so partial as to exercise a distorting influence on his representation of the men themselves. Napoleon, for example, may have been from a certain point of view the hero of the middle class, as Emerson chooses to consider him; but he was much besides, which cannot even be hinted at in a short lecture. The representation of such a hero, nevertheless, whether the character precisely fitted Napoleon or not, is highly spirited and suggestive; and the same may be said of the other lectures. That on Shakespeare is the least satisfying, the consummate art which is half Shakespeare's greatness making little appeal to Emerson. He appears also at variance with himself when he speaks of

x

Shakespeare's existence as "obscure and profane," such a healthy, homely, unambitious life being precisely what he elsewhere extols as a model. The first lecture of the series, "Uses of Great Men," would seem to have whispered the message more vociferously repeated by Walt Whitman.

Emerson was yet to write two books of worth, not illumed with "the light that never was on sea or land," but valuable complements of his more characteristic work, and important to mankind as an indisputable proof that a teacher need not be distrusted in ordinary things because he is a mystic and a poet. "The Conduct of Life" (1851), far inferior to his earlier writings in inspiration, is yet one of the most popular and widely influential of his works, because condescending more nearly to the needs and intelligence of the average reader. It is not less truly Emersonian, less fully impregnated with his unique genius; but the themes discussed are less interesting, and the glory and beauty of the diction are much subdued. Without it we should have been in danger of regarding Emerson too exclusively as a transcendental seer, and ignoring the solid ground of good sense and practical sagacity from which the waving forests of his imagery drew their nutriment. It greatly promoted his fame and influence by coming into the hands of successive generations of readers who naturally inquired for his last book, found the author, with surprise, much nearer their own intellectual position than they had been led to expect, and gradually extended the endorsement which they could not avoid according to the book to the author himself. When the Reason and the Understanding have agreed to legitimate the pretensions of a speculative thinker, these may be considered stable. Emerson insensibly took rank with the other American institutions; it seemed natural to all that without the retractation or modification of a syllable on his part, Harvard should in 1866 confer her highest honours upon him whose address to her Divinity School had aroused such fierce opposition in 1838. Emerson's views, being pure intuitions, rarely admitted of alteration in essence, though supplement or limitation might sometimes be found advisable. The Civil War, for instance, could not but convince him that in his zeal for the independence of the individual he had dangerously impaired the necessary authority of government. His attitude throughout this great contest was the ideal of self-sacrificing patriotism; in truth it might be said of him, as of so few men of genius, that you could not find a situation for him, public or private, whose obligations he was not certain to fulfil. He had previously given proof of his insight into another nation by his " English Traits," mainly

founded upon the visit he had paid to England in
1847–48, a book to be read with equal pleasure and
profit by the nation of which and by the nation for
which it was written ; while its insight, sanity, and
kindliness justify what has been said on occasion
of another of Emerson's writings :—" The ideologist
judges the man of action more shrewdly and justly
than the man of action judges the ideologist." This
was the secret of Napoleon's bitter animosity to
" ideologists ": he felt instinctively that the man
of ideas could see into him and through him, and
recognise and declare his place in the scheme of
the universe as an astronomer might a planet's.
He would have wished to be an incalculable,
original, elemental force; and it vexed him to feel
that he was something whose course could be
mapped and whose constitution defined by a mere
mortal like a Coleridge or a De Stael, who could
treat him like the incarnate thought he was, and
show him, as Emerson showed the banker, " that
he was also a phantom walking and working
amid phantoms, and that he need only ask a
question or two beyond his daily questions to find
his solid universe proving dim and impalpable before his sense."

The later writings of Emerson, though exhibit-
ing few or no cases of mental decay, are in general
repetitions, or at least confirmations, of what had

once been announcements and discoveries. This can scarcely be otherwise, when the mind's productions are derived from its own stuff and substance. Emerson's contemporary, Longfellow, could renovate and indeed augment his poetical power by resort in his old age to Italy; but change of environment brings no reinforcement of energy to the speculative thinker. Events, however, may come to his aid; and when Emerson was called before the people by a momentous incident like the death of President Lincoln, he rose fully to the height of the occasion. His last verses, also, are among his best. We have spoken of him as primarily and above all things a poet; but his claim to that great distinction is to be sought rather in the poetical spirit which informs all his really inspired writings than in the comparatively restricted region of rhyme and metre. It might have been otherwise. Many of his detached passages are the very best things in verse yet written in America; but though a maker, he is not a fashioner. The artistic instinct is deficient in him; he is seldom capable of combining his thoughts into a harmonious whole. No one's expression in verse is better when he aims at conveying a single thought with gnomic terseness, as in the mottoes to his essays; few are more obscure when he attempts continuous composition. Sometimes, as in the admirable stanzas on the Bunker

Hill dedication, the subject has enforced the due clearness and compression of thought; sometimes, as in the glorious lines beginning, " Not from a vain or shallow thought," he is guided unerringly by a divine rapture; in one instance at least, " The Rhodora," where he is writing of beauty, the instinct of beauty has given his lines the symmetry as well as the sparkle of the diamond. Could he have always written like this, he would have been supreme among American poets in metre; as it is, comparison seems unfair both to him and to them.

What we have to learn from Emerson is chiefly the Divine immanence in the world, with all its corollaries, no discovery of his, but re-stated by him in the fashion most suitable to his age, and with a cogency and attractiveness rivalled by no contemporary. If we tried to sum up his message in a phrase, we might perhaps find this in Keats's famous " Beauty is truth, Truth beauty," only while Keats was evidently more concerned for Beauty than for Truth, Emerson held an impartial balance. These are with him the tests of each other; whatever is really true is also beautiful, whatever is really beautiful is also true. Hence his especial value to a world whose more refined spirits are continually setting up types of æsthetic beauty which must needs be delusive, as discordant with beauty contemplated under the aspect of morality; while the mass never think of bringing social and political arrangements to the no less infallible test of conformity to an ideally beautiful standard.   Hence the seeming idealist is of all men the most practical; and Emerson's gospel of beauty should be especially precious to a country like his own, where circumstances must for so long tell in favour of the more material phases of civilisation.   Even more important is that aspect of his teaching which deals with the unalterableness of spiritual laws, the impossibility of evading Truth and Fact in the long run, or of wronging any one without at the same time wronging oneself.   Happy would it be for the United States if Emerson's essay on "Compensation" in particular could be impressed upon the conscience, where there is any, of every political leader; and interwoven with the very texture of the mind of every one who has a vote to cast at the polls!

The special adaptation of Emerson's teaching to the needs of America is, nevertheless, far from the greatest obligation under which he has laid his countrymen.   His greatest service is to have embodied a specially American type of thought and feeling.   It is the test of real greatness in a nation to be individual, to produce something in the world of intellect peculiar to itself and indefeasibly its own.   Such intellectual growths were indeed to be found in America before Emerson's time, but they were not of the highest class. Franklin was a great sage, but his wisdom was worldly wisdom. Emerson gives us, in his own phrase, morality on fire with emotion—the only morality which in the long run will really influence the heart of man. Man is after all too noble a being to be permanently actuated by enlightened selfishness; and when we compare Emerson with even so truly eminent a character as Franklin, we see, as he saw when he compared Carlyle with Johnson, how great a stride forward his country had taken in the meantime. But he could do for America what Carlyle could not do for Great Britain, for it was done already; he could and did create a type of wisdom especially national, as characteristic of the West as Buddha's of the East.

SHELLEY'S VIEWS ON ART

SHELLEY'S VIEWS ON ART

SHELLEY'S attitude towards fine art is not one of the most significant or the most important aspects of his mind, but, even as a single element in a rich intellect, it possesses sufficient interest to justify independent treatment, and it is instructive in a high degree if regarded as an illustration of the manner in which poets and men of letters in general look upon art, which is not that in which artistic production is usually contemplated by the artists themselves.

Shelley's views on art, it need not be said, are in no respect authoritative. Their value—and they have considerable value—is not derived from any profound æsthetic knowledge or study on the part of their promulgator. He is quite unlike Goethe, who corrected the immaturity of his first instinctive impressions of art by a strenuous course of study, and by much actual practice in artistic production. Goethe, consequently, is listened to with deference as one who has taken pains to qualify as' a connoisseur. Were he living now, the most distinguished of contemporary artists would resort to him with something of a tremor, and feel elated or depressed in proportion as his verdict upon them was favourable or the reverse. Shelley would be consulted, not as an oracle, but as a mirror. The artist would not expect to be enlightened by his dicta; but he would instruct himself by discovering the impression he had produced on a mind so sensitive, acute, and sincere. Shelley never criticises contemporary artists; but our perception of the merits of the Greeks and the men of the Renaissance is vivified by discovering how they are regarded by him and such as he.

One caution, however, is essential. Shelley would have been a better art critic in our day than he could be in his own. The revival of a feeling for pure Hellenic art in Europe may be said to date from the public exhibition of the Elgin marbles in England, which occurred as Shelley was on the point of leaving his country never to return. Up to that period Greek art could not be understood, simply because no one knew what it was. The classical tradition, which quite rightly laid it down that Greece had exemplified the perfection of art, inevitably ascribed this character of perfection to the best works then attainable, which were not, properly speaking, Greek, but Græco-Roman, many of them works of great merit, but

as secondary and imitative as any modern productions modelled upon antique examples. In like
manner, the inferior Italian painters were ranked
by public opinion much nearer to the great masters
than would now be permitted, and the tourist
visited Italy under an obligation to adore Guido
and venerate Guercino. This remark is less appli-
cable to literature, because literature possessed
the models which art wanted. Unlike the Elgin
marbles, the literary masterpieces of antiquity were
already in men's hands, and required nothing but
insight to be appreciated. It is true that the
seventeenth and eighteenth centuries, in their
blind veneration for anything and everything
classical, had put the Latin imitators too nearly
on a par with their Greek prototypes, but sounder
views were already beginning to spread. Shelley
himself was one of the few to whom this long-
delayed insight had been granted. With little aid
from art or æsthetics, he was, together with
Goethe, Keats, and Landor, busy in dispelling
former conventions, whether by the incomparable
ease and grace of his direct translations from the
classical originals, or by the spirit of myth and
personification which he imported from these into
his original verse. The same Hellenic spirit would
have made him a regenerative force in art if his
archæological equipment had been more complete.

It is not easy to say whether Shelley had received any technical instruction in art; but, as drawing-masters were in his day frequent ornamental appendages to the graver studies pursued or supposed to be pursued in schools public and private, it is likely that he had. If this had proceeded far, it is probable that he would have made some attempts to sketch the beautiful scenery and imposing ruins that so often overcame him with admiration in his foreign travels; but the only recorded effort in any respect analogous is a portrait from memory of a goblin which had visited him in a bad dream. When, nevertheless, he fell into a reverie over the composition of poetry, his hand would wander over his note-book and aimlessly delineate trees, boats, or human countenances, the latter sometimes of a strangely Blake-like character. A few of these have been worked up into elaborate drawings, displaying weird invention and considerable faculty of draughtsmanship. Of his ability as a colourist nothing can be said, for he never possessed a paint-box, and if he had, his drawings seem the vague impulse of a passing mood, which would have vanished before the exertion of depicting it. The fine feeling for colour displayed in his poems, however, leads to the conclusion that his occasional criticism upon painters as colourists must deserve

respect. Yet it may not be without significance
that his most elaborate æsthetic utterances concern
a department of art which in his day entirely dis-
pensed with colour—sculpture.

Shelley's art criticisms may be divided into three
classes—those which, whether with a view to publication or not, he wrote down with deliberate care;
those which occur casually in his letters; and, lastly,
passages in his poetry. The first section are, of
course, the most important; but they are solely
concerned with sculpture. It would seem probable
that he recorded his observations on sculpture in
Rome in a note-book which has been lost; but
three passages, on the Arch of Titus, on the "Laocoon," and on a Borghese vase, were fortunately,
though probably inaccurately, transcribed by Captain Medwin, a great snapper-up of unconsidered
trifles. According to him, the more important
notes on Florentine sculpture were written down
in the gallery itself, "in a burst of enthusiasm."
These, too, Medwin copied, and with his usual
inaccuracy; but Mr. Buxton Forman has fortunately been able to restore the text from an
authentic manuscript.

Shelley's note on the "Laocoon" is especially
interesting because it brings him into conflict with
Byron. "Byron," he says, "thinks that Laocoon's
anguish is absorbed in that of his children, that

a mortal's agony is blending with an immortal's patience. Not so." The allusion is to the celebrated description in "Childe Harold":—

> " Or, turning to the Vatican, go see
> Laocoon's torture dignifying pain—
> A father's love and mortal's agony
> With an immortal's patience blending ; vain
> The struggle ; vain against the coiling strain
> And gripe, and deepening of the dragon's grasp,
> The old man's clench ; the long envenomed chain
> Rivets the living links, the enormous asp
> Enforces pang on pang, and stifles gasp on gasp."

Shelley, on the contrary, thinks that—

" Intense physical suffering, against which he pleads with an upturned countenance of despair, and appeals with a sense of its injustice, seems the predominant and overwhelming emotion, and yet there is a nobleness in the expression, and a majesty that dignifies torture."

No one will question that Shelley was right. Byron did not, in this instance, " compose with his eye upon the object." The feelings which he attributes to Laocoon rather belong to the elder boy, of whom Shelley writes :—

" His whole soul is with—is a part of—that of his father. His arm extended towards him, not for protection, but from a wish as if instinctively to afford it, absolutely speaks. Nothing can be more exquisite than the contour of his form and face, and the moulding of his lips that are half open, as if in the act of—not uttering any unbecoming complaint, or prayer, or lamentation, which he is conscious are alike useless, but—addressing words of consolatory tenderness to his unfortunate parent."

"In the younger child," Shelley adds, "surprise, pain, and grief seem to contend for mastery. He has not yet arrived at an age when his mind has sufficient self-possession or fixedness of reason to analyse the calamity that is overwhelming himself and all that is dear to him. He is sick with pain and horror. We almost seem to hear his shrieks."

This description alone would suffice to establish Shelley's claim to speak on works of art, in so far as the interpretation of the artist's purpose and the delineation of the effect on the spectator are concerned. Technical criticism is a different matter; yet few will contradict Shelley when he declares that "every limb, every muscle, every vein of Laocoon expresses with the fidelity of life the working of the poison." At the same time, while thus enthusiastic, he anticipates, in another place, the objections that have been made to this famous work, by expressing a fear that it may be thought to transcend the modesty of nature; that is, since its perfect truth to nature cannot be questioned, that it pertains to the province of painting rather than to that of sculpture. Such criticism, even if somewhat fastidious, proves that a higher and purer ideal has been revealed to us, since even so consummate a critic as Lessing took the name of Laocoon as the title of his own treatise on the laws of art, as though it symbolised something absolutely faultless. It may, indeed, be faultless in its own sphere; but the Elgin marbles and the Melian Venus have taught us that there is something higher; and this Shelley, who had barely seen the marbles, and had never seen the as yet undiscovered Venus, divined as by an infallible instinct. It is as though modern art had been thought to have culminated with Rembrandt in the absence of any knowledge of the works of the Italians. The place and merits of the "Laocoon" must of late have become better understood through the discovery of the Pergamene sculptures of the wars of the Gods and the Giants, near in period and akin in spirit.

The Arch of Titus does not afford very much material for æsthetic criticism, and Shelley's comment upon it is mainly descriptive. Let us for a moment interrupt the sequence of these notes by citing his observation upon the figures of Victory sculptured upon the arch, from a letter written about the same time :—

"Their lips are parted : a delicate mode of indicating the fervour of their desire to arrive at the desired resting-place, and to express the eager respiration of their speed. Indeed, so essential to beauty were the forms expressive of the exercise of the imagination and the affections considered by Greek artists, that no ideal figure of antiquity, not destined to some representation directly exclusive of such a character, is to be found with closed lips."

Excluding one most beautiful piece of landscape description, a general view of Florence, Shelley's Florentine notes number no less than fifty-six. Many of these, however, are but bare memoranda of the subject of a statue, or brief anathemas on the misdoings of some miscreant restorer. It would, nevertheles, be impossible here to enter upon all or nearly all of those which deserve serious attention. We must be content with extracts from a few of the more important—enough, however, to demonstrate Shelley's artistic enthusiasm and the general superiority of his judgment to the standard of his day.

None of the Florentine antiques aroused Shelley to so high-wrought a pitch of enthusiasm as a statue of Pallas, and most interesting it would be to learn whether the charm it exerted upon him was objective or subjective. Is it really a work

of such merit ? or did it merely mirror the impassioned feeling of the poet ?—

"The face uplifted to heaven," he says, "is
animated with a profound sweet and impassioned
melancholy, with an earnest, fervid, and disinterested pleading against some vast and inevitable
wrong ; it is the joy and the poetry of sorrow,
making grief beautiful, and giving to that nameless
feeling which from the imperfection of language
we call pain, but which is not all pain, those feelings which make not only the possessor but the
spectator of it prefer it to what is called pleasure,
in which all is not pleasure." (In the "Defence
of Poetry," Shelley speaks of "that delight which
is in the grief of love.") "It is," he continues, "indeed divine, as Wisdom pleading earnestly with
Power, and invested with the expression of that
grief because it must ever plead so vainly."

This is a favourite idea with Shelley. In the
first draft of his "Hellas," Christ appears to plead
before the Father for Greece against Islam ; and
Shelley elsewhere apostrophises Liberty as

> " Last of the intercessors
> Who 'gainst the crowned transgressors
> Pleadest before God's love."

By a curious anomaly this effigy of Pallas was
in Shelley's time placed upon a Bacchic altar,

adorned with reliefs of Mænads, whose whirling forms, perhaps conventional enough, Shelley invests with the tumultuous sublimity of his own imagination :—

" The tremendous spirit of superstition, aided by drunkenness and producing something beyond insanity, seems to have caught them in its whirlwinds, and to bear them over the earth as the rapid volutions of a tempest bear the ever-changing trunk of a waterspout, as the torrent of a mountain river whirls the weeds in its full eddies. Their hair, loose and floating, seems caught in the tempest of their own tumultuous motion."

It is interesting to find this idea repeated in his " Epipsychidion " :—

> " When some heavy tress
> The air of her own speed has disentwined."

The note concludes with a remark, not æsthetic, but historico-philosophical and deeply true : " A monstrous superstition only capable of existing in Greece, because there alone capable of combining ideal beauty and poetical and abstract enthusiasm with the wild errors from which it sprang." Speaking of the effects of the naturalisation of Bacchic worship in Rome, which compelled the Senate to suppress it, he adds : " The strict morals of the Romans sustained a deep injury little analogous to its effects upon the Greeks, who turned all things—superstition, prejudice, murder, madness—to Beauty."

Modern taste might not entirely sanction Shelley's enthusiasm for the "Niobe"; but certainly this group possessed the power of inspiring in him the finest language, and awakening the deepest thoughts. After speaking of the "careless majesty" stamped upon the countenance as upon "the rare master-pieces of Nature's creation," he adds :—

"Yet all this not only consists with, but is the cause of, the subtlest delicacy of that clear and tender beauty which is the expression at once of innocence and sublimity of soul, of purity and strength, of all that which touches the most re-moved and divine of the strings of that which makes music within my thoughts, and which shakes with astonishment my most superficial faculties."

In strong contrast with this eulogy is the con-demnation of Michael Angelo's "Bacchus," which, though extolled for its fine workmanship, is con-demned as deficient in that unity which, as Shelley acutely remarks, could not well be conceived as pertaining to Bacchus in an age when his divinity was not realised. It is, indeed, true that, from the influence of degrading associations compara-tively unknown to the ancients, we find it easier to realise the divinity of the Goddess of Harvests

than that of the God of the Vintage, and easier
still to recognise the divine attributes of a Muse
or a Grace, an Apollo or a Venus. It must be remembered, in partial vindication of Michael Angelo,
that this statue was an early work, which renders
its technical merit the more remarkable. Addington Symonds, who entirely confirms Shelley's
criticism, says it is the best representation conceivable of a drunken young man. Two others
of the notes are highly interesting, not so much
from their æsthetic importance as from their
adumbration of circumstances in Shelley's own
history. The group of "Bacchus and Ampelus"—
"figures walking as it were with a sauntering and
idle pace, and talking to each other as they walk,
as expressed in the motions of their delicate and
flowing forms," reminds him of the only delightful
part of his own school experiences: "Just as
you may have seen (yet how seldom from their
dissevering and tyrannical institutions do you
see!) a younger and an elder boy at school walking in some remote grassy spot of their playground
with that tender friendship towards each other
which has so much of love." When, again, he
speaks of a statue of Æsculapius, "with the fore-
finger in an attitude of instruction" and "the
gentle smile of the benevolent lips a commentary
upon the instruction," he must be thinking of

Dr. Lind, the good physician who befriended him in boyhood, and whom he has immortalised in "Prince Athanase" and "The Revolt of Islam."

These notes on the Florentine sculptures are the only formal and deliberate appearance of Shelley in the character of an art critic. His views must otherwise be collected from expressions in his letters, chiefly relating to works of art which have recently come under his observation, and from detached passages in his poems. He was not one of those poets whose temperament is in a super-eminent degree artistic, limiting the phrase, as it often is limited, to taste for pictorial or plastic art. His sympathies were rather with the art of music. Whether his taste as a musician was sound it is impossible to pronounce, but he unquestionably derived a more rapturous pleasure from audible than from visible art; and though his own songs are, it is understood, not always the best adapted to the requirements of the composer, it is admitted that his command of verbal harmonies was superior to that of any poet of his age, Coleridge perhaps excepted. It seems probable, however, that not a little of the delight which imaginative poets of warm affections derive from music may be attributed to the circumstance that music, from its close association with the performer, imparts a human element of interest in which the other arts are necessarily deficient. As Omar Khayyam's cupbearer must be not only a minister of wine, but also a cypress-slender minister, so the music, vocal or instrumental, when performed by the right sort of person, borrows enchantment from the beaming eyes, flowing tresses, and snowy fingers of the performer, which, in a sense different from that intended by Shelley, " teach witchcraft to the elemental strings." It may be doubted whether Jane Williams's guitar would have rung so sweetly in Shelley's ears if Jane Williams had not touched it, to the accompaniment, moreover, of Mediterranean moonlight. Still, with every allowance for the effect of these accessories, it remains true that Shelley was preeminently of a musical nature, with a joy in all flitting and evanescent effects of air, sound, and cloud, and light and shadow: rather ethereal than plastic. His analogue among painters is Turner rather than Raphael, and when he treats of painters we shall see that his favourites are those whose charm chiefly consists in expression, and who exhibit the deepest spirituality.

Criticism, even when most scientific, is so largely a matter of subjective impression that nothing less than an oracle could authoritatively tell us how far Shelley's eulogies on some of the Italian painters are to be regarded as founded on a discriminating judgment, and how far the beauties he discerned were but the effluence of his own impassioned feeling. It must be remembered that he approached the shrine of Guido with a greater disposition to admire than would be possible in our day. In our time, indeed, many a young man would deem that he proved his sensitiveness to the finer shades of culture by refusing to look at anything later than the middle of the sixteenth century. It was so different in Shelley's time that he must be held to have exhibited considerable independence of judgment by declaring that, for all the unanimity of connoisseurs in favour of Caracci, he cannot admire him. On the other hand, he wanted the assistance which a truly enlightened connoisseurship might have afforded him. The early Florentine school, in particular, was little known. There was no one to direct Shelley's attention to Masaccio or Filippo Lippi, much less to Sandro Botticelli, a painter in whom he must have greatly delighted had he been acquainted with him. He did not, indeed, like Goethe, accord scarcely a day to Florence in his anxiety to reach Rome; his stay there was long, and his investigation of its sculpture at all events, as we have seen, very thorough. But his knowledge was in many respects very defective, and he never became saturated either with the spirit of Italy or with the spirit of Renaissance art to anything like the same extent as another illustrious poet who for a long time made Italy his home— Robert Browning.

The first pictures of importance which Shelley saw in Italy were those at Bologna, described in his letter to Peacock of November 9, 1818. Here Guido dominates; but one of the two specimens of Correggio which Shelley saw "gave me," he says, "a very exalted idea of his powers." The subject is "Christ Beatified," and it must be fine indeed if it is as fine as some portions of Shelley's description :—

"The whole frame," he says, "seems dilated with expression; the countenance is heavy, as if weary with the weight of the rapture of the spirit; the lips parted, but scarcely parted, with the breath of intense but regulated passion; the eyes calm and benignant; the whole features harmonised in majesty and sweetness. The sky is of a pale aerial orange, like the tints of latest sunset; it does not seem painted around and beyond the figure, but everything seems to have absorbed and to have been penetrated by its hues."

A remark by Shelley on a picture of Guido's representing the " Rape of Proserpine "—" Proserpine casts back her languid and half-unwilling eyes to the flowers she has left ungathered in the fields

of Enna "—reminds one of his own song on Proserpine and the mention of Enna in his "Arethusa."
The picture was probably not without influence on
the former of these exquisite compositions; but he
has more to say on another whose subject must
have been infinitely less congenial to him. It is
Guido's picture of Samson drinking water out of
an ass's jawbone, in the midst of the slaughtered
Philistines. Here it is remarkable and characteristic to observe how Shelley turns aside from the
principal figure—the triumphant Hebrew Hercules
—to the pathetic figures of the overthrown Philistines, treated, as it would seem, by Guido in a
spirit of tenderness congenial to his own:—

"One prone, with the slight convulsion of pain
just passing from his forehead, whilst on his lips
and chin death lies as heavy as sleep. Another
leaning on his arm, with his hand, white and
motionless, hanging out beyond. In the distance
more dead bodies, and, still further beyond, the
blue sea and the blue mountains, and one white
and tranquil sail."

This introduction of the distant sail into the
picture was an exquisite touch of poetry in the
painter, and was not lost upon the poet. Such
a touch, indeed, would, in the eyes of the poet,
redeem even a bad picture. Shelley, when judging
of a work of art, inevitably places himself at the

poetic point of view — that is, he put feeling and expression as conspicuously into the first place as the great master of oratory put delivery. We have seen that while he had quite sufficient æsthetic perception to appreciate the technical excellences of Michael Angelo's "Bacchus," these do not in his view redeem the cardinal offence of its misconception of the spirit of the Greek myth ; so that, if the two had been positively incapable of combination, he would have craved truth to poetry even at the expense of fidelity to nature. This, of course, cannot be the view of the artist himself, with whom technical rather than spiritual excellence must be the first consideration; for the latter he shares with the poet, while technical mastery is his own peculiar *differentia*, the one endowment which gives him his place in the ministry of the Beautiful. It must not be thought, however, that Shelley's conception of the office of art is in any respect didactic. He does not look for sermons in sculpture, though he might, with Shakespeare's duke, have found them in unsculptured stones. He merely regards the expressiveness and spirituality which he desiderates, when they are to be had, as the spontaneous efflux of the artist's nature, and unquestionably he who unites a nature thus productive to technical mastery must stand higher than the mere craftsman. Only in one place does Shelley attribute didactic efficacy to a picture, and then to a disagreeable one. After remarking that he can take no pleasure in Guercino's pictures, he adds that one is unquestionably powerful, but the power is of a repulsive sort. It is an ideal representation of the founder of the Carthusians :—

"I never saw such a figure as this fellow. His face was wrinkled like a dried snake's skin, and drawn in long hard lines; his very hands were wrinkled. He looked like an animated mummy. He was clothed in a loose dress of death-coloured flannel, such as you might fancy a shroud might be after it had wrapped a corpse a month or two. It had a yellow, putrified, ghastly hue, which it cast on all the objects around, so that the hands and face of the Carthusian and his companions were jaundiced by this sepulchral glimmer."

And the moral which Shelley derives from the delineation is by no means that intended by the painter: "Why write books against superstition when we may hang up such pictures?"

In one point Shelley — here in advance of his age—sympathises with the general modern feeling. He looks upon the restoration of a work of art as at best a necessary evil. "It made me melancholy," he says, "to see that they had been varnishing and restoring some of these pictures," though he must have admitted this to be sometimes necessary, as in the case of such as had been pierced by the French bayonets.   This leads him into reflections which will find an echo in the mind of every artist :—

"How evanescent are paintings, and must necessarily be ! Those of Zeuxis and Apelles are no more, and perhaps they bore the same relation to Homer and Æschylus that those of Guido and Raphael bear to Dante and Petrarch. There is one refuge from the despondency of this contemplation. The material part, indeed, of their work must perish, but they survive in the mind of man, and the remembrances connected with them are transmitted from generation to generation. The poet embodies them in his creations ; the systems of philosophers are modelled to gentleness by their contemplation ; opinion, then legislation, is infected with their influence ; men become better and wiser ; and the unseen seeds are perhaps thus sown which shall produce a plant more excellent than that from which they fell."

It will have been noticed that Shelley here names Guido and Raphael in the same breath. It will be remembered that he had not seen much of Italian art at the period when this letter was written. Experience of the masterpieces of Rome and Florence doubtless greatly affected this estimate of Guido in so far as it was relative ; but the sunny cheerfulness of such performances of Guido's as his "Aurora" on the one hand, and the tender sentiment of his Madonnas and Magdalens on the other, must always have exerted a peculiar charm upon Shelley. He probably came to see in Raphael the perfection of what he had admired in Guido, while perhaps Raphael may have been even a little too academic. Perhaps Correggio would, on the whole, have been more attractive to him than any other painter if only Correggio had preserved a larger infusion of that poetical, as distinguished from merely pictorial, feeling which imparts such value to the works of Leonardo da Vinci, Giorgione, and the earlier Titians. Unfortunately, Shelley had few opportunities of becoming acquainted with the Venetian school in its poetical prime, or with the intensely spiritual art of Umbria. To one very great artist he may appear unjust, and yet his verdict on Michael Angelo is that of the generality, although his expressions are stronger. He concurs with most persons in condemning the celestial compartments of Angelo's "Last Judgment," but admits that "every step towards Hell approximates to the region of the artist's exclusive power." His great objection to Michael Angelo is his deficient sense of beauty; but this verdict was delivered without any acquaintance with Michael Angelo's drawings, and before having seen his sculptured figures of "Day" and "Night." The precipitate judgment, however, elicits the profound remark: "To want a sense of beauty is to want the sense of the creative power of mind. What is terror without a contrast with and a communion with loveliness? How well Dante understood this! Dante, with whom this artist has been so presumptuously compared!" And after a harsh, though not wholly unjust, criticism of the "Last Judgment" as a sort of Titus Andronicus in painting, he turns to the more congenial tenderness of Titian's "Danae" and Guido's "Magdalen."

Architecture was always interesting to Shelley, and he is always interesting upon it; but he is almost destitute of technical knowledge, and can only speak of the general impression. Milan Cathedral fascinated him, as it was afterwards to fascinate Tennyson; but the elder poet seems most impressed with the exterior, the younger with the interior features of the edifice.

"The effect of it," says Shelley, "piercing the solid blue with those groups of dazzling spires, relieved by the serene depth of this Italian heaven, or by moonlight when the stars seem gathered among those clustered shapes, is beyond anything I had imagined architecture capable of producing."

Tennyson, on the other hand, though praising the "mount of marble, the hundred spires," does not stand on the earth and gaze up to them like Shelley, but looks beyond them as he stands among

Z

them, and celebrates what he beholds in a marvellous stanza :—

> " How faintly-flushed, how phantom-fair
> Was Monte Rosa, hanging there
> A thousand shadowy-pencilled valleys
> And snowy dells in a golden air ! "

This is not the cathedral, but the view from the
cathedral. The interior, which is pronounced by
Shelley of a more earthly character, evokes Tennyson's highest enthusiasm :—

> " O the chanting quires !
> The giant windows' blazoned fires !
> The height, the space, the gloom, the glory ! "

Shelley thought this interior had the aspect of
" some gorgeous sepulchre," but excepted one nook,
" a solitary spot behind the altar, where the light
of day is dim and yellow under the storied window,
which I have chosen to visit and read Dante there."
With St. Peter's, the interior especially, Shelley
is disappointed, as is said to be usually the case
upon first visits, admitting, however, the magnificence of the façade, and that the whole is " an
astonishing monument of the daring energy of
man." The truth would seem to be that this
creation of the later Papacy, standing in the midst
of a city, had neither the association with history

nor the association with nature necessary to captivate a taste untrained to the perception of architectural principles, of which, however, he is not wholly ignorant, as appears from his praise of the just proportions of the Pantheon. When he very greatly admires architecture it is generally in connection with its natural environments, and hence he is peculiarly delighted with ruins. It rejoices him to think that, "unlike the inhabitants of the Cimmerian ravines of modern cities, the ancient Pompeians could contemplate the clouds and the lamps of heaven, could see the moon rise high behind Vesuvius, and the sun set in the sea, trembling with an atmosphere of golden vapour, between Inarime and Misenum."

From his account of the ruins of the temple of Pæstum, though fully sensible of their intrinsic sublimity, he appears more impressed by "the effect of the jagged outlines of mountains, through groups of enormous columns on one side, and on the other the level horizon of the sea." It is needless to cite his famous description of the Baths of Caracalla, in his day so overgrown with ivy and self-sown shrubs and wild flowers as to have become almost an object of nature. In a similar spirit, although while writing of a sublime piece of sculpture, Shelley does not omit to celebrate the combination of irresistible energy with perfect loveliness in the equestrian figures of Castor and Pollux, he remarks that "they are seen in the blue sky of Italy, overlooking the city of Rome, and surrounded by the light and music of a crystalline fountain."

The direct references to works of art in Shelley's poems are not very numerous, and are usually concerned with sculpture rather than painting. In "The Revolt of Islam" the emancipated nations erect a marble pyramid adorned with three sculptured images symbolising Equality, Love, and Wisdom. In "Marianne's Dream" a marble portal is—

> "Filled with sculptures rarest
> Of forms most beautiful and strange,
> Like nothing human."

And in "Prometheus Unbound" there are two lines on sculpture so frequently quoted for their justice and beauty as to have become almost proverbial :—

> "Praxitelean shapes, whose marble forms
> Fill the hushed air with everlasting love."

But there is one poem entirely devoted to a single picture, one whose character was specially adapted to fascinate the imaginative spirit of Shelley : no other than the "Medusa" in the Uffizi Gallery at Florence, attributed to Leonardo da

Vinci, a subject which we have most of us lately
seen treated by Sir Edward Burne-Jones. The
first stanza reads:—

> " It lieth, gazing on the midnight sky,
>   Upon the cloudy mountain peak supine.
> Below, far lands are seen tremblingly,
>   Its horror and its beauty are divine.
> Upon its lips and eyelids seem to lie
>   Loveliness, like a shadow, from which shine,
> Fiery and lurid, struggling underneath,
> The agonies of anguish and of death."

This poem is, perhaps, the only one in which
Shelley has deliberately set himself to translate a
picture into verse, and he is, perhaps, open to
the charge of having adhered too closely to his
original. He wrote at Florence, either with the
picture actually before him, or, at least, with a
very vivid impression of it upon his recollection.
Keats's similar translation in " Endymion " of
Titian's " Bacchus and Ariadne," which, as it was
not then placed in a public gallery, he had probably had but few opportunities of contemplating,
is more successful, because less anxiously modelled
upon an original. A much more remarkable instance of the effect of a picture in inspiring Shelley
is that portrait, genuine or otherwise, of Beatrice
Cenci by Guido, which in a manner compelled him
to write his tragedy of the " Cenci." Yet there is

nothing in the play from which it could be surmised that Shelley had ever seen the portrait.

We find in Shelley, then, as good an instance as we are ever likely to encounter of the judgments on fine art passed by a person of rare gifts, endowed beyond most men with penetrative insight and with delicacy as well as intensity of feeling, but devoid of the technical equipment of a professional art critic. Of the literary value of such judgments there can be no question; they bring beautiful things before the mental sight when the originals are inaccessible. Their practical value to artists is more disputable. Artists are apt to resent the interposition of outsiders, feeling, as of course they have every right to feel, that the merit of a picture largely depends on a knowledge of a number of technicalities, only to be acquired by study and practice beyond the sphere of the connoisseur. In the writings of the pre-Raphaelite school we may discern some impatience at the interposition of Mr. Ruskin, an artist rather than an amateur, but one who had never absolutely enrolled himself in the brotherhood by sending his pictures to an exhibition and affixing a price to them. This feeling is most natural; no man conscious of having undergone a severe novitiate likes to be criticised by one who has exempted himself from such an ordeal. Artists should remember, however, two things : one, that the fame and the less illustrious rewards for which they strive depend upon the award of a public outside the limits of their profession, and that it is greatly to their advantage that this public opinion should be regulated by intellects of the calibre of a Shelley's or a Ruskin's ; secondly, which is even of more importance, that a merely professional standard must necessarily become a merely academical standard, and that a merely academical standard is in the long run synonymous with convention, stagnation, and inanity.   The creative mind must be kept flexible, prehensile, fluid ; and this object is often best attained by criticisms which, if sometimes imperfect for want of exact knowledge and technical accomplishment, at all events reveal to the artist what a world of thought and feeling lies outside the sphere of rule and tradition, and may often delight him with the conviction that he has builded better than he knew.   Guido, we may be sure, had little notion that a Cenci tragedy lay in his Cenci portrait.   In the world of art, as elsewhere, poets, to borrow Shelley's great saying, are in the last resort " the unacknowledged legislators of mankind."

Date Due
